HUNTING NORTH AMERICA'S UPLAND BIRDS

Tips and tactics for pheasants, grouse, quail,
woodcock, doves, and more

John D. Taylor

The Lyons Press

Guilford, Connecticut

An imprint of The Globe Pequot Press

For Jack and Nash and Shana . . .
For all the people and dogs I've ever had the honor of spending a
day afield with . . .
For family and friends . . .
And for Mother Earth, whose bounty graces our lives and fills our
souls with peace, joy, and the wonder of the Great Mystery . . .

Mitakuye Oyasin

The Lyons Press is an imprint of The Globe Pequot Press.

Printed in the United States of America

Designed by Compset, Inc.

10 9 8 7 6 5 4 3 2 1

The Library of Congress Cataloging-in-Publication Data

Taylor, John D., 1960–
    Hunting North America's upland birds/John D. Taylor.—1st Lyons Press ed.
        p. cm.
    Includes bibliographical references (p. 257).
    ISBN 1-58574-245-7
    1. Upland game bird shooting—North America. I. Title.
SK323.T39 2001
799.2'46'097—dc21

2001029903

CONTENTS

ACKNOWLEDGMENTS

The author is deeply indebted to the following people who helped with the creation of this book: Jay Cassell, Senior Editor at The Lyons Press, for getting this project off the ground and his encouragement during the production of it. My friend, Dennis Burkhart, for the fine illustrations within. And the state wildlife agency officials who took the time to respond to requests for information: H. Lloyd Alexander, Section Administrator, Delaware Division of Fish and Wildlife; Tommy Hines, Small Game Management Section, Florida Fish and Wildlife Conservation Commission; Todd Bogenschutz, Upland Wildlife Research Biologist, Iowa Department of Natural Resources; Randy Rodgers, small game biologist, Kansas Department of Wildlife and Parks; Fred Kimmel, Biologist Program Manager, Louisiana Department of Wildlife and Fisheries; Andrew Weik, wildlife biologist, Maine Department of Inland Fisheries and Wildlife; Vicki Heidy, wildlife staff biologist, Missouri Department of Conservation; Scott Taylor, Upland Game Program Manager, Nebraska Game and Parks Commission; David K. Rice, Chief, Conservation Education Division, Nevada Division of Wildlife; Karen Bordeau, wildlife biologist, New Hampshire Fish and Game Department; Michael J. Murphy, wildlife biologist, and Robert M. Sanford, wild turkey specialist, New York Department of Environmental Conservation; Luke Millen, Ohio Division of Wildlife; Bruce Whitman, Chief, Division of Information, Pennsylvania Game Commission; Mark Gudlin, Small Game Program Coordinator, Tennessee Wildlife Resources Agency; Steve DeMaso, Upland Wildlife Program Coordinator, Texas Parks and Wildlife Department; Dean Mitchell, Upland Game Coordinator, Utah Division of Wildlife Resources; John Hall, information specialist, Vermont Department of Fish and Wildlife; Steve Wilson, wildlife resources section, West Virginia Division of Natural Resources; and Tom Matthews, of the Game Management section, Maryland Department of Natural Resources.

Also, a sincere thank you to everyone who provided the little sparks of ideas that help create a book and anyone I might have missed. . . .

INTRODUCTION

August is the happy month. It all starts on that cool night in August, out in the country, away from the clutter of street lamps, car headlights, and the lights from a hundred new homes on the far hillside, where it is dark enough to see the stars. There, in the eastern sky, the constellation Orion, the hunter, begins his seasonal climb through the heavens.

Shana, the DeCoverly Kennels English setter puppy, and I witness Orion while coming home from a training session, a "run." The truck stops at home and Shana, panting from the kennel crate in the back of the truck, tells me she is happy to be home. She whines to be out of the crate and into the house, where there is water and food. It was Shana's first big run, quite an adventure: She learned about butterflies and grasshoppers and goldfinches. It was a happy time. I smile at the feeling, remembering other nights under Orion's magic.

One memory is of Shana's predecessor, Nash, another DeCoverly setter. Nash's father, DeCoverly's October Pal, was Shana's grandfather on her father's side.

For a moment, it is an August night 11 years earlier, and puppy Nash is bounding through the foxtail at the York New Salem state game lands having the time of his seven-month-old life. Suddenly, he slows to a gliding trot, and that finely sculpted head of his swings effortlessly to the right, fluid motion becomes stone.

A point! Nash's first point!

I stumble in, telling him he is a wonderful good boy, wondering what sort of critter is under his spell. I step, then pause. The weedy foxtail parts and a hen pheasant clatters into the sinking sun.

Whooping, I somehow remember to fire the blank pistol. Nash stands there, the dark soulful eyes sparkling, and hears me tell him over and over again how good he is, how wonderful he is. Later, in a newspaper column I wrote about the real costs of outdoor adventure, I tally up the gas and the time and the dog food and the vet bills and all that related stuff. The cost of the evening is high, but worth every penny for that one moment in time when "Nashy-boy" got his first pheasant, his first wild game. A bird dog was born.

Looking down at tired Shana, I see a bit of Nash in her eyes, the tilt of her orange belton head. I get misty-eyed knowing the real cost of the last nine months without Nash. In that moment, I would give anything to see that expensive pheasant and Nash again.

Before we come into the house, I pick some "booger lice" burs from Shana's still mostly-white puppy coat, clip the lead to her collar, and look into the heavens, longing to see those familiar three stars in the belt of Orion.

Orion, in the mythological heavens, is a hunter. He is followed by a canine companion, Canis Major, the greater of two dog constellations in the heavens. Canis Major includes the star Sirius, named the "dog" star because its constellation brings the "dog days" of August into the world.

Thinking about how dogs have followed me and I them into the bird fields, I smile, remembering another dog star that burns bright in memory. His kennel name was Briarcliff Arcturus, but I called him Jack, after a hard-working Montana mule from my guide and wrangler days. He was my first bird dog, a German shorthair. And he was a character. Despite my best efforts at ruining his training, he taught me how to hunt birds, especially pheasants, with a dog. He also introduced me to ruffed grouse, a debt I can never repay.

Arcturus is part of the constellation Bootes, the herdsman, who chases the two bears, Ursa Major and Ursa Minor, across the sky. In ancient times, Arcturus was a harbinger of storms, but in later years the star was a good omen, bringing wealth and honor. To the Zuni people of the southwestern United States, the coming of Arcturus, part of their Chief at Night constellation, was important in the timing of ceremony and the ritual appearance of the Kachina, the Zuni's guardian spirits.

In many ways, Jack was like a guardian spirit to me. He showed me a path that I had no comprehension at the time would be so filled with joy and wonder. Somehow, Jack worked his way into nearly everything I wrote during his lifetime, from trout fishing stories to deer articles. He was usually doing something goofy. What a character!

Yet the Jack I remember most is the buzz-tailed preserve pheasant hunter at Martz's Game Farm, *sproinging* like a gazelle through sorghum and foxtail fields, pointing with a sizzling stub-tailed intensity. Each year on the vernal equinox, magazine editor and publisher Lou Hoffman treated friends to a spring pheasant hunt. One day I got a call to bring Jack. And that's when Jack discovered his Valhalla. He pointed—and fetched—more than two dozen of the big, long-tailed birds he loved that first day. Although he suffered through my love affair with ruffed grouse quite well, roosters were his passion, bringing out the fire in those golden eyes.

Shana stumbles into the house and finds the water in her bowl, and her food. She eats, drinks, slops water on the floor, happy for the simple basics of rest, food, and water.

Then it suddenly occurs to me that the long wait, suffering through the end of winter and the summer heat, is finally over. It's finally here, another bird season filled with the hope and promise of wonders to come: crisp apple-tart air, the damp scent of freshly fallen leaves rotting in a wood, bright aspens turning fire yellow, and cool, green hemlocks.

* * * *

Upland bird hunting is a passion.

George Bird Evans describes it best in *An Affair With Grouse*, "It is a strange thing we know—those of us who are compelled to shoot, affected by the Hunter's Moons—a need to accumulate experiences that require days and months to achieve, which last for seconds and are gone, impossible to capture, but which saturate our bones from that moment on, like desire in reverse.

"More sweet each year it happens, it is fulfillment almost disturbing in its fullness; yearning and regret for the brief span of heaven that is October."

Steve Grooms, in *Modern Pheasant Hunting*, talks about loving pheasants. Grooms loves the way pheasants look, ". . . the forward half a rooster with its riot of improbable colors—iridescent purple and green, pure scarlet, stark white and shimmering copper—is the perfect reflection of the brassy, cocky side of the bird's person- ality. And yet, the rear half—with those muted tans, the surprisingly effective camou- flage barring, and that whimsical touch of effeminate blue—reflects the wily, elusive side of a pheasant's nature." Grooms loves the fiercely independent spirit of the bird. He admires the courage and awesome tenacity of pheasants. He stands in awe of the resourcefulness of gunwise pheasants.

Joel Vance, in *Upland Bird Hunting*, writes, "But always there are the birds. That's why we go. For the birds that squat in fencerows, that stalk the far, silent ridges, that sail endlessly in the protective arms of a prairie wind. Each has his talents, his subterfuges, his special savor on a dinner plate. Each is special, for I have lived with them, Tom-peeped their sexual antics, midwifed their births, and assisted with unashamed gusto at their executions.

"No matter what the species, there are attributes that make it worth looking be- yond the bead on the end of trim double. Birdshooting is more than birdshooting—or should be."

Other writers describe their passion for upland birds in a variety of different ways, some in subtle words, others more directly. But all of us are connected to up- land birds in unique ways.

Upland bird hunters live their sport year round, not just for a few days in the season opener, or when it's convenient. In order to enjoy a month or two of sport, up- land bird hunters feed, care, and train dogs all year; we jog to stay in shape for *the* sea- son; we scour new maps for the mystery of hidden spaces; we shoot regularly; we commune with others of like minds.

I cannot drive through a stretch of forest here in Pennsylvania without rubberneck- ing for new grouse coverts. When I fly fish, a minor passion compared to grouse hunt- ing, I am looking for new coverts. Upland bird hunting is a consuming passion that can strain finances, pressure friendships, ruin marriages, and create havoc in the workplace. Yet we go. We must go. Who knows how many autumns a gunner will have?

Throughout the rest of this book, we'll be going bird hunting. We'll watch the dust rise as we walk across September's dry corn silage fields to find a spot for doves. We'll slide, as gracefully as possible, because we're gentlemen and gentle ladies, through October's thick, golden aspen thickets, looking for a setter who is looking for ruffed grouse. We'll get tangled, listening for a Brittany's bell, in the woodcock's soft- bottomed alder hells. Milo and warm-season grasses on CRP land will brush our birdshooter britches in search of a brace of cackling roosters. We'll walk—and walk and walk—into an endless prairie chicken horizon and see how land that looks flat is really an endlessly undulating swirl of rises and falls. Then we'll climb mountains, search high, then higher for chukars. We'll savor the lush richness of the bobwhite's southern homelands and look at the other places—dry desert, western valleys that quail also call home. And in the spring, we'll stand breathless in the darkness before dawn, listening for the rattle of a tom turkey's gobble.

We'll share these experiences—with fellow bird hunters, a procession of four- leggeds in all manner of breeds. But most of all we'll come away with a sense of hav- ing experienced something incredibly unique, the wild spaces of this continent and their winged inhabitants. I hope you enjoy the journey!

THE LAND

It is in vain to dream of a wildness distant from ourselves. There is none such. It is the bog in our brains and bowels, the primitive vigor of Nature in us that inspires that dream. I shall never find in the wilds of Labrador any greater wildness than in some recess of Concord, i.e. than I import into it.

Henry David Thoreau

SPECIAL PLACES

Land is the predominant feature of upland bird hunting. It molds the human beings and dogs who tread over it as easily as it determines what birds live where and how they live—whether grouse feed on aspen buds or rhododendron laurel over the winter. Land is the cauldron that shapes the upland gunning experience into the swirling wonderment of magic that it is, or at least should be.

Bird hunters form a special relationship with the land. Not to slight those who don't hunt—many who never carry a firearm possess a very strong bond with Mother Earth—the relationship upland gunners form with land is different from the Earth relationship formed by nongunners. Possessing the decision of life and death for some of Earth's creatures, and the self-imposed limitations that go along with this, changes the gunner's perspective, especially when this decision is held in a sense of reverence, as it should be. The gunner experiences a sense of intimacy and oneness with land that the nonhunter cannot: Pheasant tracks in cornfield mud or a turkey feather among overturned leaves in the woods become clues to solving a mystery rather than natural phenomena. The turkey feather, for example, could lead to a series of scratchings where a small flock of turkeys enjoyed acorns under red oaks . . . and suddenly, a path unfolds, a story is told, and the hunter, rather than being an observer, becomes part of the story, a participant.

Land, the predominant feature of upland bird hunting, molds the human beings and dogs who tread over it as easily as it determines what birds live where and how they live—whether grouse feed on aspen buds or rhododendron laurel over the winter.

Many gunners have a hard time expressing this. Yet most recognize that the sense of *harvest* that gently permeates the cut cornfields, weedy drainage swales, the red barn and fences that a brassy, cackling Iowa cock pheasant calls home is unique.

Grouse and woodcock hunters call their special places a covert. This, by definition, is a play on words, because covert, as an adjective, means clandestine or hidden; as a noun, it is a thicket, a patch of puckerbrush. Hunt with any grouse or woodcock hunter worth his salt and you will soon see that he will find the most covert (adjective) way he can to lead you to his favorite covert (noun).

Still, covert is an idea that perhaps more upland gunners ought to share. Coverts are places, sacred in their connections to the people who create them. They have particular dimensions and boundaries. Yet most importantly, they hold a continuum of time within those boundaries, what grouse guru George Bird Evans described as a past, a present, and a future. Gunning a covert opens the door to this continuum: With the practical moment-to-moment movement of the dog, carrying the gun, sliding through the woods, you hunt in the *now* of the covert. But you also walk with the memories of the past; the things and experiences that made that place unique. And there is a sense of future there, too; a hope that, in the immediate future, you find what you seek; in the more distant future, that this special place will remain much as it is at this moment.

Coverts are sacred in their connections to the people who create them. They have particular dimensions and boundaries. Yet most importantly, they hold a continuum of time—a past, a present, and a future—within those boundaries.

* * * *

Perhaps a story or two can help illustrate this:

Dominated by two unique land features—one a place to camp; the other a parcel of land, an old clearcut covered in a second growth forest of mostly aspen—"17-Bird" is one of my grouse coverts. The geographer locates this covert in northwestern Pennsylvania, in the Allegheny National Forest (ANF), a 513,000-acre parcel of federally controlled land east of Erie. But this covert—and I hate to call it mine, because it owns me more than I own it—lives mostly in my mind.

A writing assignment to interview a young man who earned high bow, muzzleloader, and shotgun shooting honors opened the door to 17-Bird. That fall I was on a quest to experience all of the state's grouse hunting, not just what I knew near my home. Armed with information about likely grouse spots from the ANF office, especially a wide swath of tornado-damaged forest grown up in 15-year-old second growth forest, I hunted a few spots, including a likely looking hillside with a fascinating rock formation on the top of the hill. The place called to me, and I vowed to return when there was more time.

In November of 1997, that call was answered. That autumn was a hard one: Caught in the crunch of a failed relationship, the loss of an old dog, parting with a rural home, and not knowing what the future would hold, I took a lot of problems into the woods. But there was good news, too. A 2 P.M. Friday afternoon job interview preceded the rainy, 6-hour drive to the ANF. I still chuckle about setting up the backpacking tent in a suit and tie in the middle of the wet woods.

The following morning, Nash, the DeCoverly Kennels setter, and I climbed the gently rising logging road into the covert and began hunting. My memory sees Nash flowing over that ground, fluid tricolor belton, close, but in constant motion. Just a few minutes into the hunt, he slows to work bird scent, and before he can establish a point, a grouse thunders into the air. Nash, cautious, casts a glance back to me for reassurance. I nod, his signal to move on.

It was the start of a remarkable day, the creation of a new covert. The gunning log reveals that on that cool, damp morning we had 17 flushes and a number of points. We took a brace of grouse, the first bird puffing in a cloud of feathers at the shot and staying airborne for what seemed an eternity before Nash could bring it back; the second bird coming from the opening near the top of the hill, below the hemlocks on the ridge. Nash handled the grouse expertly throughout the point-flush-shot-fetch cycle, a reflection of what my "puppy" had become in nine birds seasons—a dog at the apogee of his grouse hunting life.

We camped that night among the boulder, at the top of the hill. My tent was pitched under an old hemlock's boughs, the perfect little overhang for protection from the elements. While beans, zucchini chunks, and meat sputtered in a cast iron skillet, I noticed that the flickering campfire's light cast shadows on the boulders, which were placed, curiously enough, in the four cardinal directions by the Creator's hand. The shadows danced around the boulders like the ancient spirits of an Iroquois hunting party beseeching *Orenda*, the Great Spirit, for good fortune, courage and strength. I felt a kinship with this sentiment, and suddenly the courage to let go of some of the things that had troubled me in recent days came.

With the movement of the dog, carrying the gun, sliding through the woods, you hunt in the now of a covert. But you also walk with the memories of the past; the things and experiences that made that place unique, and a sense of hope that in the more distant future this special place will remain much as it is at this moment.

A lifetime of other coverts, other places hold similar memories. I see a mental snapshot of Ross Steinhauer and his two Grouse Ridge setters, Will and Briar, sitting on the back of his blue pickup after a snowy late season hunt in Nine-Bird (from which 17-Bird gets its name) in the late 1980s.

Nine-Bird is located in the South Mountains, the northernmost tract of the Blue Ridge Mountains, which run from the heart of Virginia north into south-central Pennsylvania. In midsummer of 1863, during his trek north to invade Washington, D.C. and bring the Union to its knees, Confederate General Robert E. Lee followed the Shenandoah Valley and the western flank of the Blue Ridge chain north into Pennsylvania. However, just east of where the South Mountains start to bow northeast toward Harrisburg, near a village that served as a hub for numerous roads, Lee bumped into destiny—a scouting party for the Army of the Potomac, 4,000 Yankee cavalrymen under Major General John Buford. Gettysburg turned out to be the turning point of that conflict and indeed the war.

The South Mountains are unique, unlike any other Pennsylvania mountains in vegetation, land features, and underlying geology. The soil is eroded bedrock, poor and sandy, one reason this region, settled in the early eighteenth century, wasn't used for farming like the rich limestone valleys below. The forest is more like southern Appalachia than a typical Pennsylvania forest. And the grouse who live there behave more like southern grouse, relying in winter on rhododendron laurel swamps, witch hazel, and grapes than the birds I've seen in the aspen softwood forests of Michigan, Minnesota, and Maine, or even in the northern reaches of Pennsylvania.

Getting into Nine-Bird was always the challenge. Crossing several deep waterholes in the badly rutted dirt road that leads to the covert put the vehicle at risk, which kept all but the most stubborn souls from exploring this ground. Even when the South Mountains started being overrun by displaced pheasant hunters fleeing the pheasant-barren farmlands and looking for a new bird, the covert's obstacles were its saving grace.

Ross's truck lurches along the rutted road, around the puddles, then stops. The tailgate opens, a kennel door creaks open, and Will, Ross' youngest dog, is free, free at last! Two years old and full of himself and a desire to hunt, Will flies off the tailgate while we're still getting ready to go, and Ross must check him with a tap on the electronic collar.

Later, in the forearm-thick maples and scrubby "buck brush" oaks of the overgrown clearcut, fast-stepping Will glides to a stop and his collar sings its *ba-beeep, ba-beeep* song. I arrive first, see Will's stylish tail high and proud, his staunch presence hypnotizing a hidden bird like a veteran grouse dog. Before Ross can get close, the grouse goes up left and my gun roars. Will's first pointed grouse is soon trotting towards Ross. We smile, congratulate each other and Will, and finish the adventure—another fine day in Nine Bird. Later, we'll share New England clam chowder cooked over the Coleman camp stove (new for a sandwich and water bottle guy) in the back of Ross' truck.

Other memory snapshots come and go.

My German shorthair, Jack, taught me how to find the South Mountains' grouse. We spent a decade there, from 1983 to 1993, days etched on my soul—and on the bottoms of several pairs of L.L. Bean Maine hunting boots. I came to regard this land as holy, what the *Paha Sapa* (Black Hills) are to the Lakota people.

I saw Jack and wildlife artist Denny Burkhart's Lady, a Brittany, scouring the bottom of Gimpy. The covert was named in honor of a young friend, Mark Barnhart, who hunted it with a bum leg from a football injury against his coach's wishes. At the end of our hunt, Mark and I huffed up the steep, mile-long logging road, and S.O.B. Hill (named this only when leaving the covert) was created. I thought we would have to cut him a crutch!

Denny, Lady, Jack and I hunted Gimpy's maple-covered creek bottom, covered with rocks, witch hazel and grapevine tangles, when it was young enough to host many grouse. One day, Lady and Jack both pointed the same grouse in front of Denny. On another, Jack chased a couple of turkeys up the almost vertical side hill on Gimpy's northern front. I never saw that dog's orange collar move so fast or so vertically. He came back a few minutes later, hardly puffing, yet quite satisfied with himself. On a third hunt Denny and I followed our dogs on faith alone as heavy fog drifted through the hillside grape tangles and phantom grouse *brrrrrred* out left and right.

Dave Miller, his Lab, Casey, and Mark still share the joy of my first grouse after a long shooting slump in Dry Spell. Lou Hoffman, Denny and Lady still meander, her bell tinkling, through flight woodcock on golden October afternoons in the mirror coverts, Sliding Rock and Rock Sliding, and in Dry Spell.

A final image: two discreet headstones with hand-chiseled letters and silhouettes. One an English setter, *Nash, 1998*; the other, a German shorthair, *Jack, 1996*, markers honoring dogs of finer hearts than I probably deserved. Both dogs rest in my *Paha Sapa*, in the covert where Jack pointed his first grouse. I smile, picturing Jack standing there looking out over the Cumberland Valley, hoping that we will come down out of the mountains and get some "rooster macgoosters." Then there is Nash, sitting with front legs gently crossed like he always did, those rich brown eyes cast up to me, waiting to go on.

* * * *

All bird hunters have their own special places, each dominated by the features of the land. The special places—and the birds—are what keep us going.

For example, quail hunting friends talk about the Parking Lot covey on Maryland's Eastern Shore, the last spot of the day in a quail hunt's circle. It holds birds even if all others fail.

New England grouse and woodcock hunters, who often live in the midst of more human beings than wide-open spaces, are quick to conceal the whereabouts of their coverts from prying eyes. Some, especially when good woodcock cover is involved, will travel a circular route to enter the covert and even hide their vehicles or park away from a good covert. The competition for resources is that intense.

In the big empty west of the Missouri River, coverts grow larger, encompassing sections of land, sometimes many miles across—Kansas, Oklahoma, Texas quail country; Idaho's chukar canyons, Gambel's quail county in the southwestern desert; Utah sage grouse leks.

All bird hunters have their own special places, each dominated by the features of the land. The special places—and the birds—are what keep us going.

For example, we hunted southwestern Kansas' Cimarron National Grasslands with Elkhart native Lawrence Smith several years ago. Smith saw the Dust Bowl of the 1930s carry pieces of his Morton County home all the way to Washington, D.C. He also participated in the revitalization of this land, and had a strong sense of conserving it.

Smith enjoyed gunning scaled (blue) quail, bobwhites, prairie chickens, and pheasants in the high plains country along the Cimarron River, broken, sandy land with sparse clumps of grass, cactus, and sage. It looked more like desert than the quail country we had driven through to get there. Yet the birds were there.

Smith knew the Cimarron intimately. He showed us how blue quail gathered around certain water hole tanks and not others. The mystery was that both areas seemed to have the same features. Bobwhites along the river were similar. One patch of cottonwoods and grass cover near the dry riverbed held a 30-bird covey of quail. The next spot, which through our inexperienced eyes looked the same, would be empty. Trying to figure out the birds was an exercise in futility.

We saw where blue quail strutted under cholla cactus—when I think of scaled quail, I can't help but think of a bow-legged cowboy sauntering up a dusty street. We laughed when, after we had broken up a covey of scaled quail, the smart little buggers hopped down gopher holes to get away from the dogs.

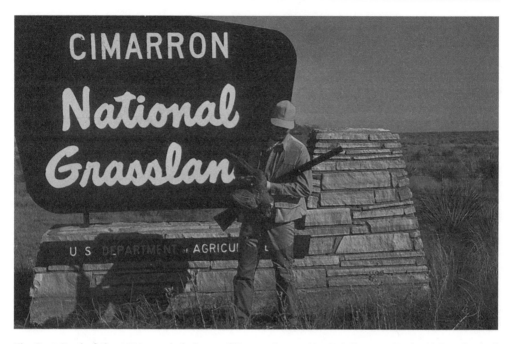

The Dust Bowl of the 1930s carried pieces of Morton County Kansas' Cimarron National Grassland all the way to Washington, D.C. However, the conservation efforts of people like Lawrence Smith, of Elkhart, Kansas, helped revitalize the land and its wildlife.

Sharing Smith's approach to these birds and his intimate knowledge of their habits, the land they lived on, other wildlife, was a study in reverence. Hearing him talk about the past gave us a sense of appreciation for the enormous conservation efforts necessary to reclaim the Cimarron from a greedy world bent on self-destruction. Sharing those hunts, walking for miles in search of prairie chickens, the ever-present wind caressing our ears with its song, was a joy with a gentleman like Smith. These were Smith's coverts. Although the geography and the vegetation were different, the idea was the same.

* * * *

Covert ownership is not a free ride. It comes with some costs.

One cost is a sense of responsibility for the covert's present and its future. You need to know the limits of your coverts. How many birds can you take from a covert without damaging it for next season? For the next 10 seasons? What impact does hunting have on the land?

Sometimes you have to play wildlife biologist to get the answers to these questions. Say a small farm holds 25 to 30 wild pheasants. Assuming the natural order of things holds true and 14 birds are roosters, and the remainder hens, how many roosters can you safely take from this farm before you damage the resource? Remember

Lawrence Smith and Dave Miller hunting scaled or blue quail, bobwhites, prairie chickens, and pheasants in the high plains country along the Cimarron River, broken, sandy land with sparse clumps of grass, cactus, and sage.

that cock pheasants are a randy lot, willing to mate with numerous females in the spring. If you are the only person that hunts the farm, you could probably safely take about a quarter of the total number of roosters before you did any damage. If there are other hunters, two might be a better bet. Now comes the larger question: How many farms like this do you need to create a season's worth of good pheasant hunting for you and the dogs? Better get the map out and start scouting.

For each species of upland bird the factors involved change and the ratios of the number of birds you can safely take from a particular place are different. For example, I limit myself to two grouse per covert annually from any public land coverts. Some small coverts are only one bird a year. While grouse biologists are quick to point out that in all probability birds taken from one area will be replaced by birds from surrounding areas, I've lost some precious coverts to too many people, too little habitat, too few birds. It's part of the responsibility of owning a covert.

Another covert-owning responsibility is being selective about those you share your coverts with, especially if it is a very special place. Often, the less said about a very good place, the better. If you're new to the sport, or if you've just come into possession of some new coverts, keep the following confession in mind so you don't have to learn these lessons the hard way.

In many ways I had a hand in the destruction of some of my favorite South Mountains places. Part of it involved being naive. Some involved underestimating the percentage of people who are takers in the outdoors. A lot of it was a lack of understanding the larger picture while being a good-hearted person who wanted to share things. Still, the bottom line was barren coverts where there was once abundance.

When I first started hunting grouse in the South Mountains, Jack and I could count on a very good hourly flush rate. Grouse were abundant then. New to the sport, I shared my coverts with several newfound friends. Some probably violated the principal covert guest rule: You don't hunt someone else's coverts. (Yes, I'm a good hypocrite, too, having adopted two deer hunting friends' spots as "my" grouse coverts.)

In addition, I wrote some articles for newspapers and magazines about grouse hunting in the South Mountains—not so much "go here to shoot a bunch of grouse" stories; but stories about what it was like to hunt grouse, and I happened to be doing this in the area. Soon, more people were gunning the limited number of coverts for a limited number of birds, a geographical reality. The forest was also aging, offering less bird habitat. One by one, the big coverts went down, first Sliding Rock and Rock Sliding, then Dry Spell, Gimpy, even Nine-Bird. Since 1993, I haven't hunted grouse in the South Mountains. By extending my range and locating new places to hunt, I found more birds and spread the impact of my hunting out over a larger area, keeping special coverts special for a longer period of time.

There are probably more questions than answers here. The bottom line, however, is that each gunner must take care of his own coverts, even if only to serve his future gunning interests.

A NATURAL HISTORY OF NORTH AMERICA'S UPLANDS

Understanding some natural history about North America, the features that make this land unique and that influence the birds and the hunting, is important for a bird hunter. Let's start at the Atlantic Ocean and travel west across North America, for a quick look at some of the land factors that influence upland bird hunting.

THE EAST

This area comprises the land from the Atlantic Ocean to the edge of what was once a tallgrass prairie, roughly western Illinois and Minnesota south through portions of eastern Missouri, Arkansas, and eastern Texas. Except for the coast, this area was originally covered by a vast forest.

Before European settlement, a patchwork of grassy openings, the result of lightning strikes or habitat manipulation by native people, punctuated this forest. Some of these openings were large enough to be called "prairies." Most of the forest, however, especially in the Appalachian Mountains, was coniferous, with white pines and hemlocks so tall they were coveted for ship masts. An oak-hickory-chestnut hardwood forest dominated the landscape of the Appalachian valleys, along the Ohio and Mississippi River valleys and in Missouri's Ozarks.

Historically, the upland birds of this region included most of today's species: bobwhite quail, ruffed grouse, woodcock, wild turkeys, and mourning doves. However, there were also three to five billion passenger pigeons using the oak-hickory-chestnut forest, and heath hens, a close cousin to prairie chickens, living on sandy scrub oak plains near the coast, from Maine to Virginia.

The greatest influences on early eastern upland bird numbers came in a one-two punch after the Civil War: Logging of much of the original forest was the left upper-cut. The right cross was the conversion of this former forestland into agricultural land to feed a growing human population.

Initially, the loss of the forest was devastating, especially to big timber species like elk, bear, wolves, cougars, and wild turkeys. Also, streams were ravaged when bare and unprotected hillsides eroded. In a short time, however, gamebirds actually benefited from the conversion of the land to agriculture. Prior to widespread agriculture, quail habitat, for example, was confined to forest openings, edges, and the coastal area. When agriculture expanded both the amount of open country and food resources, quail numbers exploded. This trend continued until the late 1950s in most areas. At that time, a rising human population and changes in agriculture that eliminated farmland wildlife habitat decimated quail numbers. Today's eastern quail numbers are probably coming back in line with what was here prior to European settlement. Human beings now edge quail out of their habitat, especially in the South, where quail were once king.

Ruffed grouse and woodcock populations experienced a similar situation. When the Appalachian conifer forest came down, settlers tried to farm the rocky hills, usually failing. Some lumber towns and tanneries (which used hemlock) flourished, creating more logging. By 1930, most of the original forest was gone. But when fresh growth sprouted, reclaiming the abandoned farms and the stumps, more new grouse and woodcock habitat was created. Some of the very best grouse gunning in the East occurred between 1920 and 1960, when the forest cut between the turn of the century and the 1930s came back in a "second growth" of 15- to 20-year-old saplings, prime grouse and woodcock habitat.

In addition, a substantial portion of the success of returning wild turkeys to their former range during the last 2 decades can be attributed to the aging of this second growth forest. Turkeys prefer mature forest to large expanses of young growth. Forests cut at the turn of the century were reaching maturity in the 1960s. This more mature forest, combined with the trap and transfer programs of conservation agencies and the National Wild Turkey Federation, restored wild turkeys to all of their traditional range and in some cases expanded that range.

The East was also the source for North America's gunning traditions. Early eastern hunters set the standards for what is acceptable in the field—why shooting quail in flight and turkeys on the ground is considered being a good sport, how dogs are to handle birds. Those early eastern gunners were following in the footsteps of the European nobles whose traditions they imported.

The real roots of wingshooting come from sixteenth-century Europe and are largely French and Spanish. Although Japanese hunters were taking birds on the wing from horseback in the 1600s, French and Spanish gunners were some of the first to note in sporting literature how they shot birds on the wing, rather than on the ground. For example, Louis XIV, the "Sun King" and France's most famous monarch, was quite a wingshot. Somewhere between succeeding his father as king at age five, conjuring up the notion that he was divine, and instigating four major wars and building the Palace of Versailles, Louis managed to be recorded shooting 32 flying pheasants for 34 shots with a flintlock. It might also be that the English owe their love of upland bird hunting to sunny Louis. After being deposed and exiled in a civil war by Oliver Cromwell's supporters, England's Charles II hid out in France for 9 years. When he returned to the throne in 1660, he brought back a passion for French-style bird shooting. Call it *noblesse oblige.*

The bulk of North American upland traditions are English and came about during the seventeenth century when titled gentry (the only economic class that could afford the luxury of sport hunting) began using flintlock fowling pieces to shoot birds on the wing, rather than stalking birds and potting them on the ground. The development of a series of behaviors and limitations about what is and what is not acceptable in the field comes directly from these gentlemen and ladies.

For a time, North American shooting manners continued to follow the European lead. This included the early days of the development of double guns, estates, and driven shoots. However, by the mid-1800s, as the distance between mother country and former colonies grew, a break occurred. This was reflected in the development of a unique "personality" in all aspects of society, from Mark Twain's writings, to George Catlin's Native American paintings, to the 1842 founding of the New York Philharmonic. By the Civil War's end in 1865, perhaps later in Canada, distinct North American gunning customs were established.

For example, individualistic North Americans gunners tended not to group for driven shoots, but approached hunting as individuals gunning private coverts in small parties or often alone. (The exception might be a South Dakota pheasant hunt.) Acceptable dog behavior is more individualistic, too, more like "rough" shooting on an English estate.

Today, the East is also where the most people live in the smallest amount of space, something that presents both challenges and opportunities for both birds and bird hunters. Challenges include trying to keep the remaining pockets of habitat, especially those that hold wild birds, from becoming housing complexes, shopping malls, or industrial parks. The opportunities include the adaptation birds like doves make to call a housing development home.

THE MIDWEST

The Midwest, "the Heartland," is often more a state of mind than a geographical description.

This is the area originally covered by the tall- and shortgrass prairies and the high plains. It includes what lies between most of eastern Montana, Wyoming, Colorado, and New Mexico and western Illinois, Missouri, Arkansas, and Texas. It also includes the Canadian prairie provinces of Alberta, Saskatchewan, and Manitoba.

The Midwest is very, very old land. The underlying geological structure of Kansas, for example, consists of one of the oldest chunks of continental crust in the world. Thrust from the Earth's middle by enormous tectonic forces, this crust became a mountain so high that it reached into a nonoxygen atmosphere. Yet within a geologically short amount of time, this same land was dropped back down to Earth and eroded by wind and water, then covered by a vast shallow inland sea, the result of a melting ice age. The erosion process and the coming and going of an inland sea continued for millions of years, building layer upon layer of sedimentary rock, in some places 2 miles thick.

The land reflects this turmoil: A good example is South Dakota's Badlands—how the broken, abrupt badlands materialize in the midst of a swirling expanse of undulating grass, sage, and mythic *tatanka* (buffalo), in the mind's eye, where the sun meets that forever sky.

Explorers traveling west in the early 1800s described the middle section of North America as both a sea of grass and a desert wasteland. Both perceptions appeared correct: Imagine a Kentuckian heading west into the great unknown in the early 1800s. Accustomed to the definition forests add to a landscape, our explorer would be very easily overwhelmed by the vastness of tall grasses that stretch to the horizon, the wind's fingers gliding over the stalks, sending endless ripples across the tops.

Rainfall determined the height of the grass. More rain falls in Peoria than in Wichita or Cheyenne. A tallgrass prairie, as high as a horse's belly in many places, stretched from western Illinois to eastern Kansas. Less rain fell on the prairie, which ran from south-central Minnesota to eastern Montana. The high plains, which get the least amount of rainfall, begin west of the Missouri River and end at the Rocky Mountains. The plains, especially in the south, look more like a desert than a place of abundance, but looks are deceiving.

A wealth of birds lived in the heartland prior to European settlement. Bobwhites were found in many areas, and scaled quail preferred the dry southwest, Oklahoma, and Texas. Wild turkeys of two subspecies were common. Mourning doves were plentiful. And in the far western reaches of the high plains, on big sagebrush flats in Montana, Wyoming, and Colorado, 8-pound sage grouse strutted over their leks in the spring.

However, the birds that most embodied the spirit of the prairie and plains were the lesser and greater prairie chicken and the sharp-tailed grouse. The muted tan colors and striations in the feathers mirror the land. The movements of both birds, especially during courtship displays, when the males fluff up pinnate feathers on the neck (like a ruffed grouse's ruff), hunch low to the ground, and step out a peculiar natural rhythm, resemble the movement of a Native American pow-wow dancer—perhaps a natural link.

Sharptails were northern birds, favoring the mid-length grass prairies found in the Dakotas, Montana, and the Canadian prairie provinces. Greater prairie chickens ranged from Kansas north into Canada. Slightly smaller in size, lesser prairie chickens favored the arid, sandy grasslands found in southwestern Kansas, southeastern Colorado, the Texas and Oklahoma panhandles, and the land east of the Pecos River in New Mexico.

Westbound travelers remarked first about vast herds of buffalo, then about the tremendous quantities of prairie chickens and sharptails they found. These birds were often dinner for those early pioneers. Also, until 1900, when this was prohibited, both species were shot, salted and placed in wooden barrels to be shipped to eastern markets. Despite this carnage the birds remained numerous. Arthur Cleveland Bent, in *Life Histories of North American Gallinaceous Birds,* records a Mr. Colvin's accounts of hunting prairie chickens on Ed Ward's Kansas farm in 1914: After witnessing a flock of 500 chickens near the state line, his guide told Colvin that these were just "rovers" and he knew of a better spot, Ward's farm. Colvin describes booting prairie chickens out of tall bunch grass and moving many birds before getting into a cane and kaffir field where, with each step, chickens would flush in flocks of 50 to 100 birds. The deeper they moved into the field, the more birds got up, 50 to 500 birds at a clip. Colvin and his guide estimated that there were 3,500 to 4,000 prairie chickens in the field.

What happened to the prairie chickens and sharptails is the same story that happened to buffalo, passenger pigeons, and the vast eastern forest. California's Gold Rush in 1849 brought more people onto the prairies, a trend that continued with the discovery of gold in the Black Hills and Wyoming in the 1860s and the coming of the transcontinental railroad in 1869.

People saw gold in the prairie's soil, too. Between the mid-1800s and 1910, much of the prairie, with its ages-old rhythm of migrating buffalo, plant decay, wind, and weather providing the raw materials for incredibly rich soil, was put to the plow. What wasn't plowed was fenced and turned into cattle pasture, especially on the plains. Between a government policy of killing buffalo to eliminate problems with the western Indian tribes and buffalo range being plowed or fenced, the annual migrations stopped, and the herds split into two—one north, one south. Without the sea of grass, the niche prairie chickens and sharptails had evolved to fill, the number of birds fell to just a shadow of what explorers found.

The tall- and shortgrass prairies did not entirely disappear. The hard soil of the Flint Hills in Kansas, for example, preserved a large tract of original prairie and a sizeable number of prairie chickens. And the high plains is definitely still there. Agriculture, however, changed the nature of the upland bird life on the prairies. Prairie chickens and sharptails filled the pockets of the original habitat remaining and adapted in some ways to land used for agriculture. Quail numbers blossomed with the coming of agriculture. Also, two new birds, both imported from Europe, came into the picture.

In addition to trying to start pheasant populations in the East during the late 1700s, Richard Bache, Ben Franklin's son-in-law, tried to stock Hungarian or gray partridges. Neither took. However, 207 pairs of Huns released in Calgary, Alberta in 1909, did. From these roots and the release of other birds by well-intentioned sportsmen's groups and others, Hun populations were introduced and took hold across much of the northern prairie country of southern Alberta, Saskatchewan, and

Manitoba, parts of Quebec, and in eastern Minnesota and parts of Michigan. Today, birds can be found as far west as eastern Oregon and Washington and as far south as Iowa, in some areas.

But the bird that would come to dominate upland hunting across most of the prairie states was the ring-necked pheasant. In 1882, Judge Owen Denny, U.S. consul to China, released 10 roosters and 18 hens trapped in China in the Willamette Valley of Oregon, then returned to China for 2 years. When he returned, the birds had spread into two adjoining counties.

During the next several decades, all of North America was involved in releasing pheasants using birds trapped in Oregon or raised on game farms. The releases were successful. Pheasants were well adapted to agricultural land, feeding in the grain fields, nesting in hay or grasslands nearby. The agricultural lands of the 1920s–1970s, small farms punctuated by pockets of wild land, especially brush and swamps and hedgerows, were tailor-made for pheasants. Also, the Soil Bank, a land set-aside program of the 1950s, created even more pheasant habitat.

Pheasant numbers soared. In the best of times, 1940–1960, South Dakota pheasant hunters bagged up to 7.5 million birds annually! Iowa, Nebraska and Kansas gunners took over a million pheasants each. However, this bounty didn't last. The link with agriculture was both blessing and bust to pheasants and quail.

The bust began with changes in federal farmland policy in the 1970s. Farmers were encouraged to feed the world and in doing so to take more from the land. Fields were double-cropped. More land was put into production, which meant the fallow fields, swamps, and hedgerows were removed to make way for larger fields, tilled by monster tractors. This evolved into the development of a corporate-style of agriculture during the 1980s, where land was looked at as a tool of production rather than a living, spirit-filled place. Smaller family farms, just the kind of places that held birds, were bought out, stripped down, and conglomerated into large tracts. As a result, bird numbers plummeted. In the mid-1980s, the Conservation Reserve Program (CRP), a land set-aside similar to the Soil Bank, took cropland out of production and put it into wildlife habitat for 10 years. This has helped rejuvenate pheasant and quail numbers in the Midwest. Its renewal in the late 1990s offers hope to bird hunters that the rebound will continue.

THE ROCKY MOUNTAINS

Prior to Lewis and Clark, John Fremont, and other early explorers of the West, little was known about land beyond the Great Plains. In the early 1800s, a Mississippi River explorer named John Carver learned about a range of mountains to the west that native people called the "Shining Mountains." They told Carver about crystals of amazing size and quantity that covered these mountains. Carver's imagination turned the crystals into diamonds. Later explorers found no diamonds in the Rockies. Snow crystals shining in the sun gave the mountains their name. Still, beaver trappers, miners, lumbermen, and today's ski resort owners—in a strange kind of circular irony—found their own kind of precious jewels in the "Shining Mountains." A bird hunter headed west from Great Falls, Montana sees peaks of nearly 10,000 feet in the distance; peaks that shine with a special kind of allure, something that calls you, draws you in closer. Bird hunters can find different kinds of riches in the Shining Mountains.

The Rocky Mountains are immense, stretching from New Mexico to Alaska. About 375 million years ago, a foundation of soft rock was pushed up from the crust of the Earth by some of the same tectonic forces that moved pieces of Kansas about. This initial foundation eroded, but sliding over it came a harder plate of rock, made of granite, gneiss, and schist. This is the basis of the Rockies you see today, reaching into the sky 10,000 feet in most places, up to 14,000 in some. Some geologists believe this rising movement is still going on.

The mountains are a barrier to prevailing western winds that move moisture-laden clouds across the land. Clouds moving up over the mountains cool rapidly, losing their ability to hold moisture. This precipitation falls largely on the western slope of the Rockies, resulting in vegetation vastly different from the plants on the eastern slope. This unique mystery of location also created strange weather patterns that shaped the mountains.

Snow, glaciers, and time have etched their presence on the Rockies. About 200 feet of snow falls on the Rocky Mountains annually. Over the course of long periods of geologic time, including a number of mini-ice ages, this snow accumulated, compacted, and formed glaciers. As ice ages came and went the thawing glaciers receded, moving downhill, and water flowed along the path of gravity. This movement carved gouges and valleys in the rocky face of the mountains. Also, seasonal freezing and thawing broke apart the rock, which eroded to form geologic features and eventually topsoil.

Plants on this hard and rugged land reflect these cycles. Alpine firs and Englemann spruce cover the high altitudes, lodgepole and ponderosa pines are below them, and in the valleys, softwoods like aspens, some oaks, and other trees color the land.

Grouse are found in the Rocky Mountains. A different species of grouse lives at every level. Sage grouse strut in the flatland sage flats below the mountains. Ruffed grouse live in the foothills among the gambel oaks and aspen. Spruce grouse dwell in the lodgepole and ponderosa. Blue grouse like the spruce and firs of the subalpine region, close to timberline. And in Canada and Alaska, ptarmigan can be found above timberline.

"Fool hens," a term which can cover spruce or blue grouse, depending on the encounter, kept many trappers and modern day explorers of the Rockies from going hungry.

I spent a summer after college working for an outfitter as a trout guide, wrangler and mule packer in Montana's Great Bear and Bob Marshall Wilderness areas, south of Glacier National Park. An Easterner who desperately wanted to be a cross between Jeremiah Johnson and Jimmy Stewart in *Winchester '73,* I only had four hours of real horseback riding time under my belt. Somehow I talked the outfitter into showing me his business for room and board wages.

One day I was leading a packstring of big Missouri red mules and horses along the muddy Morrison Creek trail. I was singing "I ride an old paint, I lead an old dam,

I'm going to Montana to throw a hoolihan . . . ," at the top of my lungs, and feeling like a real, hard-bitten cowboy. (This was the most remote wilderness in the lower 48 states, and for some reason this hymn seemed to keep those psychotic mules calm.) Anyhow, we were slogging through the early season mud when a few yards ahead, several large, dark, strange-looking birds ran out along the edge of the trail and flushed low, arcing into the lower bows of a large lodgepole. My usually lethargic horse flinched at the flush, almost jumped. As we passed the lodgepole I prayed the birds would stay put, not freak out the mules who already showed me that bright backpacks, sudden movements, and strange sounds could throw them into a buck- ing, packbox saddle-tossing rage. The birds cooperated, and the woods were soon filled with my bellowing again.

The Rockies haven't experienced the radical landscape changes that revolution- ized the upland bird habitat of the East and Midwest. Modern bird hunters can still find native birds in native habitat. However, two questions arise: Given the ongoing harvests of western timber, will mountain grouse adapt to changes in the forest, per- haps flourish in the forests that return from the clear cuts? How will the influx of more people influence upland bird hunting in the Rockies?

Timber harvests could make for an interesting new chapter in wildlife biology as time goes on and more of the mountains are logged off. (Although a large portion of the diet of mountain grouse is related to conifers, it also includes insects, seeds, fruits, and leaves.) Discovering the answers to these questions may take quite a long time, since most western forests can take as long as 300 years to regenerate, com- pared to the century it takes Appalachian forests to do the same thing. The people problem could be an issue, although it is hard to imagine multiple housing units perched over a glacier-filled cirque, and people commuting daily through blizzards and avalanches to get to work. Of course, in 1900, no one imagined vast shopping malls perched on New Jersey swampland, either. It would be nice to think that when someone mentions western grouse hunting in 2300, they are thinking about hopping into the transporter with a shotgun and a bird dog and materializing in a western Montana blue grouse covert, instead of popping into a "virtual reality" hunt.

THE GREAT BASIN

The Continental Divide, located along the spine of the Rocky Mountains, splits the flow of water on the North American continent. From the divide, water flows east to the Atlantic Ocean and Gulf of Mexico; or west, into the Pacific Ocean.

The land in between the Rocky Mountains and the Sierra Nevadas, the next major mountain range west, is "cowboy country," land you see on old John Wayne flicks, 2.25 million acres of sage wastes, alkali flats, dry creek beds, sand dunes, buttes, and badlands. The land is appropriately named. Flying over this country you sense the enormity of the saucerlike geography that begins where the Sierra Nevadas and the Rockies join. From southwestern Idaho and the eastern two-thirds of Oregon, the Great Basin covers the land south through Nevada, Utah, and into northern Arizona.

This is desolate country, with a thin fringe of vegetation. There are few trees in most areas, very little water, lots of dust, and a wind that never seems to stop. The lack of water—only 8 inches of rainfall annually—is what makes this area unique. The Basin collects this water and holds it, in places like the Great Salt Lake or the Humboldt River, until it evaporates.

Despite the barrenness of the land, it has always had a peculiar draw for people. The Shoshone woman, Sacajawea, "Birdwoman," for example, showed explorers Meriwether Lewis and William Clark the eastern path to the Great Basin in August of 1805. Lewis and Clark expected to be able to hop in hide-covered canoes and float to the Pacific from the Basin. But they found the Sierra Nevadas blocked this hope. In 1812, Robert Stuart set out with six men from fur tycoon John Jacob Astor's fort on the Columbia River and traveled east to get across the Sierra Nevadas. Stuart's Indian guide, paid in full before the trek, vanished halfway into the journey. Stuart pushed on, discovering a western passage into the Basin, South Pass, in October of 1812. Trapper Jedediah Smith located South Pass coming from the east in 1824, after surviving a grizzly bear mauling. Between 1843 and 1869, 300,000 people, some gold seekers, some settlers, poured through South Pass on their way to California.

The Paiutes, the nomadic hunter-gatherer people who called the Great Basin home when Jed Smith crossed it, have a legend about the origin of the bluebird: The Great Spirit grew gloomy each autumn because there were no colors on the trees any more, so he turned the leaves into birds. Red oak leaves became robins, aspens were goldfinches, and so on. Bluebird waited to receive his color, but was overlooked. In protest, Bluebird flew into the heavens. On the way, bits of the sky colored Bluebird a prettier color than any other bird. Science stands behind this legend, because bluebird feathers have no true pigment, but reflect the blue range of the color spectrum because of the structure of the feathers.

The Basin is a lot like Bluebird—overlooked. On closer inspection, the barren-looking land, painted sagebrush gray on the hillsides and delicate sparse grass pastels in the bottoms, is quite beautiful. It is also far from barren land. Pronghorn antelope, mule deer, wild horses, horned larks, ground squirrels, gophers, and marmots are some of the creatures who live here. Plant life, in addition to sage and grass, includes a bountiful mixture of flowers from both alpine and grassland settings, such as stonecrop, cushion pink, daisies, locoweed, and larkspur, which is poisonous to cattle.

The Basin's primary native upland birds are four species of quail: Gambel's quail, California (valley) quail, scaled quail, and mountain quail. Doves and sage grouse are also natives. Chukars, Huns in the north, and pheasants, where irrigation permits agriculture, are more recent arrivals to the Basin.

The Basin's top-knotted quail—the topknot is not a single feather but thousands of tiny feathers—are fascinating birds. Valley quail come in large coveys, with 50 birds being common; up to 1,000 bird groups have been noted in some areas. The great table appeal of valley quail created a market for gunning the birds. Thousands were sold in San Francisco during the late 1800s. Intensive farming and ranching has destroyed a lot of valley quail habitat, typically brush-choked ravines and creek bottoms, especially in the western portion of the Basin. Now, irrigation ditches covered with tule weeds, grease brush, tumbleweeds, and Indiangrass are valley quail habitat. However, these highly adaptable birds are also often seen at bird feeders.

Tom Huggler, in *Quail Hunting in America,* calls mountain quail a "wilderness" gamebird, because they don't do well on land influenced by man. Lumbering, fires, and overgrazing can be problems, but hunting is not. Largely confined to western Nevada in the Basin, mountain quail are an underutilized resource, simply because not too many people spend time hunting the birds. (Westerners prefer to gather wild protein in chunks larger than nine ounces.) Mountain quail are migratory, like elk, moving higher or lower in elevation as the weather dictates.

Named for Dr. William Gambel, an 1850s southwestern United States explorer-naturalist, Gambel's quail are primarily desert birds, yet they can tolerate extremes of altitude and temperatures. The birds can survive the desert's blast furnace heat or a 40 degrees below zero Idaho night. They have been found as low as 200 feet above sea level and as high as 11,000 foot Charleston Peak in southern Nevada. This adaptability is something that encouraged several wildlife agencies in the Midwest and East, including Pennsylvania, to try releasing the birds. (These projects failed.) Also, prior to coming to Minnesota, famed grouse researcher Gordon Gullion worked with Gambel's quail in Nevada. Gullion identified three main habitat types: *Upland desert*, dominated by catclaw, creosote bush, prickly pear cactus, yucca, and desert thorn; *Desert valley*, which includes mesquite, saltbush, tamarisk and desert thorn; and *Colorado river*, which includes greasewood, rabbitbrush, saltbrush, and sage.

Chukars are native to India and Turkey. They were imported into the United States during the late 1800s, like pheasants, and released in 42 different states and six Canadian provinces. However, it wasn't until 1935, when Nevada received its first chukar release, that the birds took hold. Chukars have become the quintessential Basin gamebird. Nevada, Oregon, Washington, Utah, and Idaho all have substantial chukar populations.

Nevada's first chukars found their new home a lot like their native habitat: arid highlands and mountainous foothills filled with seed-bearing plants, grasses, leaves, and fruits. Chukars are gregarious, like quail. A typical covey has about 20 birds that roost in eroded canyons, usually close to water. Charley Waterman, the dean of chukar hunting, calls these birds track stars because they like to lead gunners on merry chases up and down the steep slopes of typical chukar country. Chukar gunners usually describe the birds in other terms, especially when the gunners are following a dog trailing a covey up a sharp slope.

THE SOUTHWEST

Deserts are the main land feature of the Southwest, which includes portions of Nevada, Utah, Arizona, southern California, New Mexico, and Mexico. Deserts get less rainfall than the Basin does, under five inches a year, and some years there is no rainfall. Temperatures reach over 100 degrees during the day, especially during summer, and can fall to freezing by night. The landscape is rocky, weathered in strange shapes. Sand dunes roll across the land. Scorpions, snakes, gila monsters, Zane Grey cowboys, and Navajos herding sheep near their cone-shaped hogans—these are the images of the desert.

Edward Abbey's *Desert Solitaire,* a 1968 nonfiction work that describes Abbey's two 6-month stints as a seasonal ranger at Arches National Monument, now a National Park, is rife with the colors of a summer sunset in Utah. The setting of the book is a sagebrush-dominated Great Basin desert that is the coldest desert in North America.

This is one of five distinct North American deserts. The other four include the small but famous Mojave desert, located in Nevada and California; California's Death Valley desert, best known for its dagger-leafed Joshua trees; New Mexico and Texas's Chihuahuan desert, which has century plants (a tubular agave plant) that flower once a century then die; and the Sonoran desert, which extends through portions of Arizona, California, and into Mexico.

Despite the name, deserts are far from barren places; however, the plant and animal life inhabiting deserts are unique. Over 100 species of cactus call the desert home. Cacti have adapted to survive the desert by creating large dew-catching areas in their structure and putting roots deep into the soil to hold the water that is caught. Cacti nurture life much like a tree in a forest, with flickers and other woodpeckers excavating nest holes in the trunks. The continent's smallest owl, the elf owl, eventually calls these holes home. Doves pollinate the blossoms and feast on the fruits and seeds. Hawks nest in the crooks of the arms of cactus. A variety of succulent shrubs and wildflowers produce brilliant displays after winter and summer rains.

The Navajo of Arizona and New Mexico actually call themselves the Dine, "The People." Their homeland is the Dinetah, home of The People. Navajo was the term used by the Pueblo people to describe their neighbors to the West to Spanish explorers. Originally hunter-gatherers who raided the Pueblos, the Dine eventually took up farming, weaving, basketry, and shepherding the sheep and goats left by the Spanish. Dine sand paintings are temporal altars, used once to make a supplication to the Creator and a cast of minor culture heroes: Changing Woman or Earth Mother; Spider Woman, who taught the Dine how to weave; Spider Man, who warns of coming danger; even Coyote, the trickster, who can help people, although he usually just messes with them.

The Roadrunner and Coyote cartoon turns around Coyote's typical role. But the desert is full of coyotes in other forms. Abbey's George Hayduke, the main character of *The Monkey Wrench Gang,* tries to harass and delay desert-country developers—even blow up the Glen Canyon Dam—like the *saboteurs* who threw their wooden shoes (*sabots*) into the gears of early factory machines. Abbey based his heroes on real, though largely unidentified individuals. Sometimes, coyote, Abbey, and the Southwest's upland birds have a lot in common. Desert quail are a good example. They come in extremes. Chasing a running covey of cotton-topped scaled quail through cacti is one extreme. Then there's Mearns' quail.

Mearns' quail are like woodcock—eccentrics. Variously called Montezuma, Harlequin, black, and massena quail, the birds were named for Edgar Mearns, a lieutenant colonel U.S. Army doctor and naturalist who explored the Southwest in the 1880s. (Mearns, who hunted Africa with Teddy Roosevelt, is mentioned in Roosevelt's *African Game Trails.*) Naturally equipped with long legs and sharp toenails, the birds like to dig for bulbs, tubers, and worms. They also eat acorns, nutgrass, wood sorrel, sedge bulbs, sunflower seeds, beetles, worms, and other invertebrates. These shy, secretive birds form small coveys; six birds are common. Mearns' quail have a reputation of being a lot like bobwhites, tight-sitting gentlemen that will let a dog point them.

Mearns' quail are actually a subspecies of Mexico's Harlequin quail, which range in the northern Mexican states of Chihuahua, Coahuila, and Sonora at 3,000 to 10,000 foot elevation. During the past 100 years, Mearns' range in the United States shrank considerably. Currently, southeastern and south-central Arizona, including the Coronado National Forest, and west of the Pecos River, in New Mexico's Mogollon and Black mountains, is the primary Mearns' range. The birds prefer oak and pinyon pine grassland hills.

During the 1960s, Mearns' quail couldn't be hunted. The birds were even put on the endangered species list. It wasn't until some Tucson bird hunters and their dogs showed officials that the birds were not as uncommon as they appeared to be, that the endangered species listing was removed. Other native Southwestern quail include mountain, scaled, and Gambel's quail.

Doves are another coyote. As if mourning doves weren't hard enough to hit, two other species of doves, white-winged doves and Inca doves, are native to the Southwest.

Whitewings inhabit southeastern California, southern Nevada, most of Arizona, southern New Mexico, western Texas, and Mexico through Central America. They are very similar to mourning doves in many attributes, but whitewings are more specifically adapted to desert life, feeding on the tops of flowering cacti. The bird gets its name from a white band prominent on the wing.

Inca doves look like miniature, thin, "scaled" mourning doves. Only 8 inches long where mourning doves measure a foot in length, Inca doves have a pale gray to tan scaled quaillike appearance, with chestnut-colored wing primaries.

Turkeys are also native to the Southwest. Pheasants, especially where there is agriculture thanks to irrigation, are also available.

Unlike the Basin and the Rockies, the Southwest has some factors that will greatly influence upland bird hunting, especially in the future. Development, and the subsequent loss of game habitat, is a critical issue across North America; however, water has always been worth more than gold in the West, particularly the Southwest. Native people grew crops where they could, using specialized species of plants that could take advantage of the harsh desert's lack of water. Modern agriculture, created through irrigation, and the growth of the human population, thanks largely to air conditioning, demands more from an already thin water resource. What happens when the water is gone? Will the birds adapt and survive?

THE HIGH SIERRAS AND PACIFIC NORTHWEST

"Climb the mountains and get their good tidings. Nature's peace will flow into you as sunshine flows into trees. The winds will blow their own freshness into you, and the storms their energy, while cares will drop off like autumn leaves," wrote John

Muir, about his experiences in northern California's Sierra Nevada mountains. Muir, like Emerson and Thoreau, believed that in wilderness lay truth and man's ultimate salvation. As he realized the importance of the Yosemite Valley and other natural wonders of the Sierra range, he became the land's strongest advocate, a wilderness prophet, and founder of the Sierra Club.

There must be something to the idea that California is a land rife with more than grapes and almonds. Maybe it's the mountain water or elevation. Whatever the case, Muir, a Scot, developed a number of eccentricities living in the Golden State. He once climbed to the top of a 100-foot pine in a gale just to be closer to the song of the wind in the needles. He was also said to communicate with birds and pine trees. He called the sugar pine the "priest of pines." (So how nutty is talking to a dog?)

Muir also influenced President Teddy Roosevelt. Muir's activism on behalf of Yosemite, the Sequoias, and Kings Canyon eventually put these areas under federal protection. In addition, Muir prepared the soil for what would eventually become both the National Park Service and the National Forest Service.

From Mojave to Lassen, California, the Sierra Nevada range forms a 400-mile spine for the Golden State. The 14,000-foot-tall granite and basalt peaks of the mountains were formed by uplifts and drops of landmasses and volcanic activity. Wave after wave of rock strata was heaved, tossed, and eroded to create this inspiring wilderness.

Spanish missionary Fray Pedro Font named the mountains. Looking at the peaks he described them as *una gran sierra nevada* (a great snowy range). In January of 1844, explorer John Charles Fremont asked local Indians how to cross the gentler elevations of the mountains, south of Lake Tahoe. One Indian told Fremont that the trail was very hard—six sleeps in summer, and you should not go in winter. "Rock on rock, snow on snow," the Indian said. Even if Fremont got past the snow, he would not be able to get down the mountain. Fremont ignored the warning, got blizzard-bound and nearly starved. His party ate everything on four legs, including his dog, Tlamath. Still, they made it. Three years later, the Donner party tried to cross the same mountains. They weren't so fortunate. From a diary: "Mrs. Murphy was here yesterday. She thought she would commence on Milton and eat him. I do not think she has done so yet, it is so distressing. . . ." Yet the risk-taker could find wonders beyond imagination in those mountains, 3,500-year-old Sequoia trees that were up to 40 feet across the trunk, 300-foot-tall Redwoods, and in 1848, gold.

The Sierras reflect a continent's vegetation as you climb up their flanks. In the foothills, at the base of the mountains, grass, live oaks, sycamores and chaparral—the thorny shrub that gave the name chaps to the leather overpants cowboys wear—dominate the dry upper Sonoran zone. California or valley quail, mountain quail, turkeys, and doves were the original game birds found here. Chukars and pheasants followed agriculture into this area.

Moving up the mountain, you meet the transition zone's yellow or ponderosa pine (Muir was fascinated by the hum of the wind in its needles). Warm summers, cool winters, and lots of moisture are typical of the transition zone climate. Blue grouse and some mountain quail can be found in the lower reaches of this zone. The Canadian zone is still blue grouse domain. Cool summers and cold winters with lots of snow make conditions right for red fir and lodgepole pine. The subalpine belt from timberline to forest is the Hudsonian zone, where a 3-month growing season, warm summers, always chilly nights and wet soils specialize plant and animal life. Heather, Indian paintbrush, gnarled whitebark pines, and pikas—a whistling, rabbitlike mammal—are Hudsonian timberline dwellers. Above the timber, in the arctic-alpine zone, intense solar radiation can raise temperatures dramatically; there is little rain and most snow is blown away by the wind. Still, plants like rockfringe, wallflower, and prickly phlox hang on.

As the Sierra Nevadas flow north they become wetter. For example, Washington's Olympic Peninsula hosts North America's only temperate zone rain forest. The mountains follow the coastline into Oregon, Washington, British Columbia, and up into Alaska in a 100-mile-wide swatch of forest and 15,000 foot-tall peaks.

Glaciers are still forming this land. As glaciers retreat—a process that has been taking place during a warm spell over the last several hundred years—they leave land open to an ordered forest succession cycle. It begins with a pioneer of the plant kingdom, like *dryas drummondii,* a tough plant that is able to root in the sparse, sandy soil and spread out in dense mats. As generations of *dryas* complete their life cycle, they set in motion processes that will allow the next succession species to take over, releasing nutrients back into the soil and helping to create the conditions for the growth of the next generation of larger plants. Joining *dryas* in this cycle are moss, horsetails, dwarf fireweed, and other plants that can find life in tiny pockets of soil created from the retreating glacier. Alders follow the *dryas,* moss, and horsetails. Black cottonwoods, then sitka spruce, then western hemlock follow the alders.

The moisture of the Pacific Ocean makes the forests of the northern Sierra quite lush. Mosses garnish douglas firs, sitka spruce, and western hemlock with festoons of green. In some places the moss is 3 to 4 inches thick, both on the ground and around tree limbs. Ferns, lichens, and other moisture-loving plants also blanket the forest's understory. Where there is a break, deciduous plants grow and serve as browse for elk, deer, and other wildlife.

Upland gunners hunt ruffed, spruce, and blue grouse, turkeys, and mountain quail through Oregon and Washington, and ptarmigan farther north. Ptarmigan are grouse family members that are adapted to the far north country. These chunky-bodied, short-legged birds have a short tail and stubby but powerful wings. There are several species specifically adapted to living anywhere from above the timberline to willow swamps.

DOVES

The thing about doves is that they don't look as hard to hit as they are. They don't fly all that high, you get to see them coming, and they're ordinarily not all that fast. It's just that they can read your mind and learn your personal weaknesses.

Gene Hill

In 1822 Charles Lucien Bonaparte, a French ornithologist, came to Philadelphia, Pennsylvania, the City of Brotherly Love, to study birds. One of the species he encountered was a foot-long, gray-colored bird with a tannish breast and iridescent pink about the neck. It had a sleek, fast-looking body, swept-back wings and a streamlined tail. The bird struck Bonaparte in a unique way. He ended up naming the bird *Zenaida macroura,* in honor of his 19-year-old cousin bride, whose name was Zenaide. The odd thing about this is that both Lucien's and Zenaide's fathers were brothers of Napoleon Bonaparte, who brought a great deal of turmoil and war to Europe, quite contrary to the dove's image as a bird of peace.

Doves have had a split personality throughout time: Doves were a sacred bird among the Phoenicians, Philistines, Assyrians, and Egyptians. The Hebrews regarded the dove as a symbol of purity and the image of the spirit of God. The Greeks revered the doves that drew Venus's chariot. Doves were also regarded as a symbol of fertility and soil. For early Christians, the white dove represented the Holy Spirit, the Virgin, spiritual love, innocence, and sorrow. Yet Hindus regarded doves as a messenger of death or a steed of the god of love. Medieval Europe's monasteries and manors had large "dovecotes" where doves were kept for food and sacrifice.

Native people in the southwestern United States were more practical about doves. Southern Arizona's Papagos caught doves in cage traps made of split giant cactus. They also shot roosting doves with arrows. The Yavopai of west-central

Arizona rarely shot doves and other migratory birds, but relished the eggs when boiled. Hopi youths baited birds in deadfall traps. The Pueblo people associated the sound of doves calling with water, an important resource. They also attributed it to supplications for rain, and believed doves were a winnower of seeds and teller of falsehoods.

In the East, the Delawares called doves "one who prays earnestly." Potawatomi mothers used doves in a children's morality tale: When the teacher who was going to tell all the birds about how to build their nests and other important bird matters came by, Dove fell asleep and missed most of the lesson. This is why doves build such flimsy nests.

Christopher Columbus had a Noah-like experience with doves. In early September of 1492, Columbus was looking for a more direct route to Cathay (China). He left the Canary Islands, off the northwestern coast of Africa, with a crew that was scared of falling off the face of the flat Earth, almost to the point of mutiny. They sailed on through September. Then on September 23, a "tortola," a small ground dove, was spotted. The captain eventually found more birds, easing the crew's fears about landfall. The crew actually followed the flights of the doves into Samana Cay in the Bahamas.

Other Spanish and English explorers noted the presence of doves in North America without specifically recording the doves they encountered. The abundant passenger pigeon (estimated population 3.5 billion) held more of their attention. It wasn't until the publication of *Natural History of Carolina, Florida and the Bahama Islands,* by Mark Catesby, who came to the New World in 1712, that mourning doves were identified as a unique North American species. Catesby drew the bird against a setting of natural flora, much like John James Audubon, George Edwards, and Alexander Wilson would. Later references to doves included those by Thomas Jefferson and explorers Meriwether Lewis and William Clark.

In more recent times, a piece of Georgia folklore has it that when a girl first hears the call of a mourning dove in spring, she is supposed to take nine steps forward then nine backward and in her shoe she will find a hair of the man she will marry. It doesn't say how she is supposed to find this guy, though. Perhaps he's out shooting doves come September. Wanted: Good woman who knows how to clean doves. Send picture of retriever and bird gun. . . .

NATURAL HISTORY

Doves are the most plentiful and adaptable game bird in North America. Each fall upland gunners shoot about 45 million doves in the United States.

Mourning dove fossil remains date back to the Pleistocene epoch, 1.8 million years ago, a time characterized by receding continental ice sheets and the dawn of human beings.

Doves are part of the *Columbidae* family, which includes all doves and pigeons. North America has three species of doves: White-winged and Inca doves are the two southwestern species, while mourning doves are found throughout the continent.

Mourning dove colors range from dark in the East to lighter in the West. There are four subspecies: *Zenaida macroura carolinensis* that live in the East and the Midwest; *Zenaida macroura marginella,* a pale western bird that inhabits the area from southern Canada to Mexico west of the Rocky Mountains; *Zenaida macroura macroura,* a bird of the West Indies and Florida Keys; and *Zenaida macroura clarionensis,* birds that live on Clarion Island, off the western Mexico coast.

Prior to the European settlement of North America, eastern doves frequented the openings created in the forest canopy by lighting strikes. The birds also thrived in middle America's mixed habitat of prairie and woodlands and in the Far West because the birds are so adaptable.

Opening lands to more intensive agriculture during the Civil War and the years that followed boosted dove numbers. Farmlands held more dove food, especially waste grains and weedy edges for seeds. Also, Midwest shelterbelt planting efforts, designed to prevent the wind erosion seen during the Dust Bowl of the 1930s, offered more roosting and nesting habitat. In addition, the dams and ponds built to serve both agriculture and human settlement created more water sources. By 1964, there

Doves are the most plentiful and adaptable gamebird in North America. Each fall upland gunners shoot about 45 million doves in the United States.

were 37 million acres of irrigated farmland in the United States. As a result of these human activities, dove population densities increased.

Dove range has expanded since the early 1900s. Biologists note expansions in both breeding and wintering ranges, and increases in overall dove populations, especially since the 1970s. Doves today are moving into the safety of suburbia, where they can find food easily in bird feeders as well as weed seeds from road edges and on development-disturbed land. Homeowner hedges and ornamental trees like conifers make wonderful roosting and nesting cover, and water sources, including everything from birdbaths to retention ponds, are rife in suburban areas. In many areas, doves are feeding on adjacent farmlands early and late, then moving back to the security of suburbia at midday, a twist on similar human movements in bedroom communities.

Still, mortality factors take 58 percent of all adult doves and 69 percent of all juveniles annually. Hunters account for 20 percent of overall mortality. Perhaps the Potawatomi story about doves and their sloppy nests offers one account of why the average dove lives only 12 to 18 months. Yet some doves live well beyond a year. One banded bird reached 19 years of age.

MIGRATION

Doves, snipe, and woodcock are North America's three migratory upland gamebirds. Doves can fly up to 55 miles per hour, a speed clocked via automobile. This kind of wing power helps the birds migrate. Doves breed across North America, from southern Canada all the way south to Central America. The birds' winter range extends from southern New York west through southern California and northern Mexico.

Migration begins in late summer, when the birds' pituitary gland is stimulated by fewer hours of daily sunlight. The pituitary gland kicks a dove's metabolism into high gear, and the bird accumulates fat. When this accumulated fat reaches a level that will allow long flights, birds head south. Cold rainfall, falling temperatures, and southerly winds also stimulate migration. When the time is right, the birds fly at low altitudes, just over the treetops. The birds find their way by topography, winds, the position of the sun and stars, and Earth's magnetic fields, which influence an internal compass. Some research also suggests that doves use olfactory reception (sense of smell) to find their way south.

Like waterfowl flyways, six main areas are most important for wintering doves:

The Carolinas—North Carolina gets a large number of wintering birds from the eastern seaboard, while South Carolina gets birds from Kentucky, Tennessee, and central areas east of the Mississippi River.

The Deep South—Louisiana, Mississippi, Alabama, Georgia, and Florida get wintering doves from the East and the central plains.

Texas—Texas's doves come from the central area and the plains states.

California and Arizona—The bulk of the West's birds spend their winters in these two areas.

Mexico—Birds from the southern plains join with copious local populations south of the border.

Central America—Nearly 11 percent of all birds banded and collected in the United States travel into Central America.

Heading north in the spring, the birds go through the same process in reverse. Doves tend to return to the same breeding and wintering grounds each year.

Dove nests have been found in every month of the year in wintering areas, although the usual nesting time is late spring to August, with a marked decline in September. Paired doves form strong bonds and are monogamous throughout one nesting season, although they sometimes stay together on the wintering grounds, too. One nesting cycle—from eggs to young adult—takes 32 days to complete. Doves may nest as often as five or six times per year. Usually only two or three nestings are completed. High winds and thunderstorms claim most of the chicks. Grackles, crows, blue jays, and cats also cause problems for nesting birds.

FOOD

Doves are very selective in what they eat, yet their diet includes everything from tree seedlings to farm crops. The overwhelming majority of dove food is weed seeds. Choice items include sunflower seeds, ragweed, pigweed, pokeweed, buckwheat, poppies, hemp, mustard, and pine seeds. In the East and Midwest, grass, spurge, pine, goosefoot, amaranth, buckwheat, mustard, composite, flax, and agricultural crops are important foods. In the West, it is purslane, pink, borage, polemonium willow, walnut, plaintain, and cape. Of these foods, doves can metabolize between 71 and 94 percent of the energy in reed canarygrass, Indian corn, sunflowers, broomcorn panicum, sorghum, thistle, timothy, and wheat.

During migration, agricultural foods become more important. Illinois studies showed autumn dove food was 60 percent agricultural crops. In New York, agricultural food ingested by doves between spring and autumn was 76 percent. During the winter months, agricultural food is even more important. In Ontario, it was nearly 89 percent of a dove's diet. Similar findings occurred in other areas: Oklahoma, 62 to 82 percent; Missouri, 99 percent; Florida, 93 percent.

As with many upland birds, insects and other critters account for a small proportion of dove food. Doves have been known to eat grasshopper eggs, ants, scale insects, beetles, sow bugs, clover seed chalcids, and chewing lice. Yet the most common animal in a dove's diet is the snail. Seventeen different species of both live and dead snails are eaten. The main attraction is not the snail, but its shell, to satisfy calcium needs during nesting season.

Doves need to eat approximately 10 to 20 percent of their body weight daily, about half an ounce of food. Another important item for digestion is grit (sand and gravel). Doves are gallinaceous, meaning they have a gizzard that uses grit to grind food so it can be digested and converted to energy. Doves prefer limestone, cinders, chert, quartz, clamshell fragments, and other items for grit.

Doves also need water for digestion. A bird's minimum daily water requirement is 2.8 percent of its body weight. However, doves can go for 4 or 5 days without water at 70 degrees. At 100 degrees, however, the birds must drink four times as much water. Doves can get this water in about 60 seconds: however, not just any water source will do. Doves drink by filling their bills with water, tilting their heads back and swallowing. For this reason, a shallow, still puddle is best, although the birds will use small ponds, river sandbars, and other water sources.

Doves typically feed and water first thing in the morning, then find an area to rest. Later in the afternoon they return to feed and water. Males range farther to feed, up to 5 miles, while females might range just 3 miles. Occasionally, the birds make short forays at midday to feed, especially if they are migrating through an area, or winter metabolic rates require more food more often so the bird can stay warm.

HUNTING DOVES

One cool mid-September afternoon, the phone rings. Wildlife artist Dennis Burkhart is on the other end, telling me that we have to check out a new dove spot he found in Lancaster County. Denny and I have shared duck blinds, grouse woods, and other dove fields. I know that when Denny says he has found a spot, it's time to go. He has a knack for migratory birds, especially woodcock, ducks, and doves.

Lancaster County, Pennsylvania is best known for its bucolic Amish countryside. The Amish are a religious sect that refuse modern conveniences such as cars, electricity, and phones. They prefer to farm with mule-drawn plows and live simply, in harmony with Earth. However, the same pretty countryside and rich farmland soil that draws the Amish also draws "English," modern people who use autos, computers, and conveniences such as strip malls. This culture clash splits Lancaster County's personality: Some areas are quite rural, others very urban and suburban. We're headed for the boundary between those two worlds.

Lancaster doves recognize that suburban areas offer the safety of close association with human beings. Early and late in the day, however, the birds seek the abundance of food on nearby farmlands. That year it was wet, so not many farmers could cut corn silage like they usually do early in September, but some dry, cool weather was changing things.

In a long, broad, gently-sloped valley, about half a mile from a conifer-ringed housing development, was a semi-secluded corn silage field. Half the field had been harvested, most of it turned back under earth to ready the ground for a winter wheat crop rotation schedule. The remainder of the field's crop was being taken off daily in small chunks.

Denny and I arrived at the field in late afternoon with plenty of shells, some water, some dove decoys, and high hopes. Denny explained how the birds flew down the valley to feed then back up to the conifers to roost at dusk. We positioned the decoys about 25 yards into the field, loaded our shotguns, and sat on our stools to wait for the flights to begin.

Gunning a feeding field is the primary way to hunt doves. The trick is to find an area where doves are actively feeding, then position shooters to take birds coming into the field to feed.

The first birds appeared in small squadrons of three of four, as doves usually do in a feeding field, and when they sailed in close enough, we took a couple each. The shooting was slow, but steady, reminding me of a roost/feeding field shoot I shared with Denny and several other friends a few years earlier, where the birds came in much the same way. I was thinking about that place, hoping Denny appreciated it as much as I appreciated the invitation to join him, when movement low on the horizon in the field we were gunning caught my eye. At first I thought it was a big, knotted flock of starlings rising. But the wingbeats, the movement was wrong. They were doves.

The flock of about 200 doves rose up off the field, some birds joining in as it passed overhead, other birds alighting down in the field, rejoining those already feeding. To the left of the first flock, another flock of perhaps 400 doves performed the same maneuver. Other gunners way up in the field started shooting, and soon there were several huge flocks of hundreds of doves each circling the field.

I don't remember all the details of the shooting, except that it was fast, and I took a double, the birds falling neatly, well-shot, to the plowed red clay, Denny's "Good shot!" riding the wind.

The number of birds in that field was amazing. Closer to evening, I remember looking up toward the development and seeing a river of doves moving out of those conifers toward the waste grain and weed seeds laid bare by silage cutting. Conditions were perfect; the field was one of the first in the area to be cut near a major roosting area. Thousands, perhaps tens of thousands of birds were in the field that night.

We finished our 12-bird limit well before the sun sank into the West, but we stayed just to watch the birds, how they moved. It was awe-inspiring, such abundance. I remember thinking how lucky I was to see this.

* * * *

Unlike most other upland birds and waterfowl, doves were not an important source of market gunner income. The only reference comes from California, where, during the mid-1890s, the state Fish and Game Commission recorded over 5,000 doves fetching a nickel each at markets in San Francisco and Los Angeles. By 1900, 12 states had protected doves on a year-round basis and 19 others offered protection at certain times of the year. Dove seasons varied from 2 to 9 months.

Today, doves are the third most abundant bird species—*the* most abundant gamebird—in North America. Biologists estimate 475 million doves live on this continent. Hunters take more doves in the continental United States than all other gamebird species combined. Although hunters have removed 40 million birds annually since the mid-1970s, 165–207 million die of natural causes each year.

Despite these facts, dove shooting remains controversial. Some people regard doves as songbirds; others see a gamebird. This clash of ideas has led to much turmoil. William Hornaday, avid hunter and conservationist, opposed granting doves gamebird status and called dove hunting "another thorn in my flesh." Even Aldo Leopold, the father of American wildlife management, glossed over doves in his *1931 Report on a Game Survey of the North Central States,* despite the dove seasons in Illinois, Minnesota, and Missouri, which were within his study area.

Traditional dove techniques include gunning feeding fields, water holes, or roosts, and pass shooting flight lanes into these areas.

Shooting doves is a matter of practice. Skeet, trap, or sporting clays will up your odds.

More recently, North Dakota Senator Stella Fritzell received a death threat during her term of office. It was related to her espousal of dove hunting, not other more controversial issues. In Indiana in the mid-1980s, doves were designated as game-birds after years of discussion. The designation failed to end the debate. *Audubon* magazine, for example, hosted some of the debate on both sides, but eventually had to cut off the discussion after several issues. There was simply too much. During the 1990s in South Carolina, a parent/child dove hunt with the slogan "Shoot for the Future—Don't Use Drugs" resulted in protestors picketing the state capital, Columbia, and vowing to demonstrate at hunting sites. This didn't happen, but it does show how hot tempers can get when it comes to doves.

Currently, 38 states permit dove hunting: In the East, Alabama, Delaware, Florida, Georgia, Illinois, Indiana, Ohio, Kentucky, Louisiana, Maryland, Mississippi, North Carolina, Pennsylvania, South Carolina, Rhode Island, Tennessee, Virginia, and West Virginia allow dove hunting. Wisconsin is now considering a dove season. In the Midwest and Rocky Mountains, Arkansas, Colorado, Kansas, Missouri, Nebraska, New Mexico, North Dakota, Oklahoma, South Dakota, Texas, Montana, Wyoming, and Idaho allow dove hunting. In the West, Arizona, California, Nevada, Oregon, Utah, Washington and Hawaii are dove states. In Canada, British Columbia is the only province that permits dove hunting. South of the United States border, Costa Rica, El Salvador, Guatemala, Honduras, Mexico, and Nicaragua are popular dove centers, especially for traveling gunners.

Leaders in dove harvests in the United States are Texas, which has had bags as high as 7 million doves; South Carolina, 4 million; Mississippi, 3 million; California, 3 million; and Alabama, 3 million. However, the states with the highest dove harvest per square mile were South Carolina, with 132 birds harvested per square mile; Mississippi, with 70 birds; Tennessee, with 68; Louisiana, with 61; and Alabama, with 58.

States with the most dove shooters include Texas, with 425,000-plus shooters; Pennsylvania and California, with 200,000 each; and Mississippi and Louisiana, with 130,000-plus each.

* * * *

There are five basic dove hunting techniques:

Feeding Fields

Gunning a feeding field is the primary way to hunt doves in North America. The trick is to find an area where doves are actively feeding, then position shooters to take birds coming into the field to feed. That sounds simple. But there is more here than meets the eye.

First, feeding fields vary a lot across the continent. Here in Pennsylvania and throughout most of the East, cut corn silage fields are the classic dove feeding fields. In eastern Kansas, feeding fields could be acres of sunflowers. In Arizona or Texas, a feeding field could be a grain field fed by irrigation or a weedy pasture.

Also, locating birds requires a good deal of scouting. One of the best ways to locate a feeding field is to follow flights of doves using binoculars and a vehicle. Fred

Herr, another Lancaster County dove hunter, has a knack for finding good dove areas like this. A few weeks before dove season, he likes to cruise back roads between 9 A.M. and 10 A.M., looking for cut corn silage, seeded winter wheat fields, barley, and other grains. He pays particular attention when he spots doves on telephone lines or in a dead tree in the middle of a field.

Thirty or 40 doves sitting on a power line near a feeding area like a cut corn silage field is a good indicator that hundreds of birds could be using the area, Herr says. When Herr spots a clump of birds, he asks the landowner for permission to hunt the property. (An information card, with your name, address, phone number, hunting license information, and auto plate number is a handy tool for getting on private property. We'll look closer at this later on.) Herr then walks the field. "If the birds get up and go about 200 yards before lighting back down, you've got yourself a honey hole," according to Herr.

After locating several feeding fields comes the actual hunting—it's more shooting than hunting. The basic idea is to choose a spot in the field where doves will fly over you and take the birds as they pass within shooting distance. On clear, sunny days Herr likes to hunt feeding fields between 3 P.M. and 5 P.M. If the weather is overcast with a drizzle the action can last all day.

Most gunners wear drab clothing or camouflage and use natural cover, like a patch of weeds or a few stalks of standing corn to break up their outline in the field. The trick is staying very still until the moment you are ready to shoot. Mount a shotgun before you're ready to shoot incoming doves and you will see juking, dodging aerobatics that would make both the Red Baron and Eddie Rickenbacker green with envy.

Refining the game of picking good shooting spots in a feeding field is another matter. Florida outdoor writer and broadcaster Bob McNally interviewed 30-year veteran Savannah, Georgia dove hunter Jim Dillard about this for an October, 1987 story in *Southern Outdoors*. Dillard's comments about doves using a field's "structure" like big bass use a lake bottom's structure continue to make a lot of sense.

Dillard recommended that hunters who desire to shoot more doves keep the structure idea in mind. He suggested paying particular attention to field structure: gaps in the field's surrounding timber—doves often move through these areas; mid field islands, which can be perching sites for doves; the lines formed by fences, powerlines, ditches, and even farming patterns, which doves use to navigate; hills; points of cover; field corners; heavy timber, especially conifer stands, which often serve as roosts; and water holes.

Dillard also suggested staying mobile, being able to move to a better spot in a field if that becomes necessary. Sometimes moving as little as a couple of feet can make a world of difference, especially if birds use particular flight lanes in and out of a field.

Fred Herr is also cautious about overgunning any dove hunting area, especially feeding fields and roosts. A good feeding field can withstand some gunning pressure, but Herr said he has had too many experiences where lots of doves drew lots of shooters. Some of these shooters were less than sportsmanlike. They rained shot on barn roofs, made lots of noise, and ended up getting the property closed to hunting, Herr said.

In feeding fields, roosts, and waterholes, six to a dozen dove decoys can be used as both attractors and to draw attention away from a shooting position.

Roosts

Doves gather in the safety of large groups in dense cover when spending the night.

Gunning a dove roost is very much like gunning a feeding field. The basic idea is for shooters to establish positions along flight lanes leading into a roost and take birds as they return from feeding in late afternoon, or as they leave to feed in the morning. A classic roost gunning spot might be a hill in the shallow valley that leads to the roost.

Finding a roost, like locating feeding fields, is a matter of scouting. The best way is to follow birds back to the roost in the evening. Usually, doves prefer roosting in dense cover. In the East, a classic dove roost is a large stand of young conifers near feeding areas and water. The Midwest's shelterbelts are roost cover. In the Southwest, trees are replaced by cactus.

If you get permission to hunt a roost, treat it with care. Roosts are some of the most productive dove spots. They are also easily ruined by too much gunning. Shoot a roost too often, or hunt too close to it and the birds will find a new roost. Hunt a roost sparingly and only with good friends.

Pass Shooting

Sometimes when a dove gunner can't get access to feeding fields or a roost, a spot on a flight lane is available. Under the right circumstances, pass shooting can offer every bit as much action as a feeding field or roost. Things can also change quickly, doves being migratory, and today's pass shooting hotspot is tomorrow's long, empty-sky wait. Keep your scouting up-to-date.

Waterholes

Most important in the dry Southwest, waterholes are dove magnets. However, I've gunned over waterholes in the East during drought conditions and had success there, too. The best dove waterhole is a large puddle near a feeding area. A shallow-sloped creek bank or river sandbar, where the birds can light and walk up to the water for a drink can also work.

Basically, gunning a waterhole involves locating water that is used regularly by the birds—look for dove tracks and droppings around the puddle—then setting an ambush. Dove decoys work wonders here. It's a little bit like duck hunting.

Jump Shooting

Walking up doves is usually a tactic reserved for those slow times when the birds just aren't flying and you (or the dog) need a stretch. The basic idea is finding birds to flush within gun range. Some gunners prefer walking up doves to other kinds of dove hunting. The targets are more difficult, but the satisfaction of taking birds can be great in jump shooting.

You can jump shoot doves in feeding fields, if you can get close enough. Another good tactic for midday, when the birds are loafing, is for two gunners to walk a hedgerow, narrow shelterbelt, or a conifer stand to flush doves. In the Southwest, loafing areas are often patches of mesquite, saltbush, or cactus in the middle of low desert terrain. Gunners there say doves will hold in these areas until shooters are upon them, then flush up like a covey of quail, offering great shooting.

Although I've never tried it, I think it would be neat to sneak a well-used dove waterhole, just like you might jump ducks under the same circumstances.

Jump shooting doves is usually tougher than while gunning feeding fields or roosts. The shots are usually longer, trickier. Take a limit of doves jump shooting and you've accomplished something.

* * * *

Pass shooting on a flight lane can offer good dove action when you can't get access to feeding fields or a roost. But keep your scouting up-to-date; things change quickly.

Dove hunting is not gear-intensive like waterfowling, but having some comfort items makes sense.

Clothing for dove hunting should be comfortable and drab. Most gunners like camouflage, but tans and greens can work just as well. Loosely woven cotton, because it absorbs perspiration and dries quickly, is a good fabric choice, since most dove hunting is warm-weather sport.

Footwear can be anything from snakeproof boots and chaps, which are a realistic necessity in some locales, to sneakers. However, it would be hard to beat a good pair of leather hiking boots for most situations.

Some gunners like shooting vests to hold their shells and personal items. Others prefer strap vests because they are cooler. (Never keep downed birds in a game bag. There's too much heat there.) Many dove gunners like the shell aprons, or over-under utility pouches that trap and skeet shooters use, to carry ammo and spent casings.

A small tote bag—I've used an olive Army surplus mussette bag for years—that can go over the shoulder and carry gear, shells, and other important things for the hike to and from the dove fields is a good idea. Other hunters use shooting stools with pouches below. A canteen or bota bag makes a great dove field refresher.

For some reason, dove decoys are not very popular where I hunt. Yet six to a dozen decoys used as both attractors and to draw attention away from a shooting position work. In a feeding field, I like a couple of small groups of decoys on the ground about 25 yards out, as range markers and attractors. In a roost shoot, I often place decoys in dead tree limbs near my shooting position, or use a dove pole—a long, multiforked branch that can carry decoys and be set up to look like a tree in the roost. Dove poles can also be used in feeding fields.

Some other comfort items might include a small cooler to keep downed doves cool, sunglasses, a small towel to wipe away perspiration, and water bowls and jugs for hunters and their dogs.

DOVE DOGS

The basic function of a dove dog is to wait patiently with his hunter and retrieve downed game by scenting or tracking winged birds to bring them back to the hunter. Many breeds of gun dog are capable of doing this, some quite well. But for the bulk of the action, it would be hard to beat a retriever—a Lab, Golden, or Chessie—in the dove fields. Fetching downed game is what these dogs are meant to do.

A good second line of dove dogs includes springer spaniels and the versatile pointing breeds: German shorthairs, wirehairs, Brittanys, the Vizsla, and so on. These dogs usually have strong retrieving instincts and either point or roust other upland game in different settings. Jack, my German shorthair, loved fetching downed birds. Another advantage of a shorthaired dog is their ability to take heat. Sultry days that would wilt a Chessie or a Golden can be handled by a light-colored German shorthair.

It should also be noted that there are some individuals of all the breeds that do have strong retrieving desires but just don't like fetching doves—and all those feath-

Many gundog breeds can hunt doves, but its hard to beat retrievers—a Lab, Golden, or Chessie. Fetching downed game is what these dogs are meant to do.

ers coming off in the dog's mouth. Some dogs respond by spitting the bird out and walking away.

SHOOTING DOVES

Figures from the United States Fish and Wildlife Service (FWS) show that 3.1 million dove shooters made 19 million recreational trips and spent $540 million for dove hunting. A large part of this $540 million—$70 million—was for shells. FWS figures say that at this rate, on a national average, it means that 385 million shells are fired at doves per year!

A great many dove shooters across the continent heaved a sigh of relief when South Carolina gunners went on record for a study of their dove shooting habits. Hail the bravery of the South Carolinians! Bravery aside, they averaged 8.6 shots per bird bagged. Pennsylvania gunners are poorer shots, bagging a bird for each 10 shells, according to Pennsylvania Game Commission estimates.

Dove shooting hasn't changed too much in the last 50 years. Nash Buckingham had this to say about dove shooting: "All too often, however, no matter how well gun-fitted, the bird's naturally versatile and bewildering caper-cuttings bring pinned back and reddened ears to our dove gunner and his averages—rapidly deflating his ego."

Buckingham's advice for doves was this: "Don't be greedy. Swing in from behind and think only about that *one dove*. (Or any other flighting fowl for such mat-

United States Fish and Wildlife Service (FWS) figures show that, on a national average, 385 million shells are fired at doves per year!

ter.) Blot it well out, keeping swinging—and touch off. And here's a dividend tip. Just for luck—still swinging—let go of the second tube. If your initial let-off was a trifle behind, that old chant about 'the last shot got'im' might come true. You'll be pleasantly surprised and never mind which shot did the damage—you've got the quarry."

Buckingham describes his most difficult dove shot: "Picture four or five of them with gusty blasts on their tails, very low and heading directly at you across the dun-colored open terrain, with surface dust whorls making matters worse against a dark-skied background. They're hard to spot, infinitely more difficult to separate for the single try. They're sideslipping, corkscrewing and doing their best to make your gun muzzle do anything but revolve. It jumps from first one to another candidate. So you proceed to miss by a mile with your first tube and then have not the faintest idea where your second charge disappeared. What you should have done was to pick up your first customer way out in front and let him have it—twice. Remember that those doves are speeding at you at a clip almost equal that of your shot charge. So try the on-hurtling incomers farther out. It's still the hardest shot in dove shooting."

Field & Stream shooting columnist Bob Brister, a Texan, is a master dove shooter. He also gets my vote for being one of the gurus of shotgunning. (He performs all these neat tests on various shotguns and shotshell loads, most of which involve his wife driving a car towing a trailer with vertical pattern boards on it, while he shoots at the boards. For this, Mrs. Brister must have earned a fine place in Heaven.)

Brister says it's important to differentiate dove shooting from other kinds of upland gunning. High incoming angles and long crossing shots combined with high bird speeds make dove shooting more like pass shooting miniature waterfowl than grouse or quail shooting.

A summary of Brister's ideas on dove guns goes like this: Brister is largely a 12-gauge fan. His best evidence for the superiority of the 12-gauge comes from elite game shooters all over the world who have a preference for shooting 12-gauge "light game guns." For beginners, however, Brister recommends a 20-gauge autoloader to reduce kick yet handle most dove shooting situations. He also recommends a slightly longer stock on a dove gun, something solved by a slip-on rubber butt. Brister also wants a dove gun capable of rapid acceleration, because doves fly erratically, fold their wings then juke sideways, dart, dive, and otherwise throw you off.

"The easiest way to hit'em (darting birds)," Brister writes, "is to move 'to' the bird with the original gun point, watching for just a split second to see which way the dove will dart, then accelerating the barrel for a fast swing past the bird in that direction until the forward allowance looks right. Passing through makes reading the angle of flight a little more precise. This is also the only way I can satisfactorily shoot some of the new super-light guns because they are so subject to barrel stopping as the shot is fired. The accelerating swing helps compensate for that."

Brister likes interchangeable chokes: modified or full choke for jump shooting or pass shooting, skeet or improved cylinder for feeding fields and waterholes. In a double for doves, Brister would use an improved cylinder/full combination.

For loads, Brister prefers a 12- or 20-gauge load with an ounce or so of shot and 2¾ to 3 drams powder equivalent. Brister also likes the way doves fall when hit with 7½s, although No. 8s work, too. Perhaps the best ready-made factory dove loads are trap and skeet loads that throw 1⅛ ounces of shot using 3 drams powder equivalent.

Steven Bodio, a New Mexico falconer and a fine writer, has run through a number of dove guns in search of perfection—everything from an 8-pound, 32-inch barreled, Iver Johnson sidelock 12-gauge goose gun when he was a kid, to a 5-pound, 28-gauge, straight-gripped AyA Number Two sidelock. Still, Bodio seeks dove gun Nirvana in a Merkel or a Ruger with screw in chokes . . . maybe a Darne 10-gauge with special handloads of 7½ shorts. "They're all fun, all part of the quest," Bodio writes. "And I can't tell you if that's part of the nature of dove shooting, or being a gun nut, or just being alive."

"I think good dove shooters are the best game shots in the world and that they're better than the old market shooters ever were, even though I couldn't prove it," writes Charles F. Waterman. "Some of the old timers of the golden age of shotgunning really stacked up the feathered folk, but there are American dove bangers who go down into Latin America and shoot as long as they can see over their heaps of game. No complaint on that because doves are farm pests in those areas.

"Telling people how to hit doves makes me uncomfortable and I hasten to mention that all instruction is borrowed from good shots and none of it is my idea. The really good shooters generally haven't the slightest idea of how in the hell they do it and getting them to think about it will ruin their whole season. They agree on one thing: when you see a dove coming at a distance, don't start swinging on him until you're ready to shoot. Being too careful is a sure miss. Let your instincts take over. My instincts tell me to stay away from dove fields."

I think the biggest problem in shooting doves are shooters who try to swing on a dove from 100 yards out. Wait until the bird is close and you're ready to shoot before mounting the gun. Then just let your mental computer take over and calculate things like lead and swing through.

Another problem is range estimation. People want to call 75-yard doves 40-yard doves. Learn how to judge. Usually, I'm looking for color on a dove's breast before I call it close to being in range. On drab, overcast days, you just have to guess, judging the size of the bird's silhouette when the sky is cloudy. Also, spend some time shooting clay targets thrown from a portable trap before dove season so you're sharp come September. Set up the targets like incoming doves. It's fun and great practice.

My own preference in dove guns is a 12-gauge double, shooting 3 dram powder equivalent 1⅛ ounce loads of No. 7½ or 8 shot. I've used a Daly 12-gauge over-under with 26-inch barrels choked improved cylinder and modified for years with great success. I've also used a Mossberg 835 12-gauge, a Winchester Model 1300 in 20-gauge, and a Smith and Wesson 20-gauge autoloader to take doves. My current everything bird gun is a Lefever Nitro Special 12-gauge, my grandfather's gun, bored skeet.

Shotgunning is more art than science. Just about anyone can take a modern centerfire rifle with a scope and get accurate enough in a few target sessions to take deer on a regular basis. But shotgunning is not like that. It requires regular practice and an eye for the sight patterns that will break targets, then down birds.

RUFFED GROUSE

The tradition of the American ruffed grouse has been abuilding for three hundred years and has grown mainly in the Northeast, where the ruff may not be as plentiful as elsewhere but is sought by the cream of upland hunters with fine guns, tireless legs, and love.

Charles F. Waterman

Ruffed grouse are magic. There has always been a certain mysticism, a unique spirituality surrounding ruffed grouse. Ask a person who has experienced ruffed grouse first-hand—from the grouse purist, to the hiker who startles a bird along a trail—and they are quick to recount some revealing and very memorable encounters with *Bonasa umbellus*.

For example, the Ojibway or Chippewa (they call themselves Anishinabe) were among several tribes of native Great Lakes states people who believed that ruffed grouse are special creatures, imbued with mythical spiritual power, the presence of *Manitou*, the force behind the wind, the all-pervasive spirit. The Dakota (eastern Sioux) and Lakota (western Sioux) spent some time in the Lake States before being pushed on to the western prairies. They noted that grouse were magical birds because they had the sound of thunder in their wings, an ability to connect with the *wakinyan*, thunder-being spirits that lived in powerful storms.

What makes grouse so different from the average quail, pheasant or chukar? One thing is the innate wildness of both the birds and the land they live on. The places grouse dwell are usually more remote settings than the places other birds live. Compare a grouse covert in the 640,000-acre Chippewa National Forest in Minnesota's Great Northwoods, to an Iowa farm loaded with pheasants. Both are unique, but the hand of man is frequent, heavy on the farm fields. A young aspen stand

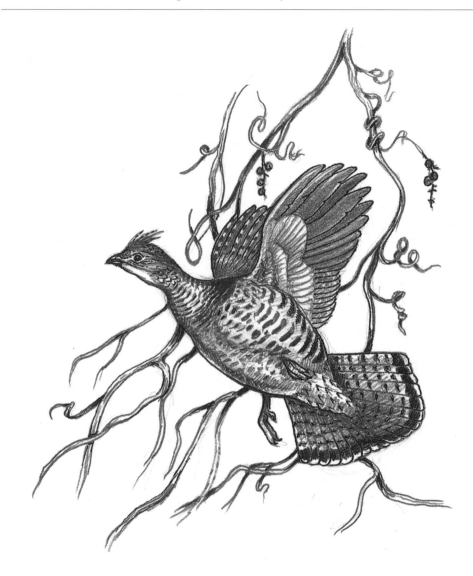

doesn't have that association. (Never mind that timber harvesting created the cut, it just *feels* more wild.) It's probably an innate cultural icon: The woods represent wild, untamed space; farmland or grasslands are closely linked with the presence of man.

The wild essence of grouse is hard to characterize without experiencing it first-hand. The best comparison is what it is like to fish for wild stream-bred trout, and know that no human hand put the fish there. Grouse can't be raised successfully in captivity and transplanted outside their natural range as can most other gamebirds. Grouse are inexorably linked to their habitat. You encounter ruffed grouse in the places where they naturally belong and on their own terms, a unique combination of past, present, and future all rolled into one. Also, you'll never shoot a grouse you

The Ojibway or Chippewa (they call themselves Anishinabe) were among several tribes of native lakes states people who believed that ruffed grouse are special creatures, imbued with mythical spiritual power, the presence of Manitou, the force behind the wind, the all-pervasive spirit.

don't earn in some way. You might shoot a limit of relatively easy birds one day. But sooner or later, you will pay for those birds in miles walked, mountains climbed, ghost birds flushing from empty points, briar gouges, bad dogs, sore muscles, long drives, little food . . . something. The balance sheet—grouse hunters rarely consider it—will always read grouse 2, hunter, 0.

The people and the dogs that specialize in hunting grouse also help make the sport unique. Dedicated grouse hunters are usually purists—some of the finest people around—yet the most demanding gunners there are. They are very fussy about such things as gun handling, hunting manners, how their dogs perform, and etiquette. Neophytes need not fear this. Lack of knowledge is not a problem for a novice who is a sportsman and gentleman. Often, purists pass along their knowledge by taking a beginner under their wing.

It takes a lot of hunting and experience to make a veteran grouse hunter and that knowledge is hard won. Few people just take up grouse hunting and get good at it. For example, I started grouse hunting in the early 1980s after a friend introduced me to a place with grouse. I read what I could about the birds, scouted, then took Jack, my German shorthair, up into the mountains before and after pheasant season to hunt. We hunted all of that first year without actually shooting a grouse. But we stuck with it. After I gained some grouse knowledge, I shared grouse hunting with a number of friends and most didn't stick with it. My barber, Ed Wallerius, was typical. He always wanted to try grouse hunting, so I took him to one of my better coverts. We covered a lot of ground quickly, flushed several birds and spotted a huge buck. But Ed didn't like all the walking and climbing hills covered with whippy maple saplings. He said he would never do it again, a choice I can respect.

Being primarily a grouse hunter, I am extremely biased about grouse dogs. A really good grouse dog can probably outperform other specialists on most gamebirds. Grouse are hard for a dog to master. One day, grouse hold for point after point. On another, they flush wild at the first tinkle of a dog bell. Some days birds will be under the dog's nose. On others, a dog pointing from 20 yards out makes them jumpy. I've seen grouse lead a dog a hundred yards through dense cover, then across a mountainside boulder field, to escape without a flush. I've also seen grouse gawk down from an aspen at a dog pointing below. Grouse dogs have to be especially savvy about bird handling because the open understory in a forest means the dog can often see a bird moving, a great temptation to break point and flush. Adaptable yet stubborn, biddable, intelligent, independent, physically strong to handle the rigors of a covert, and full of desire, intensity, and a passion to hunt are some characteristics of good grouse dogs and a rare combination to find.

Call this "Zen and the Art of Grouse Hunting," but part of the allure is the spirituality of grouse hunting. Many grouse hunters have very strong connections to the birds, the places grouse live, and the spirit of the traditions of grouse hunting. Holding a downed bird, grouse hunters speak of wanting to put the bird back into the sky, of the remorse that goes along with killing a grouse. Yet take the shotgun from the hunting equation and an essential element of the grouse experience is missing.

The physical side of grouse hunting, the walking, moving through heavy brush, the exertion, and the mental challenge involved in trying to outwit these birds

You'll never shoot a grouse you don't earn. Every easy bird is paid for in miles walked, mountains climbed, ghost birds flushed from empty points, briar gouges, bad dogs, sore muscles, long drives, little food . . . something. The balance sheet—grouse hunters rarely consider it—always reads grouse 2, hunter, 0.

The people and dogs that specialize in hunting grouse help make the sport unique. Dedicated grouse hunters are usually purists, some of the finest people around, yet the most demanding.

prepares you for a journey. It opens your mind to seeing things in a different way. There is a certain flow, a rhythm, a time when experienced grouse hunters recognize that they and their dogs and the birds are one, "in the zone," and it all happens just right. Getting there, like most spiritual journeys, is a large part of the fun of grouse hunting. Often you have to hunt a portion of a covert, or through a covert or two to get into things. But when it happens, magic is afoot.

The nature of grouse hunting demands more from a hunter than most other upland adventures. (Chukar hunting might be a notable exception.) This tends to weed out casual hunters. Grouse hunting requires a real passion to continue throughout life. Expend the time and energy necessary to understand ruffed grouse, and you will be rewarded many, many times over.

NATURAL HISTORY

Ruffed grouse are the most widely distributed nonmigratory gamebird in North America, found everywhere but the Deep South, the Great Basin, the Southwest's desert country, and central Canada's prairie region.

Currently, Minnesota calls itself North America's "house of grouse." According to Dan Dessecker, forest wildlife biologist for the Ruffed Grouse Society, "Many Minnesota grouse hunters don't know just how good they've got it." Hunters shoot more grouse in Minnesota than in any other state, averaging about 650,000 birds annually for the last several years. Yet Minnesota has only 140,000 grouse hunters, compared to other high-harvest states such as Wisconsin, with 150,000 hunters, and Michigan with 200,000 hunters. This, coupled with plenty of public hunting areas, means more flushes and more birds bagged per hunter in Minnesota.

Wisconsin and Michigan gunners annually take about 400,000 grouse each. Pennsylvania gunners have been taking between 150,000–200,000 birds annually for the last decade with an equal number of hunters. New York, Ohio, and West Virginia gunners annually average about 150,000 birds each. In the South, Virginia is the grouse leader, with about 100,000 birds annually.

Canadian grouse figures were not available; however, Ontario, New Brunswick, and most of Quebec have high grouse populations, with few hunters.

Grouse are a unique part of a larger family of birds, *Phasiandae*, which includes quail and pheasants. The grouse branch of the *Phasiandae* family includes species all over the world, from prairie chickens in the Flint Hills of Kansas, to spruce grouse in the Rocky Mountains, to capercaillie and sharp-winged grouse in Russia. The scientific name for grouse, *Bonasa umbellus*, has to do with the bird's drumming—*bonasa* means bison, a reference to drumming, and its collarlike ruff , the *umbellus*.

Twelve subspecies of ruffed grouse have been identified. In most cases it is hard to tell one bird from another, and in some areas subspecies overlap. The average

Brown or red phase grouse are found on both the Atlantic and Pacific coasts. Their coloration is a rich, rusty cinnamon brown.

ruffed grouse is 15 to 19 inches long, and weighs about 1½ pounds. A grouse's bones and body are built for quick, short flights.

Much like a hen pheasant, Grouse are covered with a camouflaging medley of brownish or gray, black, and white feathers, an adaptation that allows them to blend into the brushy, mixed-age woodlands they call home.

This unique coloration is one of the bird's most striking features. Like foxes and screech owls, grouse come in two color phases, red (or brown) and gray. Gray phase birds have an overall grayish cast, with prominently light smoke-gray tail feathers. These birds are found mostly in the continent's interior, especially in the North Country. The grayest gray phase grouse are found in northwestern Canada and Alaska. Brown or red phase grouse are found on both the Atlantic and Pacific coasts. Their coloration is a rich cinnamon brown under most circumstances, although I've seen birds that have been more of a rust color than brown. The brownest brown phase birds live in the coastal areas of Washington and Oregon, and in the southern Appalachians.

Why the color phases? Predation and location have a lot to do with it. Minnesota studies by Gordon Gullion and W. H. Marshall show that gray phase birds are less vulnerable to predation than brown phase birds. The forest floor in Minnesota and most of the North Country is a grayish hue, the color of aspen and birch leaves and needle litter. Gray grouse blend into this background. In the reddish-brown leaf

Gray phase grouse have an overall grayish cast, and are found mostly in the continent's interior, especially in the North Country.

Predation and location have a lot to do with color phases. Minnesota's gray aspen-colored forest floor holds more gray birds. Along both coasts and in the Appalachians, red phase birds blend better into reddish-brown oak and maple forest leaf litter.

litter of the oak and maple forests along the coasts and in the Appalachians, red phase birds blend into the forest floor. Although Minnesota produces its share of red phase grouse, fewer survive to breed than gray phase birds. It is easier for a goshawk to spot the off-color bird. I have also seen gray phase grouse in Pennsylvania coverts. Compared to the normal brown birds, they appeared to be apparitions flushing into the sky.

Another explanation is energy expenditure: The gray screech owls of the North Country, for example, use less energy to stay warm than the brown screech owls farther south. Coloration could also be linked to moisture. The darkest grouse are found in the Olympic Peninsula's rain forests, while some of the lightest grouse are in Utah's mountains where precipitation is less.

In most bird species, the cochlea, the site of hearing reception, is less sensitive than in mammals. Grouse are less attuned to the wide range of sounds mammals perceive, but they have 10 times more hair in receptor areas, so they can hear different intensities of sound.

Grouse rely on sight for their survival. Sight is important in mating displays, finding food, and escaping predators. Grouse can detect direction, distance, size, shape, brightness, color, depth, and motion of an object with special acuity. Grouse also have binocular vision in dim light, similar to the lizards that the entire bird family evolved from.

HABITAT

In the North Country, which includes the northeastern United States, the lake states, and eastern Canada, grouse dwell in the boreal forest, aspen parklands, and hemlock-hardwood forests. These areas have short growing seasons, very cold winters, and about 20 inches of precipitation annually. This region's climax forest of white spruce, balsam fir, paper birch, black spruce, and tamarack holds few grouse, but its early successional and transitional forests support the bulk of the continent's grouse population.

In the West, deciduous forests at sea level to 8,000 feet hold grouse. Climates vary with each mountain range, but aspen, birch, maples, and cottonwoods hold most of the birds. A contradiction to this is Idaho's thriving coniferous (mostly Douglas and subalpine firs) forest grouse population. Still, most birds prefer early successional forests.

Grouse in Iowa, Missouri, Arkansas, and Illinois live in oak- and hickory-, dominated forests. But most birds will be found in 8- to 20-year-old stands of forest peppered with serviceberry, hop hornbeam, flowering dogwood, and blackhaw viburnum. Also, narrow bottomland hardwoods along streams and old agricultural fields, abandoned 20 to 50 years ago, and growing up in cedar, oak, hickory, plum, persimmon, locust, multiflora rose, and dogwood, hold some birds.

In the southern Appalachians of Virginia, West Virginia, North Carolina, Georgia, Tennessee, and Kentucky, grouse live in hardwood forests dominated by oak, beech, black and yellow birch, and red maples. Some of these areas have highlands that resemble the vegetation of the northwoods. However, birds also survive in mountain laurel, Catawba rhododendron, and grass or heath balds, which have low-growing grasses and ground hugging shrubs like blueberries and other heathlike plants.

Overall, grouse range corresponds roughly with that of certain species of poplars, primarily quaking aspen and balsam poplar. High-quality, year-round grouse habitat is composed of a variety of different types of forest mixed in just the right way. All must be present in order for habitat to hold birds.

Grouse use different portions of their habitat for different purposes. For example, nesting cover is typically thigh-thick pole stage timber, with the nest usually at the base of a large tree. The best brood cover, where grouse raise chicks, is a mixture of herbaceous plants that is open on the ground, with green leaves, fruits, and insects available for food, and patchy overhead cover to protect chicks from avian predators. Small forest openings in their first 2 to 4 years of growth, woodland edges, overgrown fields, and berry patches typically provide the best source of brood cover.

Autumn grouse coverts are typically forearm-thick sapling forests. The best are 10 to 15 years old, but this depends on growing conditions. Some forests take a longer time to reach the sapling stage. A mix of food such as shrubs, grapes, greenbrier, and honeysuckle, and winter cover, like conifers, mountain laurel, or rhododendron, which offer protection from the cold and wind, is also important.

FOOD

Grouse are omnivorous browsers, meaning that they can eat and digest a wide variety of plant and animal foods; however, the bulk of their diet is composed of parts of forest herbs, vines, shrubs, and trees.

In the late 1940s, the New York State Conservation Department conducted one of the first and most intensive studies of ruffed grouse. In that now-famous study, Bump and his colleagues examined the crops and stomachs of more than 1,000 grouse and found over 330 species of plants, most belonging to the early succession forest, as well as insects. Some of the most prominent foods included cherry, birch, raspberry, blackberry, and hop hornbeam. Ants, beetles, caterpillars, and other animal foods were eaten mostly by chicks, but also by adults during the summer, yet accounted for only one percent of volume.

Some of the more important food sources in the North Country's boreal forest are aspen, paper birch, and cherry. South of boreal forests, sugar maple, red maple, black cherry, and other hardwoods are important. Grouse of the southern Appalachians feed heavily on all of the northern trees and yellow poplar, American holly, blackgum, and several oak species. Fruits, seeds, and green leaves are also important in the South.

The important foods for grouse hunters to know are: aspen, birch, cherry, oaks of all kinds, greenbrier, grapes, alder, witch hazel, apples, rose hips, highbush cranberry, kinnikinick, raspberries, service berry, sumac, huckleberry, dogwood, honeysuckle, multiflora rose, viburnum, ferns, teaberry, and cinquefoil.

During the winter months, especially in the frozen North, grouse need foods that are high in energy. Acorns and beechnuts offer birds the most calories to metabolize. Fruits like grapes and apples are next, followed by herbaceous leaves like clover, evergreen leaves, and finally catkins. Aspen buds offer a grouse 31 percent metabolizable energy; a yellow birch catkin, 38 percent; greenbrier leaves, 51 percent; clover, 57 percent; grapes and apples, 60 percent; and acorns, 78 percent. This is interesting because the predominant winter food in the north offers the least amount of energy, and the more time birds feed, the more vulnerable they are to predation.

SEASONS OF LIFE

At 17 weeks of age, a grouse chick is fully feathered in its adult plumage, except for two sharply pointed outer primary wing feathers that it won't lose until its second year. This is also the age at which grouse broods begin to break up and disperse, often called the "crazy flight" because dispersing birds have a habit of getting into trouble by flying into windows and other crazy things.

Brood break up actually starts in late summer, when the birds are 12 to 15 weeks old. Young birds start spending more time alone, away from the hen and apart from each other. By early fall birds are ready to move into new territories and establish their own breeding grounds.

Males go first, stopping when they reach the first suitable habitat not claimed by other males. Males may travel up to 2 miles, at about 250 yards per day. Females tend to travel farther, up to 3 miles, at a rate of 500 yards per day; however, distances of 5 miles are not uncommon for females. Some females have moved up to 71 miles from their brood cover.

During dispersal, both males and females are looking for winter cover and new breeding grounds. Grouse tend to be less selective when looking for fall sites. By the time the leaves have fallen, dispersal is all but finished. A second dispersal takes place in late winter, usually February or March, when the birds seek unfilled breeding territories. This movement could continue until May, mating season, the time male grouse drum. Drumming is a unique ruffed grouse phenomenon.

* * * *

Minnesota's Chippewa National Forest is land that President Teddy Roosevelt proclaimed the Minnesota National Forest in 1908. Two decades later the government finally purchased it from the Chippewa people, naming it in their honor. We were hunting the Chippewa out of Heig's Bowen Lodge, in Deer River, on Lake Winnibigbigosh. Bill Goudy, group director of field services for the Ruffed Grouse Society and

Characterizing the wild essence of grouse is hard to do: The best comparison is what it is like to fish for wild stream-bred trout, and know that no human hand put the fish there.

a good friend, suggested lodging with Bill and Gail Heig and their golden retriever, Sparky, for the trip. Woodcock paté and roast duck, served at dinner that first night, verified Goudy's advice.

Two days into the hunt, the dogs and I lurched along a rutted national forest road and stopped at what looked like a promising mid-afternoon hunting spot, a tamarack swamp. The swamp was ringed with alders and goldenrod in its openings. There was a 100-acre swatch of forearm-thick aspens, complete with a dense, fern-filled understory. Even the prerequisite stand of young conifers bordered the alders. I let Nash out of his kennel crate, while Jack, in his "box," yodeled about how evil I was for hunting the white dog instead of the old Kraut.

We started where the alders and aspen formed an edge. Immediately, Nash wheeled left and right in that animate liquid flow he became when the aroma of *Bonasa umbellus* washed into his shiny black nose. Twenty yards ahead, he slowed, liquid almost to stone, and I thought he was going to point. Instead, he hesitated, then moved on. I noticed something indistinct in the brush, a green mound. As I got closer, an ancient grouse drumming log materialized.

The log was 3 feet in diameter and about 20 feet long, one end buried over time in the earth, the other on a mound that might have once been the stump of the tree the log came from. Covered in dense green moss except in the middle, where it bowed to hug the contours of Mother Earth, the log had to be 100 years old. White-tipped grouse droppings filled a trough in the center of the log and sprinkled the sides. A dense canopy of alders and other tangled vegetation hung over the log. Seen as a whole, the log and brush was a natural amphitheater. In my mind, I could see green springtime, a large cock grouse standing on this log, strutting. The bird stops, ruff bristled. Toes dig into the moss, and his wings begin to *thrump-thrummp-thrummp*, the sound throbbing like the amplified beat of your own heart between your ears. I shivered in the cold Minnesota air and marveled at being in the presence of this site, thanking the Creator for the gifts offered there.

Coming out of the covert, I was talking to Nash like I usually did, like I might to another human being, when two balsam cutters from the nearby Anishinabe reservation heard and saw us. I stopped. We talked. They needed a ride back to their car, and a jump-start because their battery was going bad. It was a relief to learn later that the Anishinabe hold dogs to be sacred—dogs fathered the human race. I didn't want them to think my conversation in the middle of a wilderness with a dog was the kind of magic inspired from spirits in a bottle.

* * * *

The muffled drum-roll sound of a drumming grouse has been called "eerie and hypnotic." After becoming sexually mature and establishing a breeding territory, drummers stake out a 5-acre plot and rarely move more than about a quarter mile during spring mating season. A drummer's territory can overlap several larger 26-acre female territories.

Males drum most often at the break of day and twilight—too early for hawks, too late for owls. The sound, caused by the compression and release of air under the wings, usually 50 wing beats per drumming session, travels well in the forest. After the drumming, the males display by puffing up the black ruff around their neck, fanning their tail out, and strutting on their drumming log, wings down, like a boss gobbler. Males use one primary drumming log but can have several others.

Females are first attracted by the drumming, then the effectiveness of the male's displays. The pair mates only once to fertilize eggs, then the female leaves to nest. Year-old males usually have to compete with older males before they can claim a drumming space. Up to 30 percent of a grouse population may be nondrumming males. Drumming males impregnate several females. Drumming in autumn is triggered by less daylight, which creates a springlike response in the birds.

* * * *

Under most circumstances, grouse are most active early and late in the day. Peaks in activity occur during sunrise and sunset, as birds feed. During breeding season, hens are active up to 55 percent of the day and might leave the nest up to five times during the day for a half-hour feeding trip. Drummers reach peak activity at sunrise, and spend less time being active than females, about 40 percent of the day. Usually, males spend most of the day on their drumming log.

By autumn, grouse are up at sunrise, spend up to 15 minutes feeding, then loaf in a semialert state in a roosting area until early afternoon, when they begin moving to feeding areas again. The birds will feed until shortly after sunset, to tank up for the night.

With the coming of winter, grouse begin to grow comblike teeth about a quarter of an inch long on the sides of their toes. Called pectinations, these teeth act as snowshoes. The birds lose their pectinations in early spring.

Grouse also need to feed more often in winter to maintain themselves; however, two specialized behaviors help reduce energy use. The birds use young conifer stands to cut wind by 75 percent, which results in a 20 percent energy saving for the birds. Spruce, fir, and hemlock are the most important conifers. Older, taller conifer stands adjacent to bird cover could pose a problem for grouse, offering avian predators a hunting platform.

Snow roosts are another winter adaptation. When the snow is 10 inches or deeper, grouse plunge from a tree or burrow into the snow, to hide from predators and to keep warm. Outside a snow roost, the temperature could be 5 degrees below zero with a drastic wind chill. Under the snow, the temperature hovers around freezing, which reduces energy use by 30 percent. Grouse are not unique in this. Pheasants, quail, and other northern birds also use snow roosts.

One of the most contentious issues among grouse biologists is the grouse cycle, seasonal ups and downs in grouse populations every 10 years or so. What is known for sure is that the cycle is most prominent in the North, less in the southern portion of the bird's range. Lloyd B. Keith in *Ten Year Cycle*, notes that grouse cycles are primarily limited to the northern coniferous forest and aspen parklands. The cycle also corresponds with cycles of other species such as snowshoe hares, red fox, prairie grouse, and lynx. More recent research suggests that the cycle could be related to an influx of predators from the north. When snowshoe hare numbers fall, goshawks, owls, and other raptors head south and begin hunting, one prey being grouse. Other ideas have the cycle linked to aspens, which, as they reach a certain level of growth, or get stressed, communicate this to surrounding plants, and produce tannins and phenols that make the buds and other plant parts less digestible to animals. As a result, grouse must travel farther to get food, and are more likely to become prey. However, the cycle, although identified, is still a mystery.

HUNTING RUFFED GROUSE

The classic image of ruffed grouse hunting shows a pair of gentlemen gunners with fine double guns following an English setter through an amber- and crimson-leafed North Country covert, an abandoned field grown up to apples and aspen; alders where it's wet. The sky is usually bright October blue and tart. The dog work is flawless. Birds hold for points and flush across wide openings, and the gunners always shoot true.

The reality of grouse hunting is quite different: cold, rainy days; a lot of walking; empty points; poor dog work; a pumpgun that shoots left when it should shoot right; gunners who cuss being tangled in blackberry canes. Many grouse are killed by people who cruise back roads looking to pot birds feeding along grassy edges with .22 rifles.

Still, it's nice to hold the classic image in your mind, even if you have to pretend your 870 is a Parker and old Pasquale, the Lab, doesn't have a long, well-feathered tail.

* * * *

Joel Vance is right: A ruffed grouse will spit in your eye and give you ammonia in a Murine bottle to wash it out. Ruffed grouse are hard birds to hunt. Persistence can produce even the leggiest cock pheasants. Patience takes doves. Knowing where to go

is a key to unlocking the quail door. And chukars and the prairie birds are leg-power birds. Grouse require all of these skills and more—especially strong lungs and the balance of a mountain goat if you're gunning the Appalachians. Plan on hunting until you are mentally exhausted, all hope of seeing a bird gone, then *brrr*—out *Bonasa* goes and you stand there gun half-mounted, wondering what you should have done.

A few years back, Nash and I were gunning a hawthorn covert in southwestern Pennsylvania that reminded me of George Bird Evans country. After we were through the haws, we walked across the road and down the hill into a new covert. Within moments, Nash was acting birdy again. Suddenly, he pointed, indicating that a curious tangle of greenbrier in this beautiful aspen stand was the source of bird scent. I could see all but a little hump of the forest floor below the vines and there were no birds in sight. So I told Nash to quit fooling around. He remained staunch. When I took another step, the most perfect and easy double thundered into the air, 10 yards apart. All I could do was I stand there, chin on the ground, shotgun half-mounted, watching those birds glide into the main portion of the covert. Dry leaves, stirred during the flush, floated back down into the little depression from where the birds rose.

When the birds were out of sight, Nash, always the consummate gentleman, glanced back over his shoulder at me with a surly look that spoke of pure contempt. "You idiot," was pretty close to his message.

Seeking redemption, I urged him on, to follow up on the right bird, eventually getting another point and a reflush. This time, I smartly completed my mission, and a bird fell from the sky. Nash was fetching the bird back to me but stopped short behind a rotting log. He looked at me again, bird in mouth. Then he started digging, dropped the bird in the hole and trotted back to me, head high and proud, as if to further express his disgust in my lack of confidence in his abilities.

If I couldn't have laughed at this, I probably would have cried.

How Grouse Use Cover

The basic idea in grouse hunting is to flush birds from likely habitat so you can take them on the wing. If a dog is involved, the dog's job is to find birds and point them, or roust them into the air within gun range if you're using spaniels or retrievers. Then the dog is supposed to fetch the bird back.

The problem—call it a challenge—is that ruffed grouse know their habitat and, like whitetails, use it extremely well. Like whitetails, grouse feel safe only when there is a barrier between a hunter and the bird. This separation from danger is one key to understanding how grouse think.

One of the most successful grouse predator combinations is a pair of gray foxes. The foxes work as a team. One fox distracts the bird, the other sneaks in to take the bird. Grouse play this game often, and their defense mechanism is to keep some form of separation between themselves and danger, to stay constantly vigilant.

When hunters and dogs approach a covert, the birds think it is the fox game. They will lead you into impenetrable cover where you cannot follow, then *brrrr*—out the other side. They will take you to a rocky, grape-tangled section of ground that is hard to move across, then thunder off the edge of it as you stumble for footing. They

Like white-tailed deer, ruffed grouse know and use their habitat extremely well. Grouse feel safe only when there is a barrier between a hunter and the bird.

will lead you into an especially dense grove of trees, then flush from behind the thickest group. It's the way the game is played.

Thwarting this mechanism requires outthinking the birds. You need an ability to see a covert's textures, the way one stand of trees grows into a different section of plant growth; how a dense understory of "buck brush" flows into a more open rock outcropping; how the edge of aspens and alders along a swamp creates a different kind of density in a covert. Then, you need to figure out how a grouse will use these textures as escape routes.

On the aspen/alder edge, for example, a bird started in the aspens will probably move to the denser, lower alders and find a thick spot to flush. A gunner needs to be prepared for this. Always anticipate a flush. Assume there is a crouched grouse waiting to fly behind every bush, in every morass of deadfalls, in each slash pile.

It helps to think like a bird dog and hunt objectives, places that are likely to hold grouse—slashings left to rot in the middle of an aspen stand, for example. Seek out the objectives in a covert, then move into a shooting position. There are always little openings where you can shoot rather than trying to stumble through the objective. Grouse expect you to follow. When you stop and hold, the long pause unnerves the bird. Moving well through thick grouse cover is an art form, part of the Zen-like flow of the hunt that, when done properly, unites bird, covert, dog, and hunter as one.

Novice grouse hunters stumble through the thickets getting whipped by branches, trying to bull their way through the thick stuff and making a lot of noise. An experienced grouse hunter will slide through the same area, moving a bit slower, but much more quietly. The trick is finding those twisting, winding paths through the aspens. Think like a deer and follow the path of least resistance. You may have to wind and loop through places to get where you want to go, but you'll cover more ground and do it quietly.

Bird Movement

Becoming proficient as a grouse hunter demands an intimate knowledge of bird cover and how the birds use it. Learning to see the textures of cover within a covert is extremely important. Time of day and the movement patterns of grouse in the covert are also important. Experienced grouse gunners know how each cover feature relates to others.

For example, a 15-year-old clearcut grown up in cherry, maples, and some aspen lies adjacent to a head-high stand of young hemlocks. There are a couple of older apple trees in the cut near the hemlocks. Where do you find early afternoon grouse? Check the apples. Some birds will move from the hemlocks (a roosting area) to the feeding area in early afternoon. Also keep in mind that each area is different, each covert is different, each bit of cover is used differently. Often there are patterns, and birds move between a feeding area and a roost in a similar way in two different coverts. However, some days there is simply nothing you can do. The birds just won't be there.

Most of the grouse hunters I know prefer hunting from mid-afternoon to dusk rather than at any other time. This is when birds feed most and are most active. Early

Becoming proficient as a grouse hunter demands an intimate knowledge of bird cover and how the birds use it. Learn to see the cover textures within a covert, how each cover feature relates to others.

morning can be good, too. At midday, however, you will usually have to move grouse from roosting areas into more open cover before getting decent shooting. An exercise in frustration is trying to get a shot at birds booted from roosting cover in dense conifer stands, swamps, mountain laurel, and especially rhododendron hells.

I remember a late season January afternoon when Denny Burkhart; his Brittany, Lady; Barry Franciscus; and Jack and I had 26 flushes from birds that were using a rhododendron-filled creek bottom adjacent to a clearcut for roosting cover. Dog bells tinkled then stopped, wings roared, and hunters groaned, trying to get untangled enough from the twisted, gnarled stems of the big-leafed rhoddies to see flushing birds. The birds knew that buzzing up to the top of the plants then skimming along for 50 yards or so would put them out of harm's way.

I've never hunted grouse without a dog, because I wouldn't want to, although it can be done. Two good hunting partners can work as a team to probe objectives. A single hunter can move through grouse cover, stopping occasionally to unnerve birds for a flush. For grouse hunters without canine partners, finding downed birds is more difficult. Nothing can conceal a perfectly dead grouse like a leafy forest floor. So spend some extra time looking for downed birds. One trick to make this easier is marking where you shoot from (use your blaze orange cap), then moving in small circles around this mark, until you locate the downed bird.

GROUSE SHOOTING

Short, light, and fast-moving are the adjectives many gun writers use to portray what the ideal grouse gun should be. A lot of novice gunners have bought into this idea and ended up with expensive guns that were quite disappointing.

Consider some typical shots at grouse: The 15-yard straightaway pointed bird, the 25-yard crossing bird your partner boots up; the 35-yard winter grouse that won't sit too long under a point. All of these shots are taken in dense, brushy cover where there is usually little room to swing a shotgun. Even if you could, grouse are quick and move out of a shooting range fast. Grouse shooting is usually a quick affair, under 40 yards and in brush.

Also, you'll be carrying a gun over deadfalls and under tree branches. You'll need one hand free for balancing while walking on some Appalachian slopes. This means the grouse gun should be well-balanced and lighter than a duck blind shotgun.

Finally, connecting pellets with a speeding grouse moving through dense brush at distances up to 40 yards calls for a fast load that produces a dense pattern. Modified or improved cylinder chokes work well for longer shots and are good choices for single barrel guns. Double gun enthusiasts often have the first barrel choked skeet for pointed birds that flush close.

What would make the ideal grouse gun? The English game gun, a light, 6½- to 7-pound 12-bore side-by-side with open chokes seems like an ideal combination for grouse. World-class game shooters would agree. Most use a series of English-style game guns for everything from Scotland's red grouse to South American pigeon shoots and gray partridge in Hungary.

George Bird Evans, grouse hunting's guru, espoused the English ideal in his "gun with a history." After trying several American doubles, Evans used a 12-bore Purdey given to him by Dr. Charles Norris, of Philadelphia, for his upland shooting. Still hunting hard well into his 80s, rotator cuff injuries in his shoulders, the result of falls, required a lighter gun. Evans switched to a light 28-gauge AyA double proportioned much like the beloved Purdey.

I've followed a similar path. I have used a light, whippy, short-barreled 12-gauge over-under, a 12-gauge pump, a 20-gauge autoloader, and a 12-gauge side-by-side for grouse, all accounting for numerous birds. My preference today is to hunt with my grandfather's Lefever Nitro Special—another gun with history. It's a 1920s workingman's side-by-side without frills, a 12-gauge, with 28-inch barrels that I had rebored to skeet chokes. It's a little plump on weight, but it balances exquisitely, and I shoot it well.

Fellow grouse specialists I know like both 12- and 20-gauge doubles with open-choked 26- to 28-inch barrels. Many are in love with their lightweight stackbarrel Browning Citoris. One friend tried an English double worth a small fortune for a

The ideal grouse gun is light, quick, and fast handling, balanced with a smooth swing.

short time; but, fearing the loss of its economic value if he fell and dinged a barrel in the coverts, he went back to a Citori.

I am hard pressed to find a better grouse load than the standard high-quality trap or skeet load, a 12-gauge, 3–3¼ drams equivalent powder, throwing 1⅛ ounces of hard No. 8 or No. 7½ shot.

GROUSE GEAR

I'm particular about my hunting gear, and I like it traditional. Footwear is the most important thing. Feet take a lot of abuse hunting grouse, yet it is important to feel what is under your feet to be able to move well. Also, grouse hunting is often done in a wet environment. For these reasons, I find it hard to beat the 12-inch L. L. Bean Maine Hunting Shoe. For hunting the more rocky terrain common in the Appalachians, other hunters I've shared coverts with prefer Danner lace-up boots with lug or air-bob soles. Cordura chaps help protect legs from assorted thorns and briers. I'm not nuts about nylon or leather-faced hunting pants ("birdshooter britches") in this role, but some gunners prefer them to chaps. Also, I prefer a blaze orange shell vest over a strap vest or jacket for freedom of movement. Over a number of years, I've found it is hard to beat a tan pair of L. L. Bean cotton chinos for hunting pants. They're tough, wear incredibly well, are quick to dry, sharp looking, and very, very comfortable. A light cotton safari shirt over a long-sleeved T-shirt works well for the early season. As the temperature drops, I'll switch to a shepherd's check flannel shirt over a Duofold or polypropylene long-johns top. Capeskin shooting gloves help keep hands safe from the abuse of briars and whippy sprouts and save a lot of wear and tear on firearms, but I can't wear them until it gets pretty cold. Also, I like to wear a neckerchief for touch of class. The old timers wore ties, and the neckerchief over a buttoned collar serves a dual purpose: It keeps crud out of your inner layers and it can wipe glasses clean, mop a sweaty brow, and so on. Blaze orange headgear, usually a ball cap, tops off this rig. One of these days, when someone can make a stylish-looking fedora-style hat in blaze orange that doesn't look too goofy, I'll trade in my ball cap.

GROUSE DOGS

Here, too, I'm quite biased and particular. My dog will always be a DeCoverly Kennels English setter. Ken Alexander and business partner Bill Sordoni run a top-notch operation and produce fine dogs that are intelligent, stylish, beautiful gentlemen and ladies in the house, around children, and still first-class bird dogs in the field.

That said, I also know any breed of pointing dog that is well-trained and has a passion for birds can make a fine grouse dog. My German shorthair was an excellent

Grouse dog characteristics include: intelligence, a combination of good nose and bird sense, biddability, a sound body, style and beauty, and a passion for bonasa, which Pup gets from his hunter.

grouse hunter, despite his love of pheasants. I've hunted over very many capable Brittanys, two English pointers who were fun to watch move, and two breeds of flushing dogs, springer spaniels and Labs.

Any grouse dog should have some basic characteristics, however:

- First is intelligence. A grouse dog needs to use his noggin as much as his instincts. He needs to outthink grouse, something that is hard to do.
- A very close second is a combination of good nose and bird sense. Birds must drive Pup, fuel his inner fire so that at the end of a long day, when a whiff of grouse comes his way, he comes alive again, like a fresh dog. Also, he needs to have an innate knowledge of where to find birds, a sense that if he finds birds under a hemlock in one covert, he should look under hemlocks in other coverts.
- Biddability—a willingness to be handled and take commands is a very close third. Uncontrollable dogs can ruin a good hunt.
- Sound-bodied dogs are important to grouse hunting because it is physically demanding.
- Style and beauty—which is always in the eye of the beholder—are important.
- The final thing a grouse dog needs is a passion for the sport. It is likely that a dog will get this from his hunter. If a hunter loves grouse gunning, then Pup will reflect this, too.

WESTERN GROUSE

We can kill a big male sage grouse and feel his improbable weight (there is no bet-
ter definition of specific density than a brace of mature sage roosters, three or four
hot miles from a pickup) and smell his acrid blood, like railroad ties on a hot day,
but the birds will always remain strangers. No let me correct that. We will always
remain strangers in their land. We've never really accepted their sagebrush
ocean—"wastes," we often called them, in our journals of exploration—and so
never really accepted the birds, since they are the essence of sage.

John Barsness

The wide open spaces of western North America have been called many things:
The Great American Desert, a Sea of Grass, Indian Territory. "The empty third" of
the continent is how upland bird hunting writer Joel M. Vance described this land, as
true a statement today as it was in 1981. In the last 2 decades, however, the people
emptiness of the place has filled in some.

I like to think of the mountains as Jeremiah Johnson country, and the rest as
Lakota, Cheyenne, Arapaho, Shoshone, Kiowa, and Comanche country. I imagine
vast herds of buffalo, white-rumped pronghorn antelope bounding in the distance,
and the pointed buffalo skin lodges of beautiful, proud, strong red people there. My
heart is with them.

On my first western pilgrimage, to work for a Montana outfitter for the summer,
I stood in South Dakota's Badlands and something in the prairie wind whispered
"home." The same message reached my cold-reddened ears hunting southwestern
Kansas for prairie chickens at Thanksgiving a few years later. And in 1996, while
swimming in South Dakota's Moreau River on the Green Grass Lakota reservation, I
experienced a sense of time warp. A dozen kids from the reservation piled in my
Bronco II for a trek to the swimming hole and some horseplay. I remember diving into
the river, swimming under water, then popping up, like a muskrat, in the midst of
some boys I wanted to dunk. When I came out of the water, I saw their long black

hair, dark skin, cottonwood trees, sundance flags following the breeze, and the ancient riverbank behind the boys all at once, and it was as though I was 14, living 120 years back in time, swimming in the Little Bighorn with Wooden Leg, Black Elk and the sons of Gall and Rain-in-the-Face. *Hetch etu.* . . . The empty third is also spirit place, if you listen to the wind.

Six species of grouse—sage grouse, prairie chickens (pinnated grouse), sharp-tailed grouse, and three mountain birds—ruffed grouse, blue grouse, and spruce grouse—live in the empty third. Ruffed grouse are common throughout the Rockies, although they rarely possess the savvy for which their eastern relatives are famous.

* * * *

SAGE GROUSE

Explorers Meriwether Lewis, William Clark, and their Corps of Discovery "discovered" North America's largest grouse in 1804, at the headwaters of the Missouri River in Montana, and near the Lemhi River valley and along the Salmon River, in Idaho, in 1805. They called the bird "the Cock of the Plains." By 1827, Lucien Bonaparte—cousin Zenaide's husband, from Philadelphia dove fame—gave the sage grouse its Latin scientific name, *Centrocercus uophasianus.*

Sage grouse are found in Montana, Wyoming, South Dakota, North Dakota, Colorado, Utah, Idaho, Washington, Oregon, Nevada, California, northern New Mexico, and southern Alberta and Saskatchewan. Their range stops where greasewood replaces sagebrush in the southern deserts.

Some time during the last ice age, scientists believe seeds from wormwood plants, common to the Eurasian steppes, found their way into the fur of animals crossing the land bridge between Asia and North America, or were cast into the wind and carried to North America. These seeds took root and eventually dominated 95 million acres of western North America, including much of Nevada, Utah, eastern Oregon, southern Idaho, and portions of Montana, Wyoming, Colorado, and southern Canada.

In North America, wormwood is called sagebrush. (A quick aside: Remember Ernest Hemingway writing about the drink absinthe? It was aged in wormwood casks, which were said to add a chemical to the drink that induced mental illness.) There are 20 varieties of *Artemesia* in North America. Some are Eurasian descendents, others developed here independently.

An opportunistic plant, sagebrush thrives at elevations from 1,600 feet to 11,000 feet. Most sagebrush consists of a gnarled, woody trunk with upright branches clothed in small, delicate gray-green leaves. Each shrub produces tens of thousands of seeds in a year. Sage takes advantage of openings, and once established, maintains itself for years. A plant in California's White Mountains was 217 years old.

Sage is an evergreen, producing two sets of leaves each year. The plant can survive long winters and rainless summers by carrying on photosynthesis at extremely low temperatures and absorbing water from the soil. Surface pores on the leaves close, creating suction, like a little hydraulic pump, within the root system. Sage has evolved a variety of chemicals, secreted by glandular hairs on the leaf, which inhibit the germination and growth of competing species. Also, monoterpenoid oils within the plant retard the activity of stomach bacteria in herbivores like deer. Deer can eat sage but need time to build up the microbes required to digest it. For some wildlife, however, sage is what buffalo were to the Plains tribes: food, shelter, clothing, and more. Blacktailed jackrabbits hide in sage. Songbirds nest in it. Pygmy rabbits eat the bark. Pronghorn antelope and sage grouse eat almost nothing but sage, especially during winter.

Oregon Trail journals are rife with sagebrush complaints: how much there was, its poor burning time, and so on. Native people saw sage differently. Smudges of the camphor-saturated leaves were used as a spiritual cleanser and purifier in ceremonies in sweat lodges. Other types of sage were used to make everything from sandals and loincloths to toilet paper. The Paiutes even used sage as a hair restorer. It worked for the Paiutes, but didn't for the white entrepreneurs who tried bottling and selling sage extracts as hair tonic.

Ranchers and farmers have worked at eradicating sage for years, primarily to plant crested wheatgrass, a good cattle food, in its place. They've dragged huge chains over sage, plowed it, sprayed poisons on it, burned it . . . all to no avail, because sage is a natural succession plant in the West. Today, some ranchers are learning to live with sage as sage flats produce more grass because they retain winter snow runoff.

For sage grouse, good sage is critical, especially from October until April, when the leaves and buds of the plant are almost 100 percent of their winter diet. Ideal sage grouse habitat has a 15 to 25 percent sagebrush canopy and good grass and forbs, plants like arrowleaf, balsam root, phlox, lupine, and dandelions. This type of cover is also critical for breeding and brood rearing. Meadows, riparian areas, alfalfa fields, and other moist areas are important summer range for the birds.

Sage grouse are big birds. Males go 4 to 7 pounds and can measure up to 30 inches long. Females are smaller, 2 to 4 pounds, up to 23 inches long. The average wingspan is 40 inches. (Think young turkey or goose!)

The breeding behavior of sage grouse is somewhat familiar, thanks to television. In February, male grouse begin moving from their winter habitat—snow-blown ridgetops—to the leks. Leks are open areas, typically meadows or patches of low sagebrush, with 40-square-foot openings that function much like a ruffed grouse's drumming area. In an elaborate mating ritual, cock sage grouse fluff and spread their plumage, strut, and "boom"—inflate a sac in the breast which produces a booming or

Lawrence Smith and Dave Miller hunting the Cimarron National Grasslands.

"plopping" sound—from mid-March until mid-June. The first week of April sees the most activity. Most booming takes place at dawn and dusk.

John Barsness, in *Western Skies* (1994, Lyons Press), describes this: "They puff their chest sacs and spread their tailfeathers until you can't see their feet, moving about the grassy flats like spike-hairdoed basketballs on miniature roller skates. Once in a while they stop in front of one of the hens that wander unconcerned among them and emit a sound from their air sacs called booming, but more closely resembling (as my wife puts it) 'a baby farting in a bathtub.' "

After mating, females scratch a nest lined with feathers, leaves, and grass out from under smaller species of sage and lay six to eight smooth-shelled, 2-inch-long eggs. Incubation takes just under a month. The chicks are precocious, led from the nest within a few hours of the last bird hatching. The chicks initially feed on grasshoppers, ants, crickets, and a variety of tiny beetles, then gradually start taking sage into their diet. Sage grouse have a soft crop—a flexible pouch used to hold food—not a crop like a pheasant, which literally grinds food. Within 2 months, young grouse grow enough to be on their own, and the broods break up and scatter over a wide area. Like ruffed grouse, sage grouse congregate on winter range, then disperse again in the spring. Also, most birds return to where they were hatched.

Sage grouse live a long time; 4- and 5-year-old birds are not uncommon. And while most upland birds live less than 1 year, up to 80 percent of sage grouse survive a year. Yet sage grouse reproduction rates are lower than any other North American gamebird. Fewer than 15 percent of females will re-nest if disturbed—one reason why some areas experience drastic population peaks and valleys.

Overall sage grouse populations plummeted in the 1940s. Populations fluctuate naturally, but trends show a 40 percent decline in sage grouse numbers. Road counts on leks in one Idaho area that averaged 350 males during the early 1970s now tally less than 100 males. A more drastic decline took place in the Big Desert area of southeastern Idaho where lek counts dropped from 900 to 200 males during the last decade. Other states are experiencing similar problems: In Colorado, lek counts were down 31 percent between 1986 and 1995. Over a 37-year average, counts are down 17 percent in Wyoming; 30 percent in Utah, Oregon, and Montana; and by as much as 47 percent in Washington. Habitat is the critical factor. Wildfires, agricultural expansion, herbicides, prescribed fire, grazing, and rangeland seeding have nibbled away at habitat until 80 percent of the cover vital to these birds has been destroyed. Even with the declines in population, Idaho gunners take about 60,000 birds annually; Oregon, Montana, and Wyoming gunners about 30,000 each; Colorado, 10,000; Nevada 5,000.

HUNTING SAGE GROUSE

Sage grouse hunting is popular. During the early 1990s, for example, Idaho hosted 17,000 sage grouse hunters who contributed more than 2 million dollars to the state's economy, according to the Idaho Department of Fish and Game.

Most hunters, John Barsness writes, meet sage grouse in a random crossing out on the high plains. They want to shoot a bird so they can say they have hunted sage grouse. "The feeling is that sage grouse make an interesting novelty item—something like collecting a couple of conchs on a Bahamaian vacation—but they are not a bird to get all fussed up about." These hunters are missing the importance of the place and how the birds are connected to it. To really know sage grouse you need to spend some time in their country.

"One point is that any of us—pilgrim, surgeon, or native of the high plains— would gather different views of sage grouse from our individual meetings. They could be large, slow, easy-to-shoot relics of a wilderness past (something like buffalo with wings), or run in vast disquieting herds (something like Cape buffalo with wings), or the only grouse that migrates. The truth is they can be all three, and more," writes Barsness.

There are two types of sage grouse country: One is the parched Great Basin. The other is in the high sage valleys of southwestern Montana and eastern Idaho, where gunners can look at mountains turning white with snow in early September, beaver-pond brook trout streams, and some of the "most fertile hay meadows in the West."

There are also two sage grouse seasons for Barsness: September and late season. The key to September hunting, he writes, is to find water. A United States Department of the Interior, Bureau of Land Management map is handy to have to look for water sources. Birds will usually be found within a half-mile of water. Dry coulee bottoms are especially attractive.

Barsness' favorite time, however, is late October or November, when days are cool, the mountains are wreathed in snow, and the birds migrate towards winter cover. In the northern rangelands, the birds move out of high sage draws to valleys below. On the Plains and in the Basin, birds move uphill, from tall sage along the creeks to ridgetops, where knobs are blown free of snow by the wind. These are also the leks where sage grouse dance in the spring, and where, in October, you can often hear grouse booming at dawn.

For outdoor writer Byron Dalrymple, the issues in sage grouse hunting are the vastness of the treeless, rolling, sage country foothills, and the openness of sage grouse habitat. Dalrymple recounts how a Montana rancher suggested he scout for sage grouse like mule deer: Forget the big picture, and look for water sources such as windmills, creeks, seeps, cattle tanks, and dry creeks, which could have puddles. Check for signs, tracks, and droppings, then hunt any short sage slopes within a couple hundred yards of water. Birds like these areas for roosting. Often birds fly to water from as much as a mile out, especially when water sources are scarce—look at dawn, midmorning, and late in the afternoon. Alfalfa, which is usually being cut when sage grouse season is in, represents high living. You can often find large groups of birds around alfalfa fields. The birds will eat their fill at dawn, then rest an hour or so in the fields or in the shade of bales if undisturbed.

Glassing, using binoculars or a spotting scope to find sage grouse in distant fields, is also effective. Look for large dark spots against an alfalfa field's pale background, or heads popping up as birds walk or feed on sage. After you spot birds, figure out how to stalk them. Wyoming gun writer Bob Milek likes to glass for sage grouse in midmorning, when the birds are moving from water to daytime haunts, or in late afternoon, when they are getting up to feed again.

SHOOTING SAGE GROUSE

Measure the wingspan of a sage grouse, multiply this by its length and you get roughly 7 square feet of bird. This caused Dalrymple to wonder why he couldn't hit sage grouse as well as a pheasant.

"There's something about the rush of those huge wings, the guttural cackle, and the sight of a bird half the size of a turkey leaping gracefully into the air that transforms that big, slow-moving target into an unnerving rocket," Milek writes.

Barsness helps explain it: "The grouse started to run; black and white breast feathers coming out of shadow, then saw the dog, panicked, and spread its wings like a piece of sagebrush unfolding. The long barrel of the 97 moved up and then in front, grayed nicks barely catching sun, the bird a sort of a Pleistocene megagrouse, too large for the now. It seemed to be flying toward the place where the river flowed larger, until the shot, the grouse turning slightly and dragging its belly over a sage top, dust rising around the sage as it fell beyond, one wingtip above the brush slowly easing and disappearing."

Even if sage grouse are Pleistocene megagrouse, the birds are usually slow to get off the ground, not hard to bring down, and relatively predictable in flight. For these reasons, Barsness, Milek, and Dalrymple used both 12- and 20-gauges with varying loads and shot size. Hunters wanting to reduce weight liked the 20-gauge. For pattern saturation, a 12 might be better. For loads, No. 6 shot in a 1¼-ounce load for 12-gauges, and a 1-ounce load of No. 6s for 20-gauge came recommended. Barsness likes a 12-gauge with light shot in the early season, then switches to copper No. 4s or even No. 2s by November.

SAGE GROUSE DOGS

Barsness likes hunting grouse with dogs. He is a retriever fan, because he has shot more sage grouse over retrievers than any other type of dog—mostly because there are more retrievers in the West. The variety of birds a dog might handle in the West—from sage grouse, pheasants, and quail to waterfowl and doves—makes retrievers very popular.

Pointing dogs do their best work early in the year, when birds hold better, Barsness believes. I would have loved hunting my old German shorthair, Jack, on sage grouse. His knack for pinning running pheasants by swinging out in front of them and cutting them off would have been interesting on sage grouse.

Dalrymple wasn't keen on dogs. A dog could help find cripples; however, he believed most dogs work too fast or too far for grouse. Flocks don't lie for a point or flush close unless you totally surprise them.

FIELD CARE

"Sage buzzard" is the derogatory nickname some Westerners throw at sage grouse, "a bird even coyotes won't eat." Westerners, however, are notorious for tossing their birds in the back of the pickup after shooting to ride all day with the oil cans, spare tire, and irrigation ditch shovel, Barsness writes.

Field dress sage grouse immediately after the shot and rinse out the body cavity within a half hour. This improves the quality of the bird for table fare, something all bird hunters should strive for. Barsness also believes aging sage grouse in the bottom of the refrigerator for a week (if properly gutted and cooled) helps make the birds taste like a cross between pronghorn and dark turkey.

* * * *

PRAIRIE CHICKENS

The land looked sparse, dry, more like desert than what our eyes, accustomed to green Eastern lushness, expected of prairie country. Spiky yucca plants and prickly pear cactus dotted the November landscape with a strange olive-green color. Sage and wisps of shriveled bluestem grass seemed almost too fragile, too brittle to step on, as though they wouldn't come back next spring if you did. We—Dave Miller; Casey, his yellow Lab; Jack, the German shorthair; and I—were hunting the Cimarron National Grasslands in southwestern Kansas, hoping to get into some prairie chickens.

Lawrence Smith, a lanky Elkhart, Kansas native, was showing us how the Cimarron's scaled quail, bobwhites, pheasants, and lesser prairie chickens used "guzzlers," water collecting devices designed to help wildlife in the dry land. Smith had helped site and build the guzzlers, one of many of his efforts to return something to the land and the birds he loved. Judging from the number of pointing arrow-shaped quail tracks we saw under a nearby cholla cactus, efforts to help the birds were paying off. Then we were off into the prairie to find some chickens.

We walked, walked, and walked some more, going farther away from the bed of the dry Cimarron River, its cottonwoods and familiar brushy features; farther out into the land that, although it looked flat, folded into itself and created ravines, draws, and basins, things you never see flying over or driving through Kansas. I was thankful for Smith's help, thankful for the friend who arranged it, thankful that we were experiencing something so unique. I also half-expected to crest a little rise, hear the theme from "The Good, the Bad and the Ugly," and see Clint Eastwood, draped in a serape, squint, spit, and shoot somebody.

Then it happened. (Not Clint.) Wings fluttering, a disturbance in the cold prairie wind chewing my ears. A moment later, I caught sight of a lone prairie chicken sailing towards Dave. I saw Dave mount his shotgun, swing on the bird, and miss, twice. The bird sailed on, in that characteristic pump, pump . . . glide . . . pump, pump flight they have. And we continued walking, walking, walking.

* * * *

It might seem hard to imagine that there was a time when a traveler headed west into the Sea of Grass might flush thousands of prairie chickens in the course of a day's time, when a good day's travel was 10 or 15 miles. But it happened.

Four related species of birds, three that later became known as "prairie chickens," lived in North America: the heath hen, a bird of the brushy plains of the New England states; the greater prairie chicken, a bird of the vast open plains country; the lesser prairie chicken, adapted to the sparse, drier country of the southern grasslands and high plains; and Attwater's prairie chicken, found in the grassy prairies of eastern Texas and Louisiana.

No other gamebirds in North America have been eradicated from their historical habitat like these four birds. Prairie chicken habitat for the greater prairie chicken, *Tympanuchus cupido,* and the lesser prairie chicken, *Tympanuchus pallidicinctus,* once extended west from Ohio to Oklahoma, and south from Minnesota to Arkansas.

From the 1800s until the early 1900s prairie chickens were quite abundant. In the 1870s, Custer's 7th Cavalry, chasing the Cheyenne from northwestern Oklahoma, ate so many lesser prairie chickens that they called the birds "Old Yellowlegs." (Remembering the slaughter of Black Kettle's people on the Washita River, the Cheyenne women also thought it appropriate to use sewing awls to pierce Custer's eardrums after his "Last Stand" on the Little Bighorn. The idea was that he might hear better in the afterlife.) Iowa limited prairie chicken shooters to 25 birds per day in 1878, the nation's first upland bird gunning law. During the late 1800s, market gunners killed millions of prairie chickens, sending wooden barrels holding as many as 500 birds each to St. Louis, Kansas City, Wichita, and Memphis. The going price was 30 cents to one

dollar. Settlers also relied on chickens while traveling wagon routes, as well as after their soddies were built and they started farming the land.

Prairie chickens, in the words of premiere chicken authorities Frederick and Frances Hammestrom, need good grass and wide horizons. It's that simple. Yet prairie chickens even prospered when agriculture first came to the prairies. Grain crops were easy food sources. So long as a 60-percent tallgrass prairie, 40-percent farmland mixture was maintained, the birds had the best of both worlds. In an *American Hunter* magazine story, outdoor writer Jerry L. Holechek mentions conversations with old-timers in eastern New Mexico who said lesser chickens were incredibly abundant from 1900 until the 1920s. However, as farming increased—long growing seasons allowed wheat to be double-cropped in the name of greed on the southern plains and heavy livestock grazing upset the 60–40 ratio—much of the prime lesser chicken habitat in Texas, Kansas, Oklahoma, Colorado, and New Mexico was destroyed. The Dust Bowl drought of the 1930s almost did the birds in because it hit hardest in prairie chicken habitat. State wildlife agencies closed chicken seasons. Within a decade, the birds started regaining some losses. The Soil Bank program of the 1950s also helped restore some habitat and increase populations.

Today, huntable populations of prairie chickens remain in only a few states. The greater prairie chicken does best in Nebraska, South Dakota, and Kansas, with small, isolated colonies in Minnesota, Wisconsin, Missouri, Colorado, and Illinois. The lesser prairie chicken is limited to southwestern Kansas, Oklahoma, Texas, Colorado, and New

Mexico. The lesser prairie chicken, in particular, has experienced severe population declines in recent years. New Mexico closed its hunting season in 1996, and Oklahoma followed in 1998. Kansas and Texas are the only states continuing to offer lesser prairie chickens in huntable numbers, although the birds are declining there as well. Many states throughout the prairie chicken's traditional range are working to transplant birds and create more habitat in an attempt to increase populations. In 2000, Colorado was able to offer limited greater prairie chicken hunting for the first time since 1937.

Three areas are usually the focus of modern chicken hunting: Kansas's Flint Hills for both species, and to a lesser extent the southwestern portion of the state for lesser chicken; Nebraska's Sandhill country; and the Missouri River Breaks of South Dakota. The biggest threats to today's chickens are still the plow, mowing machines, and clean farming.

Biologists refer to both greater and lesser chickens as pinnated grouse. This reference is to the long, dark pinnae feathers on the side of bird's neck. When performing its mating ritual, the male's long, dark brown pinnae feathers on the neck stand erect, like a jackrabbit's ears.

The greater prairie chicken is larger, weighing 2 to 2½ pounds. The lesser chicken weighs a 1½ to a 1¾ pounds. Coloration is also different: The greater chicken sports dark brown barring on its breast; the lesser appears lighter, with an almost yellow cast to its plumage. Both birds measure about 18 inches long, and both have a 21-inch wingspan, with a flight speed of about 35 miles an hour . . . faster when the gold bead on a shotgun is trying to catch up to the bird.

Like sage grouse, the male prairie chicken's spring mating ritual involves foot stomping, strutting, and running back and forth, head down, tail and pinnae erect, wings partially drooped, across a lek to attract females. The lek is usually a small, flat open area, without ground cover, located in a pasture or on a long, rolling hill. Chickens also boom.

John Madson described booming this way: "(Booming) . . . is a lonely, wild sound made by a lonely, wild bird. It has the quality of an ancient wind blowing across the smoke flap of an Indian tepee. In all modern America, there is no more old-time haunting sound than the booming of the prairie grouse. It is the last fading voice of the prairie wilderness crying for help. When it is gone, it shall be gone forever. All of our television will not bring it back . . . and none of our spacecraft can take us to where it has vanished." Outdoor writer Tom Davis called booming an eerie, three-call note that sounds like "Old Muldoon." Like sage grouse, the booming sound comes from sacs in the chest filled with air.

After mating, hens lay 10 to 12 eggs, which hatch in 21 days. As broods mature in the fall, males congregate, loafing together. Like ruffed grouse, chickens disperse or shuffle when the broods break up, and the young birds form small groups of winter flocks of 50 or more birds.

HUNTING PRAIRIE CHICKENS

There are two basic methods used to hunt both species of prairie chickens. The first, pass shooting, is a lot like dove hunting. Pass shooting chickens is extremely

Lesser prairie chicken hunting is limited to southwestern Kansas and Texas. Populations of these birds are in a steep decline.

popular in Kansas, but not widely practiced elsewhere. The trick is to find feeding fields and station yourself along the edge of the field or between the feeding field and the chickens' daytime areas. Below-freezing temperatures have a tremendous impact on the birds' habits. Until a hard freeze, birds ordinarily feed on insects found in green pastures. After a freeze eliminates this source of food, the birds look towards alfalfa and cut-over milo fields. Several hard freezes prior to opening day will stimulate good flights into cultivated areas. Get there before dawn, or hunt drizzly, snowy, foggy days, when the birds could come at any time. Prime feeding areas include sorghum, wheat, oats, and cornfields, especially waste grain with stubble. Camouflage, if permitted, is also a good idea. Shooting can be fast and challenging, depending on how well you've scouted. This is also more of a group affair. The more hunters ringing a field, the better your odds.

The second method, walk-up hunting, is generally preferred by serious hunters. Chicken country is big, which means you need to cover some ground to find birds. Chickens, like doves, feed in grain fields early and late in the day. After feeding in the morning, the birds seek a roosting or loafing area rich with insects and weed seeds. The birds will fly out to feed on waste grain again in late afternoon. Daily movements of 3 to 4 miles are common. You can walk birds up in these loafing areas, usually located near feeding fields. Focus on heavy cover such as slough grass and buffaloberry thickets at midday, when birds are looking for shade and security.

"Hunt the best grass you can find, ideally with dogs, and keep walking. Even in a good year you can space several miles between shots. This can lead to daydreaming, the nemesis of the chicken hunter. Although their pace appears leisurely, chickens have a way of flushing noiselessly. One minute you're striding over the big country, thinking of women or whatever, the next there are birds in the air, and you're wondering how they got there," warns Tom Davis. Early in the season, when the birds are less wary and tend to be in singles, is the best time to walk birds up. Later in the season, when birds form winter flocks, you could flush 30 birds at a time, but this is likely to be the bulk of an area's chicken population. Also, prairie birds depend on vision to warn them of danger. They see better from high spots. When hunting a rise, two hunters should work it, one on either side. Chickens often cackle like pheasants when flushed close.

SHOOTING CHICKENS

Choosing the best guns and loads to use for chickens is a compromise, especially if you're pass shooting instead of walking birds up, or also hunting something else, like quail or pheasants. Chickens, like most grouse species, are not hard to bring down and don't carry shot like pheasants can.

Most chicken specialists like a light 12- or 20-gauge in two basic combinations: Early in the season, when shots are likely to be close, an open-choked gun with a light load of No. 7½'s is adequate. Later, tighter chokes and a heavier shot loads are called for. A good all-around compromise is a 12- or 20-gauge with interchangeable choke tubes. The improved cylinder and modified combination works for early season gunning, the modified and full for the late season. In a single barrel, a modified choke can handle most situations, especially if you switch to copper-plated shot for tighter patterns at longer shots later in the season.

Good chicken loads include a light, 1- to 1⅛-ounce load of No. 6 or No. 7½ shot in the early season. Later in the season, switch to a 1¼- to 1½-ounce load of No. 4s, 5s, or 6s.

A couple of final tips from Tom Davis: It's not unusual for the chickens that are most distant in a group to flush first, or for a bird or two to sit tight while the flock flushes. "When I heard boom, boom and then 'Oh shit!' I knew exactly what happened (to my hunting partner)," writes Davis. When they're going to fly, chickens will usually stick their heads up from the grass at a distance. Flushed from short cover or a harvested grain field, they rise high and fly for distant trees or a brushy swale. Follow the birds and try for a second flush.

CHICKEN DOGS

In 1916, the year Nash Buckingham's "De' Shootinest Gent'man" was first published in Casper Whitney's *Recreation* magazine, field trialers and quail hunters frequently sent their dogs to trainers in Kansas, Nebraska, or South Dakota for work on prairie chickens. Bountiful chicken populations created an opportunity for repeated bird encounters and produced some of the finest field trial and personal gun dogs

ever seen. (A similar situation existed in the Canadian prairie provinces for some time on sharp-tailed grouse.)

Yet today, many hunting experts say that most dogs can't handle chickens too well. Others, primarily dog people, say bring Pup along chicken hunting; the experience can't hurt.

My southwestern Kansas adventure showed that a versatile dog worked mostly on pheasants and grouse could do a very fine job on prairie birds. Jack, my shorthair, handled blue quail, pheasants, and bobwhites on the trip. He didn't have much chicken opportunity because a drought kept bird numbers down. The main dog problems were the dry country, sand burrs, jackrabbits (Dave's Lab, Casey, developed a jackrabbit fetish), and cactus, which the dogs learned to avoid after a couple of sticks. Most good bird dogs should be able to work chickens. Well-trained flushing dogs, retrievers and spaniels, can certainly help find birds and fetch downed game. But take plenty of water, a first aid kit, and dog boots for sand burr country.

* * * *

SHARP-TAILED GROUSE

In *Western Skies*, John Barsness describes how Ben, his grandfather-in-law, a Sioux who lived on the Fort Peck Indian Reservation, taught him how to hunt sharptails. Barsness used Ben's Winchester Model 1897, a pumpgun with a hammer, the first time he hunted sharptails. (Barsness ended up buying this gun from Ben.) The interesting thing was how the Model 97 was a reflection of its owner. Barsness writes, "It was without bluing, the steel the shade of a prairie September thunderstorm;" the wood dark, "worn by hands, dented by wagon seats and pickup doors, scratched by wild rosebushes and buffalo-berry. It had the same texture and color as the face and hands of the man who owned it, my wife's grandfather. . . ." Whenever Barsness used the gun—but only on wild game, and especially on sharptails—there was a special magic in the moment.

"Now I've hunted midwestern pheasants, quail a bit farther south, ruffed grouse in the alder thickets, doves that couldn't be kept out of a barley field, sage grouse that came in "herds" of 100 or more, and Huns in country where you could put up a dozen coveys in a day. But there is absolutely nothing that beats finding a September covey of sharptails loafing in the shade of a big chokecherry thicket below a plateau-top wheat field," Barsness writes in *American Hunter*.

He goes on to describe encountering sharptails in a coulee, and how each charmed moment leads to another. It all begins, Barsness writes, with the rhythm of the dog loping through the brush. Then, suddenly, the dry leaf patter quickens, and

there is a sharp *clututlutl.* Sharptails the size of hen pheasants come out everywhere. The birds clatter up in threes or fours, and sail flapping and gliding down the half mile of brush-choked coulee. One goes down. And the dog fetches the bird out of rosebushes that leave thorns in his muzzle. He wants the bird so badly he puts up with the pain.

"And this is only the beginning because the covey has scattered in singles and doubles down through the 600 yards of brush. You calm down, put the bird in your vest and spend the next half hour in one of the most pleasant downhill hikes possible. The birds come up at 20 yards or so, from each taller patch of chokecherry or wild plum, and you and the dog think life just might have merged with heaven right here, without that strange transition in between."

Sharp-tailed grouse, *Pediocetes phasianellus,* are more of a northern bird than a western bird. They are the northern prairie's complement to ruffed grouse, found in the same basic latitudes on the high plains east of the Rocky Mountains, up to the Arctic Circle. (One of the best kept secrets in North American bird hunting is the excellent sharptail hunting found in the vicinity of Fairbanks, Alaska.) The bulk of the best sharptail hunting is found a few hundred miles into Canada, then south and east to the central Dakotas and northwestern Nebraska. Sharptails fill the habitat niche—brushy grasslands intermingled with scrub and timber margins—between the flat wheat country where Hungarian partridge live (although their range often overlaps), and thick river bottom willows, alders, and cattails that western pheasants like. Sharptail habitat is generally drier and harsher, the shortgrass scrubby bottoms and badlands of the Plains, although in some areas the bird has expanded into forested areas. Adaptations for this northern range include feathered legs, an ability to feed on tree buds, and snow roosting like ruffed grouse.

Sharptails have mating rituals very similar to other prairie grouse. What sharptails lack in pinnate feathers, booming or "plopping" (they do make a low-toned mating call), they make up for in dancing. Sharptails strut across their leks with outstretched wings, lots of foot stomping, and vibrating tail feathers, which produces a buzzing sound described as being like a rattler's.

After mating, hens lay a dozen eggs in a shallow depression under a bush or clump of grass, with feathers and grass as a liner. About 21 days later, the chicks scramble after mother as soon as she is convinced all are hatched. The chicks eat insects and grow very quickly. At 10 days they can fly for short distances. A month after hatching the almost fully-feathered chicks can fly well. Within another month, broods break up and the young scatter.

Adult birds are 17½ to 19½ inches long, weigh 1¾ to 2 pounds, and have a wingspan of about 20 inches. Flight speed is 35–40 mph. Sharptails are powerful flyers and exceptionally strong on acceleration. They have dark breast meat, with more muscle than pheasants and other gamebirds.

Favored foods are the seeds of white birch, wheat, mountain ash, clover, dandelion, prairie rose and wild rose hips, sunflower seeds, chokecherry, wild cherry, poplar, alder, alfalfa, and maple. Since the coming of agriculture to the prairie, they also savor waste grain, especially wheat and buckwheat.

HUNTING SHARPTAILS

Like prairie chickens, sharptails feed early and late in the day, often flying long distances from roosting cover to grain fields. These flights are fairly predictable and pass shooting is possible; however, most gunners like to walk up sharptails.

The best time for this is September, when temperatures are cool, but the leaves are still on chokecherries, stunted ash, and buffaloberries. Brushy coulees, where the birds can find shade, especially those bordering wheat fields, are prime locations. Early in the day, birds will hold in wheat margins, along the field edges where a combine can't clip the wheat stalks too close to the ground, or at field corners where ragged wheat cutting and fence lines offer cover. After feeding, the birds will slip into the shade of dense cover, especially chokecherry and wild rosebushes, to rest. In the wheat lands of Canada, around old buffalo wallows where the ground is too wet to plow, patches of willows and poplar, called "bluffs" or "clumps," are often used. It is a common practice to drive from clump to clump to find birds. One hunter is dropped off at a long shotgun range from the clump, the other is dropped off on the other side, and they walk the birds up or use dogs.

Keep your ears open when hunting sharptails. The birds usually talk when first disturbed in cover, and by the time a hunter gets close enough to flush birds, they're chattering and running. Some writers describe these sounds as similar to a pheasant cackle. Others say it isn't a cackle. Byron Dalrymple describes the call as a repeated single syllable, "a grating, harsh monotone: *kuk-kuk-kuk-kuk-kuk-kuk.*"

Hunting sharptails later in the year is sometimes more difficult. October's birds are harder to hunt, harder to approach, because they've become wise to hunting tactics. The cooler weather also lets birds use open areas longer. However, find buffaloberry patches—especially those with bright, red-orange fruits—and you could be into birds. The cold nights increase the sugar content of the berries and the thorny bushes remain thick cover even without leaf cover. Rosebushes are good for the same reason. Be careful in your approach, though: birds will sneak over the coulee top if they spot you.

Beyond October, birds are increasingly wary and hard to approach. Brush is sparse, and birds prefer to be on top of a barren ridge, so they can spot any predators. Sharptails also tend to bunch up for winter. Barsness has seen as many as 200 sharptails in a late-November covey.

Usually, in areas where sharptail and prairie chicken seasons overlap, wildlife agencies group the birds together as "prairie grouse." However, if you want to tell the birds apart, look at tails, color, and breasts. Sharptails have a pointed tail, while chickens have short, stubby, square tails. Sharptails look gray in color while chickens look darker. Also, the barred breast feathers on a chicken are usually prominent on incoming birds, while sharptails have small V-shaped marks on the breast.

SHARPTAIL SHOOTING AND DOGS

Shots at sharptails vary with the season. Shots tend to be short when hunting brushy coulees in September. Later in the season, when handling wary birds, or if you hunt mornings when birds in are in feeding fields with short cover, shots are long.

For coulee hunting, an open-choked 12- or 20-gauge gun with light loads works well, especially over a pointing dog. Barsness likes his 20-gauge, bored cylinder and modified. Later in the season, of if other birds might be expected, a harder-hitting combination may be in order: a 3¼-dram equivalent, 1½-ounce load of No. 6s in 12-gauge, even plated shot in the late season.

As with prairie chickens, field trial and gun dogs were once shipped off to trainers on the northern prairies for work on sharptails. This also produced some exceptional bird dogs. Today, sharptails and dogs still work well together, especially when hunting birds in brushy coulees. Here, the pointing breeds, particularly the versatile breeds, could work wonders. Barsness, like a lot of Westerners, likes his Lab. Other flushing dogs could work just as well. However, anyone venturing on to the prairie in warmer weather should "snakeproof" their dog—train the dog to avoid snakes. Rattlesnakes are common. Snakebites are rare, but if you're a couple of miles from the truck and it happens, you could lose a fine dog. If your dog is bitten, keep him immobilized to slow the spread of venom through the bloodstream and get to a veterinarian as quickly as possible. Many bites, particularly from older snakes, don't inject much venom and survival is likely.

* * * *

MOUNTAIN BIRDS: BLUE AND SPRUCE GROUSE

In 1918, Arthur Cleveland Bent was traveling the country, collecting material on North America's gallinaceous birds for the Smithsonian Institution's United States National Museum. In Montana, he talked to Mrs. Florence M. Bailey, who recounted her experience with Franklin's (spruce) grouse in Glacier National Park.

Mrs. Bailey was in the Waterton Valley area when she noticed a brood of "half-grown, buffy breasted and tailless young" wandering around, enjoying themselves walking on the deep carpets of spruce and fir needles. They had plenty to eat. Black honeysuckle berries were hanging low on the bushes. And Momma was nearby, if needed. Mrs. Bailey reported to Bent that both the young and the adult female had "little sense of danger" about the encroaching human presence in their woods.

"She was the original fool hen of Montana, we were told, whom the Flatheads and the mountain Indians never kill except when in great need of food, as the birds are so tame they can be snared at will, without ammunition: as the Indians say, with string from a moccasin," Mrs. Bailey told Bent.

Aretas Saunders, a Montana hunter of the 1920s, didn't feel the same way the Salish (Flatheads) felt about spruce grouse. He told Bent: "All through Montana this bird is known as the 'fool hen' because of its lack of fear of man. It will sit still, even when close to the ground and allow one to approach very near. They are often killed with sticks or stones. When a dog approaches they fly up into the trees, and sit there. By shooting the lowest one first, I have shot several in the flock, the others sitting and waiting their turns. In Jefferson County, Montana, we had a small brown spaniel that would put them up a tree, and then stand beneath and yelp till we came. In Lewis and Clark Counties, on the upper waters of the Sun River, I once climbed a small pine,

grasped a cock Franklin (spruce) grouse by the foot, just to see if I could do it. The bird moved to a higher limb when I let go, but did not fly away. The male, even in fall, is fond of puffing out its black breast, and opening and shutting the red 'comb' over its eye, apparently by a sort of lifting of its 'eyebrows.' "

Although the Salish and Rocky Mountain fur trappers appreciated the blessings of "fool hens" when their bellies were growling, many modern hunters don't hold western North America's mountain grouse in too high a regard. This is a mistake. Even though spruce, blue, and western ruffed grouse may not get the respect reserved for eastern ruffed grouse, they do represent an opportunity for upland gunners to enjoy some unique high country gunning experiences.

NATURAL HISTORY

Blue grouse, *Dendragapus obscurus*, are the largest grouse in western North American forests. Roughly twice the size of ruffed grouse, a large blue grouse can

weigh up to 4 pounds. Male blue grouse measure about 19 inches. Females are 22 inches long.

Common from southeastern Alaska south in the Rockies and Sierra Nevadas, blue grouse are infrequent inhabitants of northern California's Sierra range. Blue grouse are also one of the few creatures that move higher on a mountain in winter and return to the valleys with the approach of mating season and summer.

Like other western grouse, the birds have their own unique mating ritual: Blue grouse "hoot." Early in March, the birds move down from the high country and the males begin hooting.

Bent and Samuel Rathburn observed a hooting male on Mercer Island in Lake Washington. The bird was 50 feet up in a Douglas fir in the densest part of the tree, close to the trunk so it was harder for predators to see. The bird turned about on the branch occasionally, facing one way then the other, drooping its wings, lifting and spreading his tail. When it was ready to hoot, the bird stretched its neck out, revealing two large rosettes, white feather patches on the neck, similar to a prairie chicken's pinnate feathers. The rosettes swelled open, showing yellow sacs of skin. (These are red or purple in the Rocky Mountains.) Then the bird began hooting. Bent and Rathburn described this as being a lot like a great horned owl's call, but softer, less powerful. Bent writes that the sound was four to six notes like "blowing into the bunghole of an empty barrel" or "swiftly swinging a rattan cane." Coastal forest birds are said to hoot more loudly than inland birds. Evidently hooting does something for female blue grouse.

After mating, cocks and hens separate. The cocks go to high rocky points near the edges of timber. Juniper and mountain mahogany thickets are especially attractive. The females nest in a dry, well-wooded area, laying up to 10 eggs. The chicks keep close to the hen for the first 2 weeks, then start feeding on their own and learn how to fly. Within a short time, they are feeding in the willow thickets of mountain streams, eating grasshoppers, plant tops, and berries.

Like ruffed grouse, blue grouse are versatile feeders. Seven percent of the bird's diet is animal matter—mostly grasshoppers, beetles, ants, and caterpillars—but also land snails. Vegetable matter makes up more than 90 percent. Most of this is pine forest material: the needles, buds, and flowers of yellow pine, white fir, Douglas fir, and western and black hemlocks. Red clover leaves, willow leaves, blueberry leaves, miterwort, birch shoots, poplar flower buds, lupine blossoms, columbine, Indian paintbrush, and pine seeds are also eaten. Berries—including mazanita berries, bearberries, gooseberries, huckleberries, serviceberries, salmonberries, red leder, honeysuckle, cherries, mountain ash, salal, and currants—are very popular in early fall. Forbs, flowering plants, seeds, and hardwood buds are also important. Riparian zones, creeks, mountain meadows, seeps, and springs are attractive to birds.

Spruce grouse, *Dendragapus canadensis,* are small, 16-inch, 1½-pound grouse of far northern short-needled conifer forests, especially where living branches reach the ground and where there are numerous small forest openings. The birds are found from Alaska south to northern Washington, Montana, and Idaho, across northern Canada to Nova Scotia, and south into Maine, Minnesota, Wisconsin, Vermont, and New Hampshire. Franklin's grouse are a subspecies of spruce grouse. Idaho's population of these birds is the southern-most in its range. In much of the spruce grouse's eastern range, the bird is fond of bog edges. However, spruce grouse can live in any large tract of conifers. The bird's favorite mixture is jack pine or lodgepole pine and spruce.

Spruce grouse courtship display is tame compared to other western grouse. It includes the usual strutting and tail fanning, but no hooting or booming or plopping. Males do make a small "drumming" sound. The male bird finds two trees, about 20 feet apart, with large horizontal branches, flies up, then dives off one limb. About halfway to the ground, the bird beats and flutters its wings, then flaps back up into the other tree. After a short interval, the bird repeats this performance from the other tree. Franklin's grouse has a double wing-clap at the end of its flight display. The sound, Bent says, is not really drumming, but more like a bird trying to break free of thick branches.

After mating, the hen spruce grouse builds a nest lined with dead grass and leaves under a spruce tree or tangle of bushes and lays a dozen eggs. The eggs are "some of the most handsomest eggs of any of the grouse," writes Bent. The smooth shells, with a slight gloss, are cinnamon to pinkish or cream buff in color and marked with chestnut brown to russet blotches and spots. The precocious young hatch after a 17-day incubation and learn to fly early.

Spruce grouse are not highly esteemed as gamebirds. (Remember that some of the same things were said about ruffed grouse in the 1600s, when first encountered in New England.) The birds' naiveté about the danger human beings pose makes them seem dumb. Also, in winter, when the birds feed mainly on spruce and balsam needles, the flesh is dark and "resinous," some say like turpentine, in flavor. However, other writers noted that spruce grouse taken during early autumn, when they feed mainly on berries, are as good as other grouse, even "sweeter and finer flavored than that of any Ruffed Grouse." Spruce grouse are found mainly along the edges of wet or swampy mountain valleys (Camas prairies), along streams, and in spruce or tamarack groves.

HUNTING MOUNTAIN GROUSE

You have to respect bullhide-tough Montana blue grouse gunners:

Dave Erikson, in a *Petersen's Hunting* story about blue grouse hunting, writes about being in the high country, when cool air followed by "a wall of rain working our way" overtook him and his partner.

"Taking our bearings from a rock outcrop, we headed for a pair of thick fir to have lunch and wait out the front," Erikson writes. Light rain and heavy winds hit them first. Rain mixed with snow came next. Then a full-fledged thunderstorm enveloped the hunters. "After nearly an hour of this, we were surrounded by two inches of snow and prospects for clearing weather didn't look good. Such is the finicky nature and quick-changing temperament of the mountains."

Reading this, I wondered how many gentleman ruffed grouse hunters with old doubles, briar pipes, and a profession would tough out an hour or so of heavy weather eating soggy sandwiches under a poncho to hunt birds. Most sports (me included) would be high-tailing it for the nearby car after 20 minutes of heavy weather.

After the heavy snow passed, Erikson continues, they shot some squirrels with a .22 pistol and went on to boot up some grouse. Then the sun broke through and they came down off the mountain. Wow!

John Barsness writes about a gentleman he sees occasionally when hunting blue grouse. This gunner totes an old double, a tattered shell vest, and hunts a Brittany. Barsness wonders if the gent sneers when Barsness and his Lab pop around the mountainside because the gent considers the retriever less than dignified as a grouse dog, be it blue, spruce, or ruffed grouse gunning. The sport usually slips quietly into another canyon without hailing Barsness. Barsness also wants to know if this guy wears a tie, as the real hardcore *pa'tridge* hunters are supposed to. The classic New England image versus reality . . . hmmph?

Well, *this* neckerchief-wearing pa'tridge gunner would tip his fedora to anyone willing to tough out serious Rocky Mountain weather to shoot some grouse.

Erikson writes that the reasons he hunts blue grouse include excellent scenery, the physical workout, and an opportunity to scout for other game like elk. He also has advice for blue grouse hunters: Fall is the most difficult time to hunt blue grouse because the birds are moving back to higher elevations for the winter. Along the Pa-

cific coast from Alaska to California, birds will be found at very low elevations in mountains. Farther inland, birds are higher. In Montana's Gravelly Range, Erikson located blue grouse above 7,000 feet, in Wyoming and Colorado, above 9,000 feet.

Concentrations of blue grouse are rare, except when the birds concentrate on a particular food source, such as berries, or in particular type of habitat. Finding blue grouse is a matter of scouting. If you can scout for birds during spring and summer, you're ahead of the game. Look for areas that have sub-alpine areas of open fir forest above a valley. In most cases you can find grouse along the ridgelines of open fir forests, but "be prepared to do some *serious* walking . . ." (This leaves me wondering if you should also have Medivac on standby.)

Most blue grouse, Erikson writes, usually hold pretty tight, often choosing to run rather than fly. Pay attention 20 yards ahead, and you will see birds as they try to outflank hunters moving through brush. If you work these runners towards clearings, they will usually make a short sprint, then flush. Flushed in an opening, blue grouse usually sail across the opening to alight in a tree. If the bird is bumped from a tree on a mountainside, it will usually drop downhill into timber. Birds feel safe in the tops of tall firs. Also, "three-dimensional hunting"—keeping an eye open for birds on the ground as well as on major tree limbs overhead—is important. Follow up on any flushes; blue grouse usually don't go far. In addition, check the crops of any birds taken. If the crop is full of anything other than needles—especially berries—focus on cover that has this item.

Other Western writers urge gunners to get above feeding blue and spruce grouse, and walk the ridges of south-facing slopes with conifers at your back, to concentrate on parklike flats and swales in trees along foothills, and brushy draws leading to creeks. Also, patches of purple elderberries, huckleberries, orange mountain ash berries, purple chokecherries, snowberries, dogwood, and Oregon grape should be investigated. Check out mixed forest habitat in grassy parks, shrub thickets, and aspen growth similar to ruffed grouse cover, too. In addition, clearcuts overgrown with deciduous trees, which offer mixed habitat for both blue and ruffed grouse, are good. You can also walk logging roads for birds, especially where the roads cut across ridges. Spurs on these roads often lead to the top of a steep ridge. Follow the ridges and work clearings and berry patches.

Spruce grouse are not hardcore conifer birds. They occupy the boreal forests and favor heavy stands of mature timber found west of the Continental Divide. Spruce grouse usually prefer south-facing slopes.

DOGS, GUNS, AND GEAR

Erikson, Barsness, and others agreed on guns and loads for mountain grouse: A light 12- or 20-gauge shooting moderate loads of No. 6 or 7½ shot was the ticket. (The standard 12-gauge trap load would be perfect.) In a double, improved cylinder/modified combinations are hard to beat, because most shots won't be too far, especially in dense spruce grouse country.

A close-working dog is Erikson's idea of the ideal grouse hunting partner. (Mine, too.) Other writers also appreciated the value of close-working dogs, especially pointing dogs. Both blue and spruce grouse will hold for pointing dogs. Naive birds could be just the ticket for a dog that needs extra bird contact.

Hunting the mountains requires a bit of extra gear, like good maps (and knowing how to use them) and a mini-survival kit, in the event you get into trouble and help is a long way from arriving. (Mine takes up a wallet's worth of space and includes a fire-starter, survival blanket, fishing line and hooks, extra matches, nylon string, and some other things.) Warm clothing for the ever-changing weather, simple high-energy food, and water could help, too. This can be carried in a game pouch, on a hip belt, or small pack without getting in the way of hunting.

5

WOODCOCK

Woodcock, to this upland gunner, offer so much, yet demand so little. If March makes the woodcock sing, then October makes them fly. When they fly, we gun, and in the gunning there is death. When they sing, we learn, and in their singing, there is life, for them and for us.

Bob Wingard, West Virginia DNR biologist

Twilight rolled over Michigan's Great Northwoods like an immense bed sheet pulled up on a cold night to keep off the chill. The darkness covered a group of woodcock hunters gathered near an alder-filled swale at the end of the day to witness a natural phenomenon: woodcock coming into night feeding cover. When the darkness seemed complete, October's golden Woodcock Moon peeked above the eastern horizon, blanching the land with a strange wash of light that was both eerie and appealing in the same moment. At the same time, long-billed woodcock, flitting like bats, came in singles, pairs, and trios to drop gently into the alders and spend the night feeding on earthworms.

Bill Goudy, a Ruffed Grouse Society official and former West Virginia Department of Natural Resources biologist, explained how the woodcock would probe the dark, moist, loamy soil for earthworms all night, then at sunrise move into overgrown fields, thick with goldenrod, to roost during the day.

A pair of birds silhouetted against the rising moon and flying low startled Barry Franciscus, a Pennsylvania bird hunter getting introduced to larger numbers of woodcock for the first time. Barry's hunting partner, wildlife artist Dennis Burkhart, who first met Goudy banding woodcock in West Virginia in the 1970s, told how the old market gunners used to wait for nights when the moon was full and bright, so they could "dusk" birds—shoot them as they came into feeding areas. He also talked

97

about how the birds would gather around muddy puddles to roost. We saw evidence of this in the afternoon, tracks, chalk droppings, and borings around a large mud puddle near an overgrown field.

Orrin Holmes and Bob Miller, two Louisiana bird carvers and *bécasse* (French for woodcock) hunters who had migrated north to experience ruffed grouse and their own birds at the beginning of the flyway, talked about the practice of firelighting woodcock in the South. Old-time gunners would take a blazing kettle of pine knot torches or a lantern into a woodcock covert at night. The light would reflect in the birds' eyes and the gunners would take them on the ground or as they flushed. Killing a hundred birds in a single night was typical.

While listening to Denny and Bill share their knowledge under the Woodcock Moon, I mostly marveled at the beauty of the night, the birds, their eccentric world, and the enormous trials they faced on their trek south.

Like Barry, I was relatively new to woodcock. I'd taken a bird as a kid hunting pheasants, and Jack and I occasionally saw birds while gunning our South Mountain grouse coverts. But my introduction to a greater understanding of woodcock began before this pilgrimage to Copper Country State Forest on Michigan's Upper Peninsula. It started when Denny and I picked up my new English setter puppy, Nash, from DeCoverly Kennels on an ill-fated day, Friday, March 13.

Bob Miller, a Louisiana bird carver and woodcock hunter, on his first trip to Michigan's Upper Peninsula. He called woodcock "a sportsman's game bird, a bird of gentlemen."

We arrived early and with some time to kill cruised a few back roads looking for places to hunt in the fall. Toward dusk, we stopped along the roadside at a large field with a big patch of wet alders, aspen, and goldenrod in the middle. Cool darkness was creeping toward us when Denny said to roll down the windows, to look and listen. We might see a male woodcock or two performing their mating dance and singing.

From the center of the field came a nasal sound, *bzeeep . . . bzeeeeeep.* A moment later, a curious little bird rose from the alders, the last rays of the western sun illuminating its long beak and the golden rusty colors of the bird's breast. Up, up into the sky the bird flew, a corkscrew flight for a full minute. Then it stopped, fluttering back down into the alders as though it were wounded. The performance was repeated several more times. I could imagine a female, impressed with the display, slinking into the bird's lair. We spotted three grouse along the roadside that night, too, fine omens for a new puppy's arrival.

NATURAL HISTORY

The American woodcock, *Scolopax minor* (which means lover of swamps or bogs) is a peculiar bird. Trying to characterize woodcock is like trying to describe its anatomy. Woodcock have ears lower than its brain, eyes well back on the sides of its head, and it hears pretty well with its bill—strange ways compared to other upland gamebirds.

Charles Waterman says woodcock are a caricature of other gamebirds: a snipe's beak, a quail's breast, flimsy legs, and the eyes of "a lost waif." Arthur Cleveland Bent called the woodcock a "mysterious hermit of the alders . . . a recluse of boggy thickets . . . wood nymph of crepuscular habits."

Actually, in some cases, woodcock are not considered an upland bird, but a shorebird, more like a rail or snipe, than a grouse. Grouse are gallinaceous, meaning they have a crop that grinds food like aspen buds for digestion, just like pheasants, quail, and doves. Woodcock, however, have no crop. But they do hang out in upland bird habitat.

According to Dr. Charles Norris, author of *Eastern Upland Shooting,* a classic look at the uplands, even what you call woodcock depends on where you live. Other names for the bird include: 'cock, timberdoodle, bogsucker, night partridge or pewee (in Virginia), night peck (North Carolina), mudsnipe, woodhen, marsh plover, wall-eyed snipe, woodsnipe, mud bat, Bushschnip (Pennsylvania Dutch), long bills, night *bécasse,* Labrador twisters, and Indian hens (south Missouri).

American woodcock were no strangers to the first Europeans in North America. The European woodcock, which can be twice as large as the American version, was common. The word woodcock comes from the old English term for the European woodcock, *wude-cocc* or *wuducoc,* sometimes called *wudesnite.*

Biologically speaking, American woodcock are small, chunky-bodied, long-billed gamebirds. Woodcock weigh 5 to 9 ounces, with the females larger than the males by a third, and are up to a foot long.

The woodcock's unique courtship display, the nasal *peeeent* or *peeenk* calls and the corkscrew mating flight, is called "singing." This 30- to 60-minute ritual takes place at dusk and dawn or throughout the night when the moon is full. Each male stakes out his own singing ground, which can range in size from 1 to 100 acres, usually an abandoned field, a forest cut, or an opening of some sort. The corkscrew flight lasts up to 60 seconds and is followed by more calling to attract a female. Woodcock sing from their arrival on the breeding grounds in March until late May or early June.

The bird's coloration is an adaptation to blend into the forest floor—mottled brownish-black sides, a tannish-creamy rust breast, and underbelly the color of dead leaves.

Like all creatures, woodcock are adapted to their niche in life. Woodcock are worm-eating machines, consuming 100 worms every 24 hours. To put this in human terms, a person would have to eat 80 to 100 pounds of meat a day to keep up with a woodcock. Much of the bird's anatomy is adapted to the search for worms: The woodcock's 2½-inch-bill is used to probe rich, loose soil for earthworms. Nerve endings sensitive to vibrations in the bill help detect the movement of worms in the soil. The very tip of the bill (probiscus) is flexible and can grasp a worm. Also, the bird's ears are below and in front of the eyes, closer to the ground. Its large eyes are set well back on the head to spot predators coming from behind and are adapted to gather more light when the birds feed, which is primarily at night. Its brain is under and around the eyes and ears. All of this sounds weird, but for a bird that spends most of its life bent over looking for worms, it makes sense.

Although worms are 90 percent of the bird's diet, woodcock also eat insects and some small seeds. They will often probe in anthills for worms. Chief feeding time is between dusk and sunrise; however, on overcast days woodcock will feed all day long.

Woodcock range covers most of the area east of the Mississippi River. The core of the breeding range is the northeastern United States, the lake states, and southeastern Canada. Winter range is centered around the Gulf of Mexico and southern states bordering the Atlantic coast: Arkansas, eastern Texas, Louisiana, Mississippi, Alabama, Georgia, Florida, South Carolina, and North Carolina.

Woodcock nest early in spring over most of their range. The development of chicks is rapid and they can fly within 2 to 3 weeks. By 5 weeks, the birds can take care of themselves. By fall chicks may be larger than their parents. Nest mortality to predators is 30 percent and juvenile mortality is only 10 percent, much better than other birds. Norris notes early writers mentioning how woodcock mothers carry chicks between their thighs to escape danger. Norris had several witnesses, but it is not confirmed.

Woodcock cover is young forest, 10- to 20-foot trees linked to rich, loamy, damp soil with earthworms. Think of a damp, spongy, lowland grouse covert with alders, especially near a swamp or bog.

Black alder-infested runs bordering grown-up abandoned agricultural fields are prime. Pastures with alders—if you can safely hunt them—are excellent. Cattle usually improve a 'cock covert: The dung boosts soil fertility, and hoof prints are miniponds, holding moisture. When grass becomes dense in the understory of a covert, birds can't bore, and the covert will fade. Other likely covert spots are sycamore scrub and low willows if the ground is moist and partially covered in green grass; overgrown apple and pear orchards; bayberry bushes mixed with red cedars; the edges of thickets; small springs; ravines with patches of green grass by a spring; greenbriar

Barry Franciscus with a Michigan woodcock. Woodcock range covers most of the area east of the Mississippi River. Breeding range covers the northeastern United States, the lake states, and southeastern Canada. Winter range is centered around the Gulf of Mexico and southern states bordering the Atlantic coast.

thickets; even farm-county irrigation with timber in the right age. Within a woodcock covert, look for alders, crabapple, young aspen, and white birch as indicators that the soil is prime, where woodcock will hunt for worms. "Chalk," whitewash woodcock droppings, and borings, pencil-sized bill holes, will indicate birds using the area.

Resting areas might be entirely different from feeding areas. Usually, they are close by. Woodcock prefer light overhead cover to rest in midday, a drier spot than where they feed. Often, birds use goldenrod fields adjacent to swampy areas as day-time roosting areas.

Woodcock rarely fly during daylight unless they are disturbed. When flushed, the birds rise to the top of alders, often juking left and right to avoid obstructions, then banking and dropping down into nearby cover, usually using what one writer called "helicopter pads," small openings in a covert's canopy, to land again.

Woodcock are slow flyers. A grouse clocked by the New York Department of Conservation hit 47 miles an hour. Doves can fly as fast as 55 miles per hour. Top woodcock speed is 30 miles per hour, with 15 miles per hour more common.

Also, the peculiar sound the birds make when flushing—Norris called it "a querulous, musical, and characteristic whistle—a sound no other bird makes"—are the result of the first three primary feathers. Little more than quills, these feathers are used by artists and often called "printers" feathers.

Like doves, woodcock are migratory gamebirds. However, woodcock migration is much slower than dove migration. Woodcock move as little as 25–35 miles a day, up to 200 miles per week, under the full moon in October or March. Migrating birds fly low; 60 feet is average. The birds travel singly, in pairs, or in small flocks. The first mi-

Sam and Jerry Nace, two Pennsylvania buschnip *hunters admire a bird. Woodcock are worm-eating machines, consuming 100 worms every 24 hours. To keep up with a woodcock, a person would have to eat 80 to 100 pounds of meat a day.*

grants to reach wintering grounds are females. During the middle of the migration, males and females are equally mixed. At the end of the migration, males, often called Labrador twisters for their habit of being wiry and fast flying, are the bulk of the birds. Migrating woodcock tend to follow waterways, but mountains and other geographical features also influence flights.

How long woodcock remain in certain areas during migration is difficult to determine. For example, in Cape May, New Jersey, along the Atlantic coast, birds headed south pile up on the New Jersey side of Delaware Bay and wait until the south winds are favorable for the long flight across the bay. The opposite happens in the spring. Similar staging areas are southern Nova Scotia and Cape Charles, Virginia. Freezing temperatures can drive birds south. When worming areas finally freeze in the North Country, they are pushed south.

More than 1.5 million woodcock make the trip south on two flyways—one following the Mississippi River, the other the Atlantic coastline—each fall. There are about 600,000 woodcock hunters in the United States. In 1985, 827,000 woodcock were taken by 350,000 hunters in the East. Today, that figure is down to about 250,000. Declining habitat for eastern woodcock has been a significant problem. Even in the 1930s, Norris was concerned about the future of woodcock. He looked at hunting control as a means of increasing woodcock numbers, as did many of his time, and noted that staggered seasons as birds move down flight lanes (in practice today) would help conservation efforts. Norris also noted how Britain had done things with plantings to improve woodcock coverts, something that the Ruffed Grouse Society and others are now involved in.

Typically, Louisiana might get as much as 50 percent of the fall flight, Arkansas 15 percent, Mississippi and Texas 10 percent, Florida and Alabama 5 percent, and other states 5 percent.

WOODCOCK HUNTING

Woodcock hunting as an upland gunning sport was not practiced much in North America until the 1820s with the coming of the much more reliable percussion cap ignition system on fowling guns. Europeans had been hunting woodcock for some time. John Holt, an Englishman, once took 23 woodcock for 25 shots with a *flintlock*. (Information like this is very useful to spout when juking timberdoodles have your partner's shooting twisted like a pretzel. Expect a return, of course.)

The first notice of woodcock in North America was by Father Paul Le Jeune, in 1634. In the early 1700s the American woodcock's table qualities were being touted, and in the late 1700s, Latham was describing the bird's flight song. Also, a 1791 New York City game law forbade the shooting of heath hens, partridge, quail, or woodcock. Before laughing about Manhattan mudbats or Bronx bogsuckers, remember that within 25 miles of old downtown Boston in those days, gunners were taking 50 woodcock a day.

Frank Forester, who came to the United States in 1831, found New Jersey's "Drowned Lands" of the Walkill River, near Warwick, some of the best woodcock coverts in North America. Gunners there shot 93 'cock before midday on one occasion. On another, a gunner named Krider and a friend shot 63 birds by 10 A.M. Forester and a partner took 125 birds in a day there. Later, he would protest the summer shooting of woodcock and become a pioneer in early woodcock conservation efforts.

By the late 1800s, some woodcock gunners were more interested in profit than table fare or sport. One estimate had 1,800 birds a week going to New York City alone. Other techniques were "firelighting" in the South, and dusking or skylining, shooting birds as they returned to roosting or feeding covers.

By the 1900, however, sportsmen and conservationists put an end to most market gunning. And by the 1930s, federal migratory bird regulations further protected woodcock. Dr. Charles Norris notes in *Eastern Upland Shooting* that he was able to find an average of 2.73 birds per hour between 1929 and 1932, and 4.37 birds from 1933 to 1935, near where Forester shot and in his Pennsylvania and New York coverts.

* * * *

Woodcock are not an especially hard bird to hunt. Rather than connive intricate schemes to elude hunters like a pheasant, woodcock use their forest floor coloration to blend into their surroundings and let danger pass by. Heavy winds or too much hunting pressure are about the only things that make woodcock really jumpy and wild-flushing. These sedate birds seek nothing more than a warm, sunny hillside to rest on after a long migratory night flight.

The difficult parts of woodcock gunning are finding good coverts and timing. Some natural history is worth repeating here: Woodcock and alders go together like ruffed grouse and aspen. The soft, black, muddy soil under alders holds more worms, about 26 per cubic foot, than most other soils and this is why woodcock are attracted to alders. Another important factor is the understory of a woodcock covert. It should be open with small clumps of grass here and there; Canadian bluestem is one grass that 'cock prefer. When grass becomes dense in the understory, birds can't bore, and they will abandon the covert.

Springtime, when 'cock are doing their courtship flights, is a good time to be scouting for new coverts. Chances are that in addition to local woodcock, flight birds will frequent these coverts. Also, any area that you've seen 'cock in during the fall, should be investigated again. Sometimes, you hit a limited sample of flight birds, a fluke of migration. Other times, finding a couple of birds on a hillside in the fall leads to the discovery of a great covert farther down the valley below. Check it out.

Woodcock start heading south when worms become unavailable. This doesn't happen instantaneously, overnight, but in small pockets, microclimate by microclimate, area by area. In the north, where most woodcock breed, higher elevation uplands freeze first, which pushes the birds into alder bottomlands. When these areas freeze, the birds start heading south.

Timing this event is impossible. There are general dates hunters use in various locales, but they could be days, even weeks off the mark, depending on a number of woodcock variables. This is why hardcore woodcock hunters watch things like the weather across the lake states and southern Canada and moon phases.

Generally speaking, clear, warm weather tends to prolong woodcock migration. Wet seasons tend to scatter 'cock, while drought tends to concentrate birds. Flight birds tend to like hillsides, especially those covered in small alders, birch, and poplars. Local birds are more likely to be found in bottomlands. Small, fast-flying males, usually wilder than most other flight birds, can signal the end of the flights.

Generally, woodcock use north–south flowing streams and rivers to find their way south in autumn, north in spring. The birds follow these waters, but not like trains on a track. East–west flowing streams, under the right circumstances, can have loads of woodcock when a north–south stream covert will be empty.

The best weather for woodcock is a moderately warm, pleasant day after a mild rain, with no strong winds. The birds will rest on or near feeding grounds during the day, especially in areas that have patches of goldenrod adjacent to feeding areas.

Woodcock droppings, "chalk," and boreholes are the best indicators of the presence of woodcock. Fresh chalk is like sloppy whitewash. Old chalk is dried out and means you're a day or two too late. Also, if you're shooting females or young-of-the-year, good hunting is likely to continue as males go last in migration.

* * * *

For years, woodcock were a bonus bird for quail hunters in the south. However, with more free time and larger disposable incomes, it is no longer uncommon for woodcock gunners from the north to follow the birds south during the winter months.

Louisiana, which gets half of the fall flight, is the primary southern 'cock destination. The Atchafalaya River basin is the heart of Louisiana's woodcock country. St. Landry, Pointe Coupee, and Iberville parishes are the epicenter. Also, Lake Ponchartrain, near New Orleans, and Lake Charles are good bets.

The boggy fringes of upland habitat (tree-lined rivers and creeks) in Mississippi and Alabama, East Texas, southern Arkansas, and western Florida (panhandle only) are also good spots.

Southern outdoor writer Bob McNally suggests checking creek bottoms and hardwood swamps with high spots where the birds can stay dry. Woodcock will shun bottomlands if they can't get at worms because there is too much vegetation or the ground is too wet. Ideally, a boggy spot with short grass and fallen leaves, and alders, myrtles, poplars, and willows growing along a trickling stream is where the birds will be.

Watch for snakes, especially if you're hunting with dogs. Creek bottoms and the sides of live oak ridges are often rattler and cottonmouth country. Many gunners hunt only the coldest days, when rattlers and cottonmouths are inactive. However, snake-proof boots or chaps and snake-avoidance training for the dogs can be essential.

H. Lea Lawrence, another southern outdoor writer, discovered outstanding spots for woodcock on Mississippi River islands in Arkansas, Kentucky, and Tennessee. Soil on the islands is right for lots of worms, and the main migration route for central flyway birds is right down the Mississippi.

* * * *

SHOOTING WOODCOCK

Denny Burkhart and Bill Goudy are two of the most efficient woodcock predators I know. This is meant as a compliment: I respect their woodcock abilities in the same way I admire a goshawk's ability to zoom through tight timber and take grouse. *Woyonihan!* . . . I respect you.

The key to Bill and Denny's uncanny knack with 'cock is their knowledge of the birds. They know what woodcock are going to do before woodcock do it. Having this kind of knowledge allows a gunner to capitalize on a flush and be in position for a good shot. Watching Bill and Denny move through a covert, handle the dogs, and move into position to capitalize on a flush is a thing of beauty. They know their stuff. Learning this takes many seasons and lots of birds, a luxury new hunters may not have.

Pointed birds will usually hold for a long time, allowing a hunter to move around and be in position for a flush. Woodcock cover is usually dense and thick. The trick, as with grouse hunting, is to move to a position near the point where you can move and swing a shotgun. Shots are not likely to be far, 25 yards and under in most circumstances.

Dr. Charles Norris writes: "It is the judicious use of the first barrel which fills the game pocket in all covert shooting. I have shot for a week in Nova Scotia and had not been able to use the second barrel a dozen times.

"In all covert shooting it is better to kill the bird quickly than to wait until it gets further off. Delay often results in the bird getting behind an obstruction. Furthermore it is gaining headway all the time. Also quick shooting gives a better chance for the use of the second barrel in case there is a miss with the first. Quick shooting does not mean snap shooting, but dwelling on the aim with the idea of letting the target get further off is an almost sure way to miss."

When 'cock rise in front of a point, they're usually not going very fast; 15 mph is typical. This can also throw off gunners accustomed to grouse or pheasants. Woodcock approached from outside a covert are likely to fly into the covert when flushed. Birds pushed to the edges of a covert are more unpredictable.

Initially, when the bird rises, it will juke its way through the dense underbrush and appear to be going 100 miles an hour. But when it clears the top of the alder or aspen canopy, there is a magic moment when the bird seems to pause slightly at the top of its flight. This is an excellent time to shoot. After this pause, woodcock tend to fly off, usually in a straight line, for another part of the covert. The birds will usually look for an opening in the covert's canopy to land in then wander from that point.

Follow up on any woodcock you shoot at. They don't fly far, usually less than 100 yards, and can be flushed a second time. If you missed, you'll have a second chance. If you hit, you could collect a bird that you thought got away.

For guns and loads, Dr. Norris recommended a "perfectly fitting gun" (remember that he had two matched sets of Purdeys) that gave an optimum pattern at 20–25 yards. Coming out the business end of his Purdey, the 12-gauge 2¾ to 3 dram equivalent 1-ounce loads of No. 9s did the trick. He recommended ⅞ ounce of shot for the 20-gauge. And for birds that are close, Dr. Norris recommended using the "edge of the pattern."

Denny Burkhart has shot a 20-gauge Windsor Churchill for a number of years. Denny is a very instinctive shooter who rarely practices. Most of his woodcock shooting, he has told me, is basically a quick poke at a fleeting bird. But he can hit what he shoots with the Churchill.

More than 1.5 million woodcock make the trip south on two flyways, one following the Mississippi River, the other the Atlantic coastline, each fall. Declining habitat across their range is a threat to these wonderful birds.

Bill Goudy shot a 12-gauge Remington Special Field autoloader the last time I hunted with him. He was just trying the gun out then and seemed to like the short barrel and straight stock. Bill, like Denny, is a very instinctive shooter.

WOODCOCK DOGS

Historically, flushing dogs—specifically cocker spaniels—were European woodcock specialists. American woodcock, however, are best appreciated with a stylish, well-trained pointing dog.

Dr. Norris suggested that the ideal woodcock dog "work to the gun," within sight or sound of its bell. "That does not mean the ideal dog is slow or pottering; on the contrary, he should be busy, industrious, active, and keen, and investigate all good holding ground. The dog that will not go into heavy cover or seeks the easy way will never be good on woodcock. The woodcock dog should work at as fast a pace as the surroundings permit. The idea that the woodcock dog is an old, superannuated, worn-out animal is quite incorrect."

Most of the good woodcock dogs I have hunted with did exactly this: They hunted to the gun, usually within earshot of the gunners, but they also ranged out to suit the dynamics of the cover when necessary. All were intelligent dogs, although somewhat wiry and high-strung at times. But the most important factor was a genuine love of woodcock hunting. I'm especially thinking of the way Denny's Lady, a Brittany, moved in woodcock cover. She was animated, alive, flowing, dancing magic in 'cock cover. In the grouse woods, she was interested, but it just wasn't the same. I contend that dogs pick up that fire and passion from their owners. Jack certainly caught my love for pheasants. Like Lady, he came alive in the pheasant fields. Nash shared my passion for grouse.

Old-timers preferred to break their dogs on woodcock to the exclusion of other birds. When plentiful, the birds sit well for a point, and they can be an excellent bird for working a young dog. However, some dogs don't like to fetch woodcock. Dr. Norris suggested sewing a dead woodcock up in a rabbit or fox fur pouch to encourage Pup to fetch. You toss it, then when Pup fetches it, you gradually cut away more fur. (Right . . . and I'll bet your wife would go for a dead-woodcock-in-fox-fur-sock chew toy laying around her house, too.)

* * * *

On another day up on the Upper Peninsula, when the afternoon sun had vanquished the morning's shadows and warmed the Earth under clear skies, the woodcock hunters gather around Bill Goudy's maroon van to compare notes and make plans for lunch.

Stones from the covert are gathered into a fireplace ring, charcoal briquettes go into the center of the ring, and a grill grate is laid across the stones. Everyone contributes a pair of woodcock. The birds are plucked and washed while the charcoal burns down and, one by one, they find a spot on the grate. Shortly, the browning skins turn a crispy golden color. The smell of cooking 'cock rises like an offering to the Red Gods. Then the birds are removed and distributed back to the hunters enjoying the sunshine, cool water, snacks, and fruit amidst tired dogs.

"What did you put on these birds, Bill?"

"All natural Michigan flavor!" Goudy replies.

Eaten with fingers under the sweet but cool northern sun and cobalt skies, these woodcock will come to define what woodcock should taste like for me. They are superb, wonderful, absolutely fantastic . . . perfect.

Will there be more? Will there be other times like this? These are questions I ponder while pulling a woodcock breast away from the bone with my finger.

Since the early 1960s, woodcock singing ground surveys conducted by U.S. Fish and Wildlife Service (FWS) biologists have shown declines in woodcock numbers, especially in the Eastern flyway, which includes the northeastern United States and from Quebec east in Canada. The losses on the Eastern flyway total 60 percent since 1967. FWS points to long-term habitat losses as the primary culprit for this decline. Throughout the Northeast, more and more acres of wetlands and swampy areas are being turned into shopping malls and housing developments.

The central flyway is holding its own—for now. However, a 1996 FWS woodcock status report showed singing ground surveys declining for both central and eastern regions. We'll look at this more closely later in this book, but it is worth thinking about now. What will become of our woodcock resource, especially in the Northeast?

6

BOBWHITE QUAIL

Wherever you find him—in a ragweed slough in Iowa, on peanut ground in South Carolina, in a clover field in Kentucky—the bobwhite is one cool, tough customer. He is challenging to hunt and just plain hard to hit on the wing, unless you catch him in the open. Even then, he will only be a short brrrrrrrrrrrr from heavy cover, where he will instinctively go when put into the air.

Tom Huggler

Only ruffed grouse gunning can compare in traditions to hunting bobwhite quail. The immediate mental image is a pair of fedora-topped gentlemen gunners, in worn yet dignified canvas coats and toting old doubles, walking into a brace of high-tailed pointers, one pointing, one backing. There is a tension, an expectation, in the scene . . . until a 20-bird covey roars out of a weedy pine plantation understory. Four reports, three birds down, and Ho'ace sends the Lab waiting in the shooting wagon to fetch the birds, while the pointers and gunners move on. . . . That's how it is supposed to be.

In some places where bobwhites are hunted this scene is somewhat close to reality (albeit a manufactured reality). In others, it's an orange ball-capped "regular guy" out with his autoloader and his Brittany. They comb the edges of a milo field and a weedpatch for the covey that hangs out at the fence corner. West of the Mississippi River and south of the Corn Belt—more "big hat" country—it's a pair of sports alighting from a custom four-wheel drive, cutting three pointers loose and heading into the mesquite and cactus to find, in good years, more than 20 coveys a day that don't act much like Gentleman Bob ought to.

So bobwhites, depending on where they are hunted, are shape-shifters: one thing in one place, another in a different place.

NATURAL HISTORY

During the last 40 million years, more than 30 different species of quail—including more than 1,400 North American subspecies, most south of the United States border—evolved in different habitat niches. New World quail differ from partridge, grouse, pheasants, and Old World quail because they have saw-toothed beaks and the males lack spurs. Also, North America's quail originated in the tropics, moving north to populate North America, unlike ruffed grouse, strictly a northern hemisphere bird, which moved south to populate North America.

The main focus of quail hunters in North America, the northern bobwhite, *Colinus virginiana*, weighs between 6 and 8 ounces and is 10 inches long. The birds fly at speeds of 28 to 40 miles per hour, although many gunners swear quail move even faster.

Bobwhites first came to the attention of Europeans in the early 1600s. In 1614, Captain John Smith mentions lots of quail in Virginia. In 1637, a man named Morton notes finding "quailes . . . bigger than the quailes of England." William Penn claimed that quail were an important food source to the first settlers in Penns Woods (Pennsylvania).

It wasn't until agriculture opened up large portions of the East to brush however, that quail became the focus of sportsmen. The typical nineteenth century farm consisted of a patchwork of crops mixed with brush and weedy native plants—early succession habitat. This edge habitat set the stage for an explosion in bobwhite numbers. Eastern quail numbers peaked in the 1860s in the North, and around 1900 in the South, although some areas of the South experienced a longer high period. Agriculture coming to the Midwest during the late 1800s created the proper habitat for quail and a second population explosion, which lasted through the middle of the twentieth century, occurred there.

Today, bobwhite range is primarily east of the Rocky Mountains and south of the lake states. Although many northern states have remnant populations of wild bobwhites, prime quail country is south of the Mason-Dixon line. There are more than 20 distinct strains of bobwhites in North America, most in Mexico. Four types of bobs interest gunners: Eastern, Plains, Texas, and Florida.

Mating season takes place from late March through May. Photoperiodism, the influence of sunlight on hormone production, causes the males hatched the previous spring to develop testes, the females, ovaries.

Bobwhites are monogamous and stay with the hen after mating to help raise the chicks. The hen typically lays 14 eggs in a nest near a brushy fencerow, the edge of a woods, a brush pile, a thicket, or a swamp. The nest is usually made under grass bent over to form a roof-like shelter for the chicks. However, 60 to 70 percent of all nests fail due to bad weather, predators, habitat destruction, and other reasons. If a nest fails, the female will nest again with another male.

After a 24-day incubation, the young quail hatch. Most leave the nest almost immediately and can fly at a very early age. The chicks eat mainly insects—beetles, grasshoppers, bugs, and caterpillars. Insects are also 44 percent of the adult's diet in spring and summer, a habit that branded quail as the friend of farmers, because they ate so many potato beetles.

By fall, the young birds are ready to form new coveys and establish their own territory. Quail have a shuffle, a dispersion of young birds into new habitat, like ruffed grouse. The young birds form new coveys of 10 to 15 quail, although the covey can reach as high as 20 to 30 birds. The 50-bird covey is largely mythical.

FOOD AND COVER

Shortly before the first rays of a rising early November sun strike soybean leaves, a single male bobwhite, nestled butt-to-butt with his coveymates near a fence corner tangled with blackberry canes and Johnson grass, in a brushy creek bottom, stirs and calls *Bob-white . . . bob-bob-white.*

Two answers come back: one, a soft *quoi-leeee* call from a young hen who had been separated from the covey by a marauding farm dog; the other from another male. The covey rejoins and walks to the edge of the bean field, where a woodlot offers chunks of acorns left over from the squirrels, and the border between the field and woodlot has weed seeds, and perhaps a couple of stray beans.

Food is plentiful, and the covey fills their crops in a short time. Then they retire to loaf and preen along the alfalfa field. Later that afternoon they return to the field border and woods to feed heavily before heading back to the security of the roost before nightfall.

This daily movement of quail from roosting area, to feed, to loafing area, and back to feed again in late afternoon is typical. Bobwhites generally feed most heavily before sunset. Many veteran bird hunters quit hunting about an hour before sunset so the birds have an opportunity to tank up on food prior to sundown, believing that this will give the birds a break from the usual hazards of foxes, owls, hawks, and cold weather.

About 86 percent of the adult bird's diet consists of vegetable matter. The reverse is true of birds 2 weeks old and younger: 87 percent of their diet is protein-rich insects. Mature birds eat less than 1 ounce of food daily, but a proper variety of food must be available at all times during the year to keep the birds healthy. Bobs are gleaners and seed scavengers. Most of what quail eat is weed seeds, waste grain, and insects. Berries and other small fruits are important, but quail don't disturb fruit or grain until it falls to the ground.

Quail eat more than 1,000 food items. Some of the more important plant life includes wild seeds, legumes, forbs, nuts, including partridge pea, lespedeza, chickweed, beggar lice, ragweed, foxtail, wooly croten, smart weed, Johnson and panic grasses, deervetch, filareee, thistle, sassafras seeds, ash seeds, pine seeds, and shattered acorns. Crops such as wheat, soybeans, milo, corn, and sunflowers draw attention. Berries like mulberries, blackberries, wax myrtle, persimmons, grapes, muscadines, huckleberries, and dogwood berries are also good. The birds also ingest grit to grind food in their gizzards and bits of greenery that furnish vitamins, minerals, and moisture.

How quail utilize the food they eat is critical. Dr. Robert Robel, a Kansas State University researcher who studied the winter caloric needs of bobs, discovered that quail use 44,700 calories a day just to maintain themselves. More calories are burned to avoid predators, search for food, and so on. On a 5-degree day, a bird will need 64,600 calories to maintain its body temperature. Seeds—even high-energy foods like sunflower, ragweed, and dogwood—only provide 4,000 calories per gram. A quail's crop holds a bit more than 2 grams. So the bird must fill its crop six times in a day to get the basic 44,000 calories necessary for raw survival. Quail empty their crops in about an hour and a half, which means the birds would have to feed much of the day just to maintain itself.

For quail, the availability of cover is equally as important as having something to eat. Prime quail habitat is a mix of covers in relatively close proximity to each other. Edges, where different types of habitat—each filling a different need for the quail—

come together, are important. Bobwhites have small travel areas, so two habitat requirements, such as food and cover, should be in close proximity.

How the covers relate to each other is almost as important as having cover available. For example, if quail must travel from brushy roosting and escape cover across a fall-plowed field to get to high-calorie food like corn, it makes the birds more susceptible to predators. This will influence the number of birds an area will maintain. Large timber tracts or a quarter section of corn provide escape cover and food, but each is only useful around the edges, where other quail habitat overlaps. Grassy areas adjacent to cornfields, fencelines bordering grain fields, and hedgerows or woody draws bisecting farm ground are the types of cover quail need in close proximity to each other. Top quail habitat is a delicate balance of cropland, nesting cover, woodlands, and fencerows or waterways which serve as travel areas.

Six basic types of cover have been identified as important to bobwhites:

Nesting and brood cover—Two-thirds of all quail nests are found in grass. Two-year-old broomsedge or other grasses that grow up high and in clumps are ideal. Some hayfields are used. Brushy cover along hedgerows inaccessible to cattle, roadsides and roadside fencerows which are not grazed or hayed, and similar areas are preferred nesting covers. Once chicks hatch, a mix of bare ground interspersed with annual weeds and an abundance of insects is needed. A mixture of grasses and early successional plants (weeds) are feeding areas for both broods and adults.

Roosting cover—Bobs prefer a grassy bed with southern exposure, especially if the weather is bad. Broomsedge, bromegrass, alfalfa edges, and wheat stubble are important in the South; bluestem, Indiangrass, canarygrass, switchgrass, buffalograss, and cordgrass are important in the Midwest; and foxtail is prime in both the Midwest and Northeast.

Loafing cover—This cover offers protection from predators, and at the same time is a place where birds can bask in the sun, loaf, and preen. The best loafing areas are located near feeding areas: meadows, cropped alfalfa or grain fields, pastures, mown orchards, and farm lanes are prime. In the Southwest, soapweed is a good loafing cover. In the South, broomsedge offers birds the same protection.

Security cover—Quail need security or escape cover close to feeding and loafing areas. If threatened, the birds can run or fly into the more secure area. Typically, brushy timber makes the best security cover. Both canopy and ground cover are important—some overhead protection mixed with openings for the birds to flush from. In the South, dogwood thickets, blackberry tangles, weedy fields, grapes, and hardwood saplings mixed with young pines are security cover. In the Midwest, woodlots, fencerows, brush piles, creek bottoms, osage-orange hedgerows, plum thickets, multiflora rose, or autumn olive patches can work. (Nebraska wildlife officials say brushy areas are one reason why southeast Nebraska and the Platte and Republican Rivers and their tributaries have abundant quail populations.) In the Southwest, quail call "mottes," islands of mesquite and cactus in the midst of a grassland, security cover.

Winter cover—Critical in the northern portions of bob's range and the Midwest, winter cover is thick, dense, brushy growth that cuts wind and offers thermal shelter for birds. It is imperative that this type of cover is located very near food sources. Red cedar windbreaks, for example, provide winter cover, since snow will bridge the branches, leaving a protective canopy for quail.

Pocket cover—Big expanses of cover are not always best. Tom Huggler, in *Quail Hunting in America*, writes that some of his best quail coverts are small patches of good cover, like small swampy spots, fencerows, and thickets. These, if located properly, can hold a covey of quail when larger areas won't. However, keep in mind that as quail are pushed into fragmented islands of less desirable habitat, they become more vulnerable to predation, weather, and hunting pressure. Keep pockets to yourself, a treasure.

HUNTING BOBWHITES

In 1927, Edward H. Forbush described bobwhite quail hunting for Arthur Cleveland Bent and the United States National Museum in this way: "As a popular game bird of the open country Bob-white has no rival. Probably about 500,000 sportsmen now go out annually from cities east of the Rocky Mountains to hunt this bird. This necessitates a great annual expenditure for hunters' clothing, guns, ammunition, dogs, and guides. It adds to the revenue of farmers and county hostelries. In some of the southern states Bob-white pays the taxes on many farms where the farmers sell their shooting rights to sportsmen. Perhaps there is no bird to which the American people are more deeply indebted for both aesthetic and material benefits. He is the most democratic and ubiquitous of all our game birds. . . . He seeks the home, farm, garden and field; he is the friend and companion of mankind; a much needed helper on the farm; a destroyer of insect pests and weeds; a swift flying game bird, lying well to a dog; and, last as well as least, good food, a savory morsel, nutritious and digestible."

This idea still applies throughout much of the Midwest and East. There are 1.5 million quail hunters in the United States, by United States Fish and Wildlife Service counts.

Quail numbers have been falling for the last 50 years. Some of the decline is linked to seasonal ups and downs. Quail, like doves, are prolific breeders, responding to favorable habitat and weather with large populations. Yet a hard winter and a wet, cold spring can negate this abundance. These fluctuations don't, however, explain the large-scale decline of quail across the United States: In 1970, 35 million bobs were taken by hunters. A decade later, this number dropped to 22 million bobs. During the 1990s, 15 to 20 million birds were taken annually. The South was especially hard hit. From 1966 to 1993, bobwhites declined 62 percent across the South.

Most of the decline is linked to changes in land use resulting in quail habitat loss. For example, in 1940, in Havilah Babcock's native Virginia, 64 percent of the land was farmland. By 1982, only 37 percent was farmed, with little idle cropland and far more cattle than 42 years earlier. This pattern repeats itself in state after state. Still, bobwhites are the second most popular nonmigratory gamebird in the United States, the most popular in the Midwest and South.

"Today's bobwhite . . . may dash for cover at the sound of hunters' voices, a car door slamming, or a dog whistle. He finds escape cover so thick it can rival bamboo. On the wing, he can zigzag through the thick stuff with the ease of any ruffed grouse, and because he is one-fourth the size of these noble birds, he is harder than any to hit. He will hide under thorny rows of multiflora rose defying all efforts to get him off the ground. He may run away from the dogs, then flush twice out of range. He knows when to freeze, when to run, and how to sidestep the multi-hunter drive," writes Tom Huggler, in *Quail Hunting in America*.

Bill Steinhauer is a 59-year-old hospice executive who has hunted Southern bobs with Elhew pointers since the 1970s. Steinhauer talked about a Beaufort, South Carolina low country lease he had, and how the birds used 15-foot-tall rows of broomsedge forest and a hillside to shield their escape, just like grouse use aspen. Invariably, Steinhauer said, the birds would buzz out the side of the broomsedge he wasn't on rather than sit like proper quail should. An afternoon's hunt moved a number of coveys, but offered only a couple of shooting opportunities.

Gentleman Bob has even taken to going underground: Huggler tells how Dick Bishop, of Iowa's Department of Natural Resources, had his Brittany point a patch of nothing on bare ground. They couldn't find a bird and started walking away from the point when Bishop's dog began digging . . . and came up with quail feathers. Then the bird flushed—Bishop missed, of course.

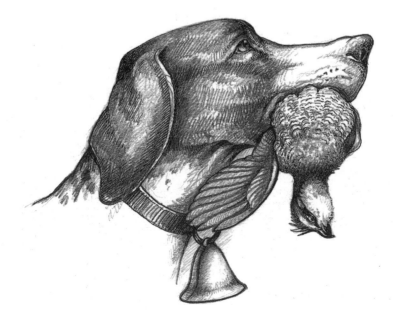

"Hunting pressure," Huggler continues, "perhaps coupled with an increase of predators—mostly raptors and coyotes—has no doubt contributed to the making of a new breed of bobwhite. He is smarter with survival skills that are pinprick sharp. Biologists call this culling of the less intelligent the *process of natural selection*. Quail that survive the hawk's stoop and the hunter's gun pass on their genes to their offspring. In the world of huntable game, this phenomenon has produced races of brainy bucks, super pheasants and, to some degree, savvy quail. I say 'to some degree' because as long as there are bobwhites, the covey will form the basic unit of interaction. The covey helps the species to survive, but it can be the bird's Achilles heel."

* * * *

Outwitting modern bobwhites is a matter of finding the right cover and hunting it effectively. The basic idea in quail hunting is to work a pointing dog through good bird habitat. Flushing dogs can and are used, but quail are traditionally the bailiwick of the pointing dog.

The right cover is an edge—the intersection of roosting, feeding, loafing, or escape covers. Weeds adjoining crops, weeds next to brush, a woods in the middle of a pasture, these are prime bobwhite real estate. Edge cover can be linear, like a brushy fencerow or crop field, or irregular, like a creek bottom, slough or wet spot a farmer can't get into.

Huggler recommends letting the dog work at his own pace, working each area thoroughly. Gunners need to slow down, too. Keep your head up, be thinking and looking ahead for the intermingling textures in cover; keep your eyes open for running birds. Hunting quietly is also more important today. A car door, a dog whistle, and talking will alert birds. Hunting with a partner or two or alone does not seem to boost the odds of getting into birds.

During the early portions of the bird season, when food is most abundant, quail could be anywhere. By midseason, however, crops are harvested, fall plowing removes a lot of the birds' loafing cover, and hunting is a bit easier. Late season offers the most challenging hunting.

Generally, the best weather for a quail hunt is a cool, dry day with a light breeze. Wind makes birds jumpy. (Hunt into it.) Rain keeps birds on the roost later. It also makes scenting conditions for dogs poor. If you have to hunt in the rain, go slow. Cold and snow causes quail to leave the roost later in the day. The birds will also spread out more to feed, because feed is usually harder to find. Midday is a good time to hunt late-season quail. Hunting in front of or behind bad weather can be outstanding because the birds will feed heavily before and after storms.

Shape-shifting *Colinus virginianus* assumes three unique identities in North America:

Bob South

Nash Buckingham stories should be required reading for both literature courses and gentlemen and ladies to whom quail are fine sport. "Mr. Buck's" stories have an exuberant elegance to them that reflect this writer and his times. Offering a glimpse into the gauzy romance that once was quail gunning in the South, Buckingham's world was the height of charming graciousness, an existence filled with genteel people living graceful and deliberate lives. His descriptions of faithful servant and friend Ho'ace, or Captain Ev and Cousin Charley, are vignettes cast in the romantic light of gorgeous prose. When he writes of places like the Brick House, built in 1850, near Saulsbury, Tennessee, you feel the texture of its walls. In his descriptions of tables spread with fine Southern cooking, you see steam rise up from the gravy-smothered quail, smell the sweet honey of the yams, the cracklin' bread and brown gravy. Your mouth will water. . . . Today, all this feels very story-bookish. Yet it was real: Nash Buckingham lived it.

That being said, there is little similarity between Buckingham's early to mid-1900s quail experience and what today's gunner will find. The Old South—Virginia, the Carolinas, Georgia, Florida, Kentucky, Tennessee, Alabama, Mississippi, and Louisiana—became the New South, part of the Sunbelt, with a lot more people, corporate agriculture, and little land left to wander. With these changes, Nash's bobwhites have been diminished. In Georgia, for example, 135,000 hunters took nearly 5 million birds during the 1962–1963 season. Ten years later, 112,000 hunters took 2.5 million birds. By the 1982–1983 season, 64,000 hunters shot one million quail.

Virginia recognized a problem with quail numbers in 1988. The state legislature and Virginia's Department of Game and Inland Fisheries established a group to both identify the sources of the quail decline and come up with a means to restore bobwhites across the state. Some of the more important problems contributing to Virginia's quail decline included: "cleaner" farming practices; an increased reliance on cool season livestock forage; decreased use of prescribed burning (resulting in poor bird cover, even though the total pine forest acreage remains close to 1940's total); greater pesticide use; the influence of pen-reared quail on wild quail; the impact of predators in fragmented habitats; and a lack of consideration for wildlife in federal farm programs.

Quail harvests in the South are the lowest of all the quail states, with a large percentage of these birds coming from commercial operations and leased-land hunting. Some areas still have a little private land available for the asking and some public hunting ground.

Bill Steinhauer described modern South Carolina quail hunting as gunning either a "desert" (crop fields) or a "jungle" (everything from the field edge into the interior of a woodlot or brushy area). Controlled burning, used in the past to keep the understory of longleaf pine plantations open for cattle and hogs, isn't done much anymore, Steinhauer said. Quail thrived in the weedy early succession plants found under the pines. However, modern timber management uses hybrid pines, intolerant of burning. Also, landowners don't want to worry about fires getting out of hand. He also lamented the loss of private land open to hunting for the asking. During the 1970s, he had access to lots of land with plenty of birds. As the small farmers who owned these "patch" farms passed away or sold their land, these areas disappeared.

Steinhauer's gunning log shows the decline in his area's quail numbers: In 1982, he found about seven coveys a day. By 1988, he was down to four coveys a day. In 1999, a covey or two was the average, although he admitted he doesn't hunt as much as he used to.

This is not to say that good quail hunting can't be found in the South. However, Charles Waterman's 1972 prediction that the future of Southern quail hunting was in leases and preserve-style hunting, that the man out with his dog for a short hunt in his spare time will be out of luck, certainly came true.

Today, you have to pay for access to good quail hunting, usually a lease of some sort. Also, in most cases, the best quail hunting (in terms of numbers) will be on commercial quail operations. Done properly, leases—the purchase of private property hunting rights—can be beneficial to both wildlife and gunners. Leased lands, depending on how the lease is arranged (some are gentlemen's agreements sealed with handshakes, others are as complex as corporate mergers and involve just as much money) can be effectively managed to increase quail numbers with a cooperative landowner.

Steinhauer said one lease he participated in was primarily managed for deer and waterfowl, with quail as an aside. Farms surrounding the waterfowl area offered plenty of good quail hunting until the land changed ownership.

Plantation-style quail hunts, complete with shooting wagons, scouts on horseback, and gunners riding to well-bred pointers, offer a glimpse into Nash Buckingham's world. Amenities are many and copious, in the fashion of true Southern hospitality. But most plantation hunts are expensive. Waterman compared the per pound cost of game collected on a plantation to an African safari! Plantation hunting has its moments, though, especially in the opportunity to experience something unique.

Bob Midwest

If Nash Buckingham can characterize the Southern bobwhite tradition, Joel Vance speaks best for Bob Midwest. Vance is gritty, raw, funny, "an aging, but incredibly virile" Mark Twain of quail. Vance's quail wagon is a Chevy pickup. His Brittanies ride up front, so they can snuggle next to the boss, instead of some cold dog crate in the back. Vance is everyman in quail hunting, a populist, not landed gentry. He stumbles through his Missouri quail coverts with an old L.C. Smith double, cusses his misses, and genuinely loves his Brittanys, bobwhite quail, and the land of the Midwest . . . home.

Bob Midwest country covers more than 450,000 square miles in Nebraska, Iowa, Missouri, Kansas, Indiana, Ohio, and Illinois. It offers the some of the best—in terms of quality, not quantity—bobwhite hunting available in North America. Combined quail harvests for these states average about five million birds annually. Most bob hunting is on private property, on corn, soybean, sorghum, and milo farms of less than 500 acres each.

Quail numbers are also falling throughout the Midwest. In Missouri, for example, quail harvests in the late 1990s have been poor. Between 1967 and 1997, more than 100,000 Missouri bob hunters averaged about two million birds annually. However, in 1997, Missouri quail harvests were 650,000 birds, 670,000 in 1998. Quail hunter numbers dropped, too, to 58,000. Roadside quail and brood counts also reached record lows in 1999. Roadside quail counts were 60 percent below the long-term, 15-year average. Brood counts were 69 percent lower than the long-term average.

Despite these drastic declines, the average daily bag in 1998 was 1.8 birds, only 18 percent below the average for the previous decade (1987–1997) when hunters averaged more than two quail per day. Also, quail hunting continues to provide a substantial amount of recreation, with 367,000 days spent afield during the 1998 hunting season.

One high spot in the Midwest has been Nebraska: Long-term trends from 1945 to the early 1990s show a gradual increase in the number of bobwhites.

The same problems affecting quail in the South, especially the loss of good habitat due to changing land use practices, have also hammered Midwestern coveys. Herbicides and pesticides destroy cover and the insects young quail need for growth. Between the early 1960s and 1980, thousands of miles of fencerows and prime quail habitat in Kansas were removed because "clean" farming's intensive agriculture requires larger fields. More recently, corporate agriculture's approach to hunting with permission is often "keep out."

Midwesterners are also discovering leases and commercial operations. Quail, when viewed as a crop like soybeans and corn, can pay for themselves if given the opportunity. And this may be the salvation of Midwestern quail.

Bob Southwest

The bright spot in quail gunning in the twenty-first century is the 400,000-square-mile Southwest, especially Texas and Oklahoma. The Southwest's quail country was "discovered" during the mid- to late-1980s by Midwestern and Southern quail hunters looking for greener pastures. Although Texas and Oklahoma quail hunting had been quite good for many years, mesquite and cactus quail didn't start looking too good until gunners accustomed to maybe 10 coveys on a really good day, stumbled across 20-plus coveys on average days.

A number of people have examined the Southwest's quail hunting, few better than *Field & Stream*'s well-respected shooting writer, Bob Brister, a Texan and a shotgunner at heart.

"These are just very wild birds in country crawling with coyotes and bobcats where a slow quail doesn't live long enough to reproduce. And they're also a different breed of bobwhite," Brister writes. (*Colinus virginiana Texanus* is literally smaller, just under 6 ounces, and paler than other subspecies. Bobs of the north Texas plains and Panhandle are the larger *Colinus virginiana Taylori,* just under 7 ounces.) "Perhaps because of their low-brush habitat *Texanus* bobs seem more prone to fly lower and make more hawk-smart evasive moves behind ground cover than other subspecies. But they'll also provide every shot imaginable in upland bird hunting."

Texas's best quail country is south of San Antonio, where "vast grassy plains interspersed with grain fields and brush hold concentrations of quail that are difficult for outsiders to believe," writes Brister. Rainfall determines which areas are best in a given year. Another prime area is the huge swath of sandy soil habitat paralleling the coastline south from Corpus Christi to the Rio Grande valley. This goes 100 miles inland, and bobs are usually plentiful due to climate conditions that produce heavy dew.

With 913,000 hunters and 97 percent of the state in private property, Texas is lease country. Texas Game and Parks recommends checking the local chambers of commerce, classified newspaper ads, feed and sporting goods stores, and with commercial outfitters for lease opportunities.

Bobs are Oklahoma's most popular gamebird. Harvests during the 1990s have ranged from 990,000 to 3.3 million quail. Oklahoma's 60,000 hunters currently average two million quail each fall. Weedy areas, small fields with brush along the fencerows and draws, and cattle operations where a small number of cattle are kept on large amounts of land, are prime Sooner State quail habitat.

Brister recommends some specialized gear for Southwestern quail hunting. Although the odds of being bitten by a rattler are low, he likes snakeproof chaps which double as anticactus devices. He also wears a thick leather glove on his left hand (he shoots right-handed) to move aside brush and thorns.

SHOOTING QUAIL

Rick Pope, a Texas banker and All-American skeet team member, who set a world record by breaking 386 consecutive skeet targets, averages 85 percent on quail. Pope believes other gunners can do the same, writes Ray Sasser, in a *Southern Outdoors* story on Pope.

Pope says hitting more quail starts with how you carry a shotgun: Hold it vertically, instead of horizontally, with the butt at the point of your hip, the muzzle at eye level. When birds flush, your right hand (for right-handed shooters) does all the work. It becomes a fulcrum. Bring the gun butt to your shoulder and the barrel is already at eye-level. Pope said this method is very efficient after you've practiced a bit.

On a covey rise, shooters have about 3 seconds before birds are out of range. Pope focuses on the first bird off the ground. Slower birds can be handled with second and third shots.

Pope likes a light, quick 20-gauge for the mild recoil, choked skeet, because its optimum pattern is 21 yards and most shots are under 25 yards; although choke tubes can tighten up patterns for windy days. Pope shoots 1 ounce, 2½ -drams equivalent loads of No. 8s. He also keeps 2¾-dram, No. 7½ loads handy. The best quail practice, says Pope, is calling for gun-down, low house No. 7 skeet targets.

Brister, analyzing quail guns and loads for *Field & Stream*, found that tailoring the gun and load to the shooting situation best handled today's quail shooting: "There are two distinctly different worlds of quail shooting," Brister writes, ". . . the classic one and the real one." One day he was hunting birds with a "wasp-waisted" 28-gauge double on a preserve that was "plenty of gun, swinging sprightly and shooting a tad high." Two days later on the "briar-thickened banks of an irrigation canal" he was stuffing 3-inch shells into a 20-gauge over/under because long shots and a rising north wind could cripple birds. On the same hunt, he ended up switching to a 12-gauge English light game gun with light No. 7½ trap loads, a combination offering a 12-gauge pattern with 20-gauge handling.

Brister believes a preserve is a good place to learn the basics of quail shooting such as how coveys flush, timing shots, and picking only one bird in a covey. Quail shooters usually fail in shooting too fast, Charley Waterman writes, and end up standing there with an empty gun while birds are still in range. Slow down: Quail flights average 25 miles per hour. There is plenty of time on a covey rise to make two shots within 20 yards. Brister also believes that 70 percent of effective quail shooting is gun mounting. It is important to hit quail in the front, so a good quail gun should throw two-thirds of its pattern above the point of aim.

Waterman likes a six-pound 20-gauge, with 26-inch barrels choked skeet or improved cylinder and modified, with a ⅞-ounce load of No. 7½s, 8s, or 9s. Brister, in most quail situations, also uses a 20-gauge, although he takes a 12-gauge light game gun along for special circumstances. Improved cylinder is a good all-around choke choice. For close quail—singles or birds in thickets—No. 9 skeet loads open patterns. For longer ranges, No. 7½ or No. 8 trap loads work well.

Brister also recommends shooters develop an increased awareness of gun safety when quail hunting. Pay special attention to zones of fire, because quail often come back on a shooter, and you could swing through a partner while following a bird. Wear blaze orange, too.

QUAIL DOGS

Robert Abbett's painting, *Waiting at Hawkeye*, where the three taut-muscled pointers in the back of a pickup truck are dying for a chance to be cut loose to run free and hunt, is the idea that pops in my mind when someone says quail dog. A quail dog is a square-headed, long-joweled, rake-ribbed pointer, tough yet fragile, like a sprinter. And each time the dog rides home, bloody-tailed, scratched and spent, you marvel how those thin legs, delicate hindquarters, the muscles and sinew, could go full-bore like that all day. It's wonderment.

Old-timers often talked about how quail could withhold their scent to hide from bird dogs. There may be some truth in this. Researcher Forbush told Arthur Cleveland Bent about how a quail he was studying flattened itself out to hide from a dog. The bird, caught on bare ground, squatted, and slowly, quietly settled its body down close to the ground. This was ". . . followed by the widening of the shoulders and an indrawing of the head, and, shaking out his feathers, he squatted on the snowy ground as 'flat as a pancake.' " The dog never scented the bird.

Other research affirms the idea that the average bird dog misses a lot of quail. According to "Efficiency of Dogs in Locating Bobwhites," a research paper from Tall Timbers Research Station in Leon County, Florida, even a dog with a "choke-bored nose" may not be as efficient as people give them credit for being.

Tall Timbers research says that dogs and hunters can expect to find about 40 percent of the birds actually present in an area. Over a period of 6 years, teams of two men and two dogs were assigned to hunt 40-acre patches of prime quail cover on a 1,300-acre area at Tall Timbers. (Where do you sign up for this kind of research?)

Biologists already had a good estimate of how many birds were on the area before the hunters and dogs went in. The dogs and hunters thoroughly combed their areas, covering about 15 acres per hour. They only found 40 percent of the quail in an area. This ranged from a high of 71 percent, to a low of 19 percent. On subsequent hunts in the same area, the range of quail found was 46 percent to 32 percent.

Tall Timber biologists summarized the value of a dog in this way: More methodical hunting of an area was more efficient than a dog. But then the truck wouldn't smell "doggy" 6 months a year, there would be no burrs to pick, no thump of a happy tail on the side of your leg, no wet kisses after drinking from a mud puddle, and life would seem infinitely less meaningful.

The standard quail dog, the horizon-raking pointer, doesn't exist. The best quail dogs vary their range according to conditions and are most effective out to 75 yards, Charley Waterman concludes. A slower-working dog is better than a faster dog, something Tall Timbers research would seem to point out, too. Pointers are supposed to be favored in the South for their ability to handle warm temperatures. Setters are considered "brush busters," able to take cooler weather than pointers. Brittanys are good, and German shorthairs are something between a pointer and plodder. Yet I've hunted with pointers who were close ranging and shorthairs that smoked the horizons. The bottom line: The best quail dog is the one that finds you birds.

Waterman also warns about snakes. Noting that Florida's eastern diamondback can drop a horse, he wrote that a dog's reflexes were the best defense against snakes because the dog avoids a full dose of venom. I'll admit that being a Yankee, a DeCoverly Kennels setter man, and hunting those infernal north-country grouse has warped my judgement, but I would take snake country more seriously than that. Train dogs that might encounter snakes to avoid them and be very careful. Losing a good dog and treasured friend that way would be horrible.

7

WESTERN QUAIL

Although Gambel's quail is a plump and delicious morsel for the table it is an exasperating bird to hunt. It loves the thickest and thorniest cover and frequents the roughest and hardest country, through which it runs, and keeps on running, faster than a man can follow; often it will take refuge in a rocky creek bed or canyon, where it is hopeless to follow.

Arthur Cleveland Bent

The Bronco II was living up to its name as it bucked, snorted, and kicked its way along a single-track side road that cut through miles of yucca, sage, cholla cactus, and sparse little patches of gama grass. Inside the truck, my hunting partners, Lawrence Smith and Dave Miller, cinched their seatbelts tight, pulled their caps snug, and gripped the truck's appropriately-placed "Omigod" handles. The dogs—Dave's Lab, Casey, and my German shorthair, Jack—were hunkered down behind the suction cup grate that went between the windows and was supposed to keep them in the rear. (It didn't work unless you plugged up the "holes" by the wheel wells with hunting accoutrements.) Me, I just went with it . . . I let the truck do its thing, up and over the ruts, never mind the strange sounds coming from the suspension. You can afford to do this when the vehicle is still under factory warranty.

The five of us were headed to one of Smith's scaled quail coverts in southwestern Kansas's Cimarron National Grasslands. We rounded a corner and came to a stop in front of an oil derrick. The derrick looked like a giant see-saw, the way it swung back and forth, in that perfectly rhythmic, methodical, machine-like way mechanical things have.

Smith's style of hunting was to flush a covey of scaled quail, then hunt the singles, especially since we had dogs. Smith, like a lot of Western bird hunters, doesn't use a dog, especially in a land where scenting conditions are poor at best, and sand

burrs, cactus, and sandy soil will chew up a dog's feet. So we left the dogs in the car—to the tune of German shorthair yelping—and went after a covey of blue quail Smith knew of near the pump and its nearby guzzler. The 18-inch-wide, 8-foot-long, tin-roofed troughs collect some of the scant 15 inches of rain the Cimarron gets annually and hold it for all kinds of wildlife. Smith helped the U.S. Forest Service build, install, and maintain a number of the Cimarron's 85-plus guzzlers.

The blue quail covey was nearby. Dozens of three-toed tracks peppered the sandy soil below a cholla cactus near the guzzler. So we followed them out into the yucca, sage, prickly pear, and fragile-looking stalks of grass. Strange little slate-blue-colored birds with a cottony white crest peeked at us from behind sage, then dashed between clumps of sage and cactus. There was more scurrying, quail sounds, then a roar . . . 10 birds flushing. The covey went in all directions, most birds about 75 yards out.

Dave Miller checks a "guzzler," a water-collecting device, for quail tracks on the Cimarron National Grassland. Scaled quail and bobwhites frequently covey around guzzlers.

Now it was the dogs' turn. When I last looked back, prior to the covey flush, the dogs were past the barrier and bouncing around in the front of the truck. I didn't want to look any more, remembering how a lonely young shorthair terrorized a house so it looked like burglars had visited. Jack hated not to be part of things, especially when shooting and birds were involved. Both dogs probably marked a couple of birds down from the truck window. So when I opened the door, both bolted for the wide open spaces and the birds.

Jack pointed something behind a yucca plant. I moved in, and a cottontop sprinted out from behind the yucca, then jumped into a packrat hole. Stubborn Jack wanted that bird. It was hard to get him away from the hole and on to other birds. But when he pointed again, I shot, and he was soon fetching back my first scaled quail.

The second blue quail covert was similar to the first, only this time there was a livestock tank instead of a guzzler and a few more quail. And while we were gone, one of the dogs (couldn't have been mine) ate one of the scaled quail we'd bagged from the first covey. There were no feathers, no licking of chops, just one bird gone and two guilty-looking suspects.

We learned something about scaled quail that day, too. They are a tough, resourceful bird, beautiful to look at, hard to hunt, a treasure in hand. We were also thankful for the things we were learning about southwestern Kansas. Through Lawrence Smith's eyes, we could see land as it once was, images of Dust Bowl horrors and what it must have meant to both people and wildlife, and the ever-present opportunity for the rebirth of land once damaged. We gained a great deal of respect for Smith, and those like him, who put such effort into restoring the area and took great pride in maintaining it.

Scaled quail are just one of the five species of western quail available to gunners. The others include California (valley) quail, mountain quail, and two desert birds, Gambel's quail and Mearns' quail.

SCALED QUAIL

Scaled Quail, *Callipepla squamata,* also known as scalies, blue quail, or cottontops, are natives of the Chihuahuan desert and the surrounding arid country with sparse grasslands in the southwestern United States and northern Mexico. This includes southwestern Kansas and east-central Colorado, south through western Oklahoma and Texas, as well as most of New Mexico and Arizona. The birds have also been introduced and established in central Washington and eastern Nevada.

One of two western quails where both males and females look similar, scalies have no topknot plume, but a white-tipped crest. Scaled quail wear mostly slate bluish-gray feathers—except on the underside, where grayish-black feathers give the bird's breast and abdomen a scalelike appearance.

Scaled quail country in southwestern Kansas.

When you think of scaled quail, think of a six-ounce, 10-inch-tall, bowlegged Oklahoma cowboy, who can run like Flo-Jo, and when it comes to eluding hunters, has the impish sense of humor of Coyote, the Native American trickster. An old Texas joke about blue quail: One gunner was telling his buddies that he had hunted scaled quail for five seasons before he realized they could fly.

Scaled quail habitat is open valleys, plains, or foothills that have a mixture of bare ground, low herbaceous growth, and scattered brushy cover such as mesquite, soapweed, acacias, mimosas, scrub oaks, and other semidesert shrubs. The land is dry, up to 15 inches of annual rain. The birds may be found on rocky, brushy slopes, draws, gullies, canyons, on sandsage grasslands, and sometimes on shortgrass plains, pastures, and cultivated fields. If shrub cover is lacking, blue quail use structures such as corrals, feedlots, and buildings for shade, resting areas, and escape cover.

Like bobwhites, scaled quail are monogamous ground-nesters. A successful nest, usually built in a protected, shady spot, will hatch 10 to 14 chicks. Other nesting locations include under shrubs, grasses, old machinery or junk, and overhanging rocks. The nesting period extends from May through September in most areas.

Proper nesting habitat is important. Quail are most vulnerable to predation during nesting season. Nesting cover should offer concealment, but not be so dense that quail can't escape when danger approaches.

As young quail mature they join with other family units to form winter flocks, generally from 20 to 200 birds. Scaled quail, like bobwhites and ruffed grouse, go through a fall "shuffle." Young-of-the-year birds may travel 10 to 25 miles. As winter progresses, the number of birds in the flock decreases due to predation—first-year mortality for blues is 70 percent or more—hunting, weather-related deaths, and other causes. Interchange among winter coveys is common. In the spring the coveys break up and the birds pair to begin the reproductive process again. Large fluctuations in population size are common from year to year. Low scaled quail numbers follow several years of drought, when the birds may not reproduce.

Like bobwhites, scaled quail home range is about a quarter-mile from a guzzler or other gathering point—researchers say scaled quail favor man-made structures like dilapidated buildings, abandoned cars, farm machinery, or barbed wire heaps. One Texas study of covey movements showed that the average covey uses a total of 160 acres. In Oklahoma, a study of 10 winter ranges averaged about 52 acres each.

Scaled quail are largely seed-eaters, feeding early and late. Many different seeds are eaten, but native woody plants and forbs are preferred. These include croton, bristlegrass, sumac, mesquite, sunflower, ragweed, snakeweed, and cholla cactus seeds. Seeds from grasses and field crops are also consumed. Other plants high on the cottontop menu include hackberry, catclaw, Russian thistle, deervetch, filaree, lupine, locoweed, and the juice of prickly pear cactus.

Green herbs make up a larger portion of the bird's diet in winter and spring. Young plant shoots, a source of moisture, are important to quail preparing for the breeding season. Insects are a hatchling's primary food. After the first month, plant material becomes more important.

The cottontop's daily routine is similar to bobwhites: The birds roost tail-to-tail in a tight circle, in groups of two or more, on duff with grass less than 16 inches high.

Roosting cover is free of overhead cover. Small shrubs, forbs, and other suitable cover is important as roosting cover.

Cottontops leave the roost at daylight and feed nearby from midmorning to midafternoon. Then the birds preen, dust, and loaf in shade near water. Biologists discovered that blue quail need a minimum of one loafing area per 70 acres of other ground, and a source of water. The best loafing cover provides overhead and ground-level protection, has a central vegetation-free area, and offers many avenues of escape. Good scaled quail loafing cover includes scattered pockets of mesquite, skunkbush, sumac, shinnery oak, cholla, and sandsage. Brush piles and abandoned buildings, corrals, and equipment may substitute for natural cover. The birds are out to feed again in the afternoon, then walk or fly back to the roost (usually a grassy hillside with southern exposure). Water is also important. Although scaled quail generally get enough water from dew, vegetation, and insects, the birds concentrate around cattle tanks, irrigation ditches, ponds, and streams. Free water may become a critical factor for the survival of young birds during dry times.

HUNTING SCALED QUAIL

Swift afoot, scalies often prefer to run rather than hide or fly. The birds seek out areas that are open at ground level to put this ability to use. Think you have a covey pinned, and the birds will vaporize into the landscape, frustrating hunters and dogs alike. When flushed, cottontops often fly 100 yards, glide to the ground, and continue running before hiding in the handiest cover available. Flushed birds also tend to fly higher than other quail, as high as 50 feet, something discombobulating to gunners.

The basic idea behind scaled quail hunting is putting birds in the air—either as a covey or as singles. In southwestern Kansas, we had the best success breaking up coveys then following up on the singles with dogs. But there are no hard rules with scaled quail.

Cottontop gunners evidently take on the unusual characteristics of their birds. Texan John Wootters is a good example. Wootters, recounting numerous adventures where quail outwitted hunters, believes that 6 ounces of quail with a brain the size of a small lima bean are out to get him. He might be right, too. "Another diabolical cottontop trick is to flush raggedly a bird or two at a time, spaced at precise intervals necessary to empty every shotgun in the vicinity before the main body of the covey gets up and away safely," writes Wootters in *Petersen's Hunting.* I've seen grouse do the same thing.

Wootters tells of a "Texican" technique for hunting scalies: Cruise ranch roads and *senderos* in trucks, looking for birds on the ground. When a covey is spotted, it is Santa Anna's full frontal assault on the Alamo revisited. "Most of the shooting will come on the initial rise; chasing blue quail singles is good aerobics, but very rarely produces much meat," writes Wootters.

"Everything from the prickly pear cactus to mesquite trees brandish spines, spikes, hooks, stickers, daggers, harpoons. Most of these can penetrate denim jeans—or even nylon-faced brush pants—about as easily as they could Saran Wrap." Wootters takes care of this with good, old-fashioned Texas leather riding chaps, a buckskin shirt, and leather gloves. "Thus accoutred, I can burst through the roughest brush at full speed, sending startled javelinas, cactus pads, limbs, and terrified quail flying in all directions!"

Humor aside, since movements are about the same for both bobwhites and scalies: Roost, feed, water, loaf, feed, roost—catch birds in the edges of these covers and you're going to find quail. It might take a bobwhite hunter a while to catch on to the textures of the cover, but it is the same basic idea. Hunt feeding areas first thing in the day. Visit water, where birds will be loafing in shady areas, in mid- to late-morning. Also, Wootters found that damp, cool, cloudy days are best in terms of dog work and quail bagged.

In New Mexico blue quail country, Tom Huggler observed three levels of vegetation: First were the tall plants, like cholla cactus, mesquite, barrel cactus, Spanish bayonet (yucca with 10-foot spires), and the tallest vegetation, the up to 20-foot-high century plant with sharp spears of green and purple sawlike teeth. Brush was the next level. It grew both high and low, and included saltbush, Mormon tea, creosote bush, lechequella ("a foot-stabber"), locoweed, and Apache plume along

Dave Miller checks a cholla cactus for scaled quail tracks in southwestern Kansas. The birds use cholla cactus as food and cover.

waterways. Then there were the grasses: side-oats grama grass, tabosa grass, and sacaton. The birds used each type of cover differently. Grass, for example, was nesting and escape cover.

Bobs and blues are natured differently, Wootters believes. Blues, somewhat like pheasants, have to be crowded hard to be forced into the air. If you can find a way to pinch a covey, do it.

Byron Dalrymple also found that blue quail are trickier. The denser the brush, the more likely the birds are to run. Yet in thin cover, birds go up out of range. Some birds don't like to climb hillsides, others pop up over the ridge and flush off the other side by the time the sports get to the top. He also had blue quail buzz in and out of eye-high brush like ruffed grouse using mountain laurel.

Hunting has little impact on cottontops. Population ups and downs are linked more to land use—especially cattle grazing, farming, and weather factors like precipitation and winter severity—than hunting.

SCALED QUAIL SHOOTING AND DOGS

Blue quail shenanigans will drive your well-adjusted, competent pointing dog absolutely batty in about half a day. A few dogs—very few—learn how to handle blues, leaving the hot body scent to circle widely and nail the covey as it trots through the brush, chuckling at the frustrated hunters in its wake. My impression, however, is that such canine geniuses are born, not made, and as a rule, local hunters don't bother much with pointing dogs in typical south Texas blue quail habitat. Retrievers, on the other hand, are a godsend in cottontop country; without one, you'll probably lose a quarter to a third of the birds you knock down, and you'll have to forego even thinking about doubles. Blue quail are noticeably tougher than bobwhites, and if a cripple comes down with both legs intact it will require a quick second shot and/or a quick, savvy dog to bring it to hand.

—John Wootters

Huggler gunned scalies with his setters and with Brittanys trained to hunt very close, 20 yards or so. The close Brits worked because they upped the percentage of birds that were bagged, not because they were able to handle running birds better. Many hunters, Huggler notes, focus on 3-hour early and late hunts, and rest their dogs at midday when heat can be uncomfortable.

Hunting running birds didn't seem to bother my shorthair Jack because he was well accustomed to Pennsylvania ringnecks, every bit as cagey and leggy as scaled quail. He was also one of those dogs who cut running pheasants off at the pass for me. (Bless you Jack!) Casey, Dave's Lab, did all right, too. The main problems we had on the Cimarron were sage and dry conditions making scenting difficult, sand burrs that required dog boots, and Casey's jackrabbit fetish.

Scaled quail are notoriously tough birds. Lawrence Smith shot a 12-gauge hump-backed Browning autoloader with an improved cylinder choke and No. 8 skeet loads. Huggler used a 20- and a 12-gauge. Wooters likes a 20-gauge, with an ounce of high-velocity No. 8s.

In southwestern Kansas, we found bobwhites and scaled quail along the Cimarron River.

Scaled quail country is rife with things that stick, like prickly pear cactus. Boot your dog against cactus and sand burrs.

"Hitting scaled quail is another matter," Huggler writes. "You have to shoot fast. . . . Without a dog you will probably lose 50 percent of the birds you knock down. Even a good dog won't find all the cripples, and that is because the heat and lack of humidity will stifle your partner's ability to scent game."

VALLEY (CALIFORNIA) QUAIL

The Maidu were largely a hunter-gatherer people, known for their beautiful baskets. They lived along the Sacramento, Feather, American, and Bear Rivers, in northern California, close to the Nevada border, and moved from place to place as the season and harvests dictated. The Gold Rush of 1848–1849 destroyed the Maidu (pronounced my-do) way of life with disease and violence and reduced the tribal population, but something of the Maidu lives on in their stories.

One Maidu legend, for example, tells how valley quail came to inhabit the hills and canyons they called home: The Maidu came to their region's hills, canyons, and streams carrying their food, supplies, and young in woven baskets and slings of rabbit fur. They stayed for a while, but, as was their custom, it was soon time to move on. When they left one morning, a small boy was left behind.

Seeking his relatives, the boy wandered the canyons and streams. In the midday heat, he crawled through the oaks and manzanita in the foothills crying "Wa-ka-ka, wa-ka-ka!"which means give me a drink of water, uncle. But no person heard his cries; only the sky and the Earth knew his plight. Then the boy was changed into a valley quail. To this day, you can hear his call in the hills of Maidu land when valley quail talk.

NATURAL HISTORY

California quail, *Callipepla californicus,* also known as valley quail, became the state bird of California in 1931. Even at that time, valley quail were particularly abundant, probably more numerous than other birds, according to the California Department of Fish and Game. Since the turn of the twentieth century, intensive farming and ranching has ruined a lot of the birds' native habitat. The birds were even gunned for market, usually sold in San Francisco. Even so, during the early 1900s, huge flocks of valley quail covered woodpiles and fields to such an extent that supply seemed inexhaustible.

Valley quail inhabit 70 percent of the Golden State, where suitable habitat remains. This is usually broken chaparral, dry washes, woodland edges, coastal scrub, farms, and parks. Like coyotes, valley quail have also become suburbia's backyard bird, helping themselves to food and water set out for pets.

Beautiful to look at, the male valley quail has a black throat and face bordered by white bands and a white forehead. The female is duller, lacking the head markings. Both sexes have a forward-curving distinctive plume or topknot. Their call, heard often during the morning and late-evening feeding, is three notes, with the middle note highest: *chi-Caa-go.*

Valley quail are found in a wide range of habitat zones. However, the birds prefer the mixed woodlands, chaparral, and grassy valleys of California, Oregon, Washington, Idaho, Nevada, and Utah, with some birds in British Columbia. Most populations north of southern Oregon and east of California are the result of introductions.

Valley quail are not migratory and seldom move far from their homes in brushy foothills or streamside habitat. The birds tolerate a relatively broad variety of climates, from cool, wet coastal areas to arid desert. Most valley quail live in the foothills and valleys where low trees or shrubs have openings of weeds and grass near water. The birds also like coastal scrub, broken chaparral, and the edges of woodlands, especially riparian woodlands, farms, ranches, and parks.

Unlike most other quail, valley quail roost 15 to 25 feet up in a dense growth of trees or shrubs at night. Brushy thickets are used during the day for loafing and escape cover. The birds also form large coveys. In most cases, a covey will be 10 to 30 birds; however, as many as 150 birds could be in a single covey.

Valley quail are largely seed eaters. Leafy green vegetation is also important, with only small amounts of animal matter in the spring and summer. The birds usually feed in open areas adjoining the roost where forbs and weeds scatter seeds on the ground and offer greens. Clover, filaree, lupine, and fiddleneck are important to the birds. Acorns are relished when available. Drinking water is essential during hot weather, especially for chicks. Adults can live on the moisture in food. Brushy cover within 50 feet of feeding areas and near a source of water is prime valley quail habitat. Valley quail build nests in a slight depression on the ground or in tall, dense weed or grass cover. Usually, the nest is well concealed at the base of a tree or shrub, near a fallen tree or under a brush pile. Nests are also often located along fencerows, in road ditches, or in pastures close to water.

A GALLERY OF GAMEBIRDS AND GUNDOGS

RUFFED GROUSE
Grey Phase
Red Phase

WOODCOCK

MOURNING DOVE

EASTERN WILD TURKEY

RING-NECKED PHEASANT

PRAIRIE CHICKEN

SHARP-TAILED GROUSE

MOUNTAIN QUAIL

BOBWHITE QUAIL

MEARNS' OR MONTEZUMA QUAIL

SCALED QUAIL

CALIFORNIA QUAIL

GAMBEL'S QUAIL

HUNGARIAN PARTRIDGE

CHUKAR PARTRIDGE

BLUE GROUSE

SPRUCE GROUSE

SAGE GROUSE

FLUSHING BREEDS
Black Labrador Retriever

Golden Retriever

English Springer Spaniel

POINTING BREEDS
Brittany Spaniel

German Shorthaired Pointer

English Setter

English Pointer

Illustrations by Denny Burkhart

HUNTING VALLEY QUAIL

Placerville, the seat of El Dorado County, California, is just over the hill from Sutter's Sawmill, where, in January of 1848, James Marshall found gold in the South Fork of the American River. This triggered the "Gold Rush" that would drive the Maidu from their original ways, and place the town, originally called Dry Diggings, into the annals of American history.

Placerville is the epicenter of a lot of early California legend. By the late 1850s, Dry Diggings became Hangtown, an allusion to the town's swift justice for claim jumpers. It also attracted outlaws: Joaquin Murieta, "The Robin Hood of El Dorado," who stopped Wells-Fargo stages and shared his loot with the poor; Black Bart, a bank clerk dissatisfied with his salary, held up stages, too, and was never caught; and Mickey Free, a minor outlaw who, while waiting his turn on the gallows, ate peanuts and danced a jig on the trapdoor while others were hung. When the Miner '49ers who didn't strike it rich or turn to a life of crime settled down, they called Placerville home. Most became farmers or loggers. Pears were a big crop until after World War II, when blight forced orchards to switch to apples. Today, the orchards attract both valley quail and hunters.

Valley quail represent 75 percent of California's total quail harvest. The 8- to 12-ounce birds are hunted in chaparral, oak woodlands, and streamside habitats in lower elevation foothills and valleys.

Roger Marlow hunted the Eldorado National Forest for valley quail, writing about it for *Sports Afield*: "Teaming up with a good pair of boots is better than most California marriages," Marlow writes. "They become close friends, these boots, they never talk back or demand alimony, and often you keep them in the garage for years after you've bought a new pair, just in case."

William Curtis, a 40-year valley quail veteran, described some of his hunting techniques in an *American Hunter* story. Curtis believes valley quail are predictable. They may act like rabbits in thick brush, but once they decide to stay put, they will stick tighter than any other bird. Twice, Curtis has seen birds hunkered in wild grapevine tangles picked up by a hunter's hand. When tossed into the air the bird flushed.

Valley quail are homebodies, seldom straying farther than a mile from the area they were hatched unless the water supply is poor. In four decades of hunting, Curtis saw changing habits, largely the result of hunting pressure and suburban sprawl pushing quail farther back into brushy terrain.

Early season is the best time to find valley quail, Curtis notes. The birds will water early, prior to 9 A.M., then go feed on seeds, greenery, insects, berries, and acorns. Until they have been spooked a few times and shot at, most valley quail won't hold tight. Chamise and buckbrush are good habitat in canyons, especially if canyons have live oaks for roosting.

Tom Huggler chased valley quail all over their range. The birds are not the sprinters that scaled and Gambel's quail are. He found California's birds preferred chaparral-covered hillsides. Nevada's valley quail liked brushy streams and irrigation ditches with tule weeds, grease brush, Indiangrass, and tumbleweeds. Oregon's birds were farm-oriented in the western part of state, and linked with desert lands in the East. Idaho birds dwelt in the Snake River's stream bottoms. In western Washington, cutovers growing back to brush were home to the birds.

Valley quail form the largest concentrations of birds found on farms and ranches in the West. Many landowners create a relationship with valley quail, feeding the birds in winter. Valley quail are also frequent visitors to suburbia. Coveys of 500 birds are common in these areas in winter, the result of several large coveys grouping. Wherever they are found, the birds like escape cover, brush, thick grass, or low trees nearby. Their roosts are in impenetrable cover on the ground or in tall shrubs or low trees. In winter, they like evergreens. The birds are opportunistic feeders, switching back and forth from grain to wild feed quite easily.

Huggler recommends hunters locate a few coveys before going after them. Valley quail have small home ranges. Look for signs, dusting bowls, and tracks. Check water (cattle tanks, ponds, streams, and irrigation systems) for tracks and droppings and call to locate birds.

Most valley quail will be in brush until midmorning. Locate loafing areas, water, and roosts nearby, all the better if these covers are connected by brushy corridors. Usually the birds will be in brush until midmorning. After this, check loafing areas and, later in the day, feeding areas.

California studied the influence of hunting on valley quail populations for 4 years and discovered that as much as 40 percent of the known fall population could be taken without damaging the overall quail population.

SHOOTING AND DOGS

"Valley or California quail," Huggler writes, "are as deceiving a target as any gamebird I have hunted. Have you ever seen a red-winged blackbird chase a rival? Well, valley quail fly like that, cutting and dodging through the cover. These fleet-winged quail seem faster than bobwhites, but I have no proof to back it up. They flush low and stay low, taking advantage of stream bottoms, trees, and brush to mask their flight. They will zip right through shirt-shredding cover, and if you are using flushing dogs or pointing breeds not steady to shot and wing (like my setters), you will have to check your swing now and then to avoid shooting the dogs."

Curtis liked shooting lightweight, quick pointing doubles, bored improved cylinder and modified. No. 7½s and No. 8s were the ticket for him. Marlow agreed with Curtis's choices. Huggler's shotgun was a lightweight, fast-swinging, skeet or improved cylinder gun throwing skeet and trap loads of No 8s.

Pointing dogs seem to be able to handle the birds when they sit tight. Actually some good dog work can occur if the birds are willing to stay put. Flushing dogs and retrievers can also be helpful in finding birds, if trained to hunt to the gun.

MOUNTAIN QUAIL

Huggler characterizes mountain quail in this way: "If the bobwhite is a gentleman, the mountain quail ain't . . . They are not very accommodating birds. To hunt them effectively, you better be in good shape and have a good shooting eye. Those who go after mountain quail may well be rewarded, for here is a true wilderness gamebird. Whereas the other quail species often thrive in habitat cultivated by man, mountain quail are nearly always affected negatively by human progress."

Mountain quail, *Oreortyx pictus*, are North America's largest quail. Major mountain quail hunting states include California, Colorado, Idaho, Nevada, Oregon, and Washington. The bird is a resident from southwestern British Columbia, western and southern Washington, and central Idaho south through the mountains of California and northern and western Nevada to Baja California.

Mountain quail look somewhat similar to both valley and Gambel's quail, only they are larger birds, up to 11½ inches, and heavier, as much as 8 ounces. They are the second North American quail where both males and females wear the same basic plumage. The long black plume looks like a feather, but it is actually two feathers, one slightly longer than the other, split apart.

NATURAL HISTORY

Mountain quail dwell higher up in the hills than do valley quail, although the range of the two birds occasionally overlaps and hunters sometimes find the birds together.

Mountain quail inhabit open montane forests with a well-developed brushy understory, steep slopes around the edges of mountain meadows, and logged or burned-over forests, from 1,500 to 10,000 feet. Typically, this is brush, scrub oak, and thicket country. In California, mountain quail breed from the chaparral up to the lodgepole pine forest, preferring areas with much shrubbery and a low percentage of canopy cover. During winter, mountain quail come to lower elevation habitats of mixed trees, brush, and herbs that produce mast and seeds.

While feeding, mountain quail forage on the ground and in low shrubs, eating leaves, flowers, and the buds of succulent vegetation; mast; pine seeds; tubers, roots, and bulbs; seeds and fruits; and insects. Some particular forbs and grasses that are important include filaree and legumes, lotus, lupine, locoweed, clover, bromegrass, fescue, needlegrass, and ryegrass.

Mountain quail begin pairing off during February and March. Their nesting success is also linked to rainfall that begins in April and supplies the birds with extra nourishment in their dry land. Good rainfall during this critical April period means a good hatch in the fall. Little rainfall can mean few young birds.

After mating, mountain quail lay 10 eggs in a nest on the ground, in a well-concealed site. Some favored nesting sites include under fallen pine branches, in weeds or shrubs, at the base of large trees and rocks, and off paths and roads. Nests will always be near water. It is imperative for young mountain quail to have access to nearby water. The birds raise a single brood annually, which hatches between May and July.

HUNTING MOUNTAIN QUAIL

"Mountain quail are, for the most part, an underutilized resource. Hunters rarely impact their numbers to any degree and have little, if any, bearing on the

mysterious population swings to which this gamebird is accustomed," writes Huggler. "Most researchers believe that severe winters and excessive periods of drought contribute heavily to the bird's ups and downs. Man-made changes in their habitat could be the other reasons. Lumbering, fires, and overgrazing, for example, are chief threats to mountain quail welfare. At any rate, reduced numbers in recent years in portions of their primary range—the Western United States—have resulted in fewer hunters seeking them. Hunters also stay home because, at times, mountain quail may appear unpredictable, be difficult to find, and are equally hard to hit on the wing."

Mountain quail are migratory, which makes them hard to find, especially during autumn. The birds move up and down the mountains and foothills, according to weather and food variables. During the summer months, mountain quail have been found as high as 8,300 feet. During winter the birds are as low as 2,000 feet.

Fall migration begins in September and peaks in October. (The spring peak is mid-April.) In most cases the birds walk because their flights are limited to about 1,000 feet at a time. Some birds travel far during migration, 25 miles in the case of one bird. But most go less than a mile.

Important mountain quail habitat during fall migration is mixed chaparral plant species (grass, scrub, low evergreens, and other trees with leathery leaves). Look for this vegetation on a 20-degree-plus slope with moderately open brush and tree cover. It will probably hold birds. Coastal and desert habitat, however, is somewhat different from California habitat. Coastal mountain quail habitat leans toward higher bush densities, 20 to 50 percent covered with trees, shrubs, and grasses. Look for birds on a southern exposure, out of the wind. Desert habitat leans toward lower brush densities. Check the mouths of canyons, just below the snowline, for birds. Also look for cottonwood, willow, wild rose, rabbitbrush, bunchgrass, and mountain sage.

Mountain quail and ruffed grouse have some things in common. Mountain quail are also adept at keeping trees, shrubs—whatever they can find—between the hunter and their line of flight. That's why brushy slopes and dense stream bottoms appeal so strongly to the birds.

Huggler recommends two approaches to hunting mountain quail. One is breaking up the covey. Locate a covey through scouting—look for droppings, tracks, and feathers around waterholes, feeding areas, and thick loafing cover, like a stream bottom—and flush the birds, then use a dog to find or walk up the singles. The birds tend to stay in the center of the tree. Mountain quail coveys tend to be smaller, six to nine birds. But those successful in breaking a covey can reap rewards; singles have a reputation for holding tight.

A second alternative, one that is standard for many mountain quail hunters, is to get above a mountain stream bottom with heavy cover and walk it out. This can be a single person operation, two parallel partners, or a divide-and-conquer approach with two hunters, one at the far end of the canyon, the other moving birds, perhaps with dog. Huggler ranks the divide-and-conquer approach the most effective because someone will get some shooting action regardless of how it's done.

Focus on mid- to late-morning for hunting mountain quail. This gives the birds time to get off the roost and start foraging. Most mountain quail roost in a tree, up to 10 feet tall. Escape cover is usually close.

Shooting mountain quail can be challenging. Huggler writes of having trouble hitting the birds at first, until he started thinking of them as woodcock, something he was familiar with, then he started connecting. Most mountain quail gunners find a 12- or 20-gauge choked between skeet or improved cylinder and shooting a one-ounce skeet or trap load of No. 8s or No. 7½s plenty of medicine for mountain quail.

As for dogs, California hunters in one study were only finding five percent of the 2,000 mountain quail in a study area because only one in five hunters used a dog. Any of the pointing breeds trained to hunt close, or a flushing dog or retriever used as a flusher could be a big benefit in both finding coveys and locating downed birds.

* * * *

DESERT QUAIL: GAMBEL'S AND MEARNS'

It's nice to know that the more things change, the more things stay the same. Take Gambel's quail, for example. Their penchant for running is legendary. This, however, is not a product of modern times. In 1932, Arthur Cleveland Bent noted, "What few I have shot have required more vigorous leg exercise than they were worth and usually had to be shot on the run." Gambel's just like to run.

Bent notes that in Arizona's Salt River Valley he talked to Herbert Brown, who repeated to Bent an express agent's account of trapping Gambel's quail for market: The express agent said that between 1889 and 1890, 3,000 *dozen* Gambel's quail were shipped out of lower Salt River Valley for San Francisco and other California markets.

This paled to the take of 6 weeks in the fall of 1894, 1,300 *dozen* quail. According to the express agent, the quail were trapped, their throats cut, and the birds sacked and shipped by express to the markets. One quail trapper caught 77 *dozen* in a single day, using eight traps and barley for bait. The next largest catch was 11 *dozen.* For their hard work the trappers were originally going to be paid $1.12 per dozen, but they only realized 60 cents per dozen.

My questions are: How did these guys round up that many quail in the space of even several square miles of territory? How did they handle all these birds once they had them? How fast did they run between the traps and the wagon that hauled all these birds to the rail station? Also, what sort of desert cactus hallucinogens were involved, both before and after doing all this?

Humor aside, mass slaughter of this sort was one of the reasons the Arizona legislature amended the state's (then a territory) game law to make trapping quail illegal.

Many authorities on Gambel's quail say hunters should skip their boots and wear sneakers to deal with these birds. Gambel's quail, *Callipepla gambelli,* also called desert quail due to their preferred habitat, are found in Arizona, California, Colorado, Hawaii, Idaho, Nevada, New Mexico, Texas, and Utah. Gambel's quail are residents from east-central California, southern Nevada, southern Utah, western Colorado, and northwestern New Mexico south to Mexico and the Rio Grande Valley of western Texas. Gambel's fill the quail habitat niche between bobwhites in the East and the valley and mountain birds of the Far West. The vast open deserts of the Great Basin and the Southwest are home to Gambel's quail.

Gambel's quail look very similar to valley quail: Gambel's stand about 11½ inches tall. The male Gambel's differs from a California male by exhibiting a prominent black patch on a creme white belly and a reddish head top. The female has a creme white belly, as opposed to the California's brownish belly. The bellies of valley quail also have a scaled appearance that Gambel's quail lack. Both sexes exhibit forward-sloping (apostrophe) plumes. Valley and Gambel's quail calls are similar—*chi-Caa-go.*

Gambel's quail are birds of desert scrub country, land dominated by desert hackberry, mesquite, catclaw, buckhorn, and cholla cactus. Gambel's quail need open water or succulent vegetation for survival, and often live in hackberry and mesquite thickets close to a water source. Chaparral and riparian areas from sea level to elevations above 6,500 feet hold interest.

Gambel's quail, like valley quail, are largely seed-eaters. One study found that 44 percent of the bird's diet was forb seeds, 14 percent shrub seeds, 3 percent grass seeds, 5 percent animal foods, and 34 percent leafy vegetation. Some of the more important foods include: deervetch, filaree, mesquite, paloverde, lupine, white-thorn, mimosa, saguaro, calowrightia, and insects (largely ants). Lotus, lupine, locoweed, and filaree were 50 percent of the Gambel's diet in California's Mohave Desert. Succulent foods are used to maintain body moisture.

The birds follow the basic pattern of life of all quail. They leave the roost in early morning, feed, water, loaf, then return to feed in the evening before roosting. Gambel's quail roost in shrubs or low trees, where shade, brushy escape cover, and succulent vegetation are available within about 1500 feet. Home range for Gambel's quail is small, between 19 and 95 acres in most cases. The birds do, however, make one trip daily for standing water and may move up to 3 miles to get it.

Gambel's mate in early spring. The success of the mating season is directly linked to the amount of rain received in winter months. A minimum of 5 inches is necessary to prompt the proper growth of green plants in the spring. The abundance or lack of green plants makes a world of difference in quail numbers. Enough rainfall ensures healthy adults, ready for the vigors of nesting.

After mating, the hen lays up to a dozen eggs in a well-concealed scratched-out depression on the ground, usually under tall grass, mesquite, sage, or other shrubs. Occasionally, Gambel's nest above ground in woodpiles, rotted stumps, or the abandoned nests of thrashers, roadrunners, or cactus wrens. Both sexes share egg-tending duties. Within 24 days, the chicks are hatching and ready to follow Mom around, eating bugs.

As more people fill the Sun Belt with new air-conditioned homes, Gambel's quail are more frequently a backyard visitor to feeders and water.

* * * *

If Gambel's quail are the track stars of the desert, then Mearns' quail, also called Montezuma, Harlequin, Massena, and "fool quail," are the homebodies. These shy, secretive birds, one of three subspecies of the Harlequin quail found in Mexico, rarely form coveys of more than six birds, and they rarely range more than about 200 yards from where they were born.

Although their range has shrunk considerably during the last century, Mearns' quail, *Cyrtonyx montezumae,* are present in most of the mountain ranges in northwestern Mexico, southeastern Arizona, southwestern New Mexico, and southwestern Texas. The range of Mearns' quail overlaps almost entirely with the evergreen oak woodlands—oak and pinyon pine grassland hills from 3,500 to 9,000 feet.

The male Mearns' has a distinctive harlequin marked face pattern. Tom Huggler describes the look as "wearing more eye shadow than a middle-aged streetwalker" and "a Russian Easter egg." Mearns' quail sport a slight crest, but not like a scaled quail's erect crest. Heavy white spotting on the bird's flank feathers remind me of guinea fowl. The females are duller, and both sexes are short-tailed. Squatty, the birds are shorter than bobwhites, 8 inches, and weigh 7 ounces. Mearns' quail communicate with a soft whistle or whinny similar to a screech owl's call.

Mearns' quail feed exclusively on the ground, using their long curved claws to scratch and dig for bulbs and tubers. Up to 75 percent of the birds' annual diet is bulbs from Oxalis and flat sedge. However, acorns, pinyon nuts, seeds and spines of prickly pear, acacia, seeds of legumes and spurges, grass, mountain laurel berries, arbutus, cedar, and insects like weevils, caterpillars, bugs, crickets, and hoppers, are also included in their diet. Unreliable acorns crops become important during years when they are produced. Mearns' quail are not dependent on free water. The birds utilize moisture in the foods they eat. Foraging generally begins low on the slope in the morning and progresses uphill during the day. Crops are usually full by late afternoon when the quail will work their way back down to the base of the slope.

As with Gambel's quail, winter monsoon rains are linked to Mearns' breeding success. Mearns' habitat is best described as open woodland consisting of evergreen oaks and junipers. A good perennial grass understory is essential, as is a tree cover greater than 20 percent. Mearns' rarely venture farther than 45 yards from the edge of the trees and are frequently found in association with clumps of catclaw mimosa.

At night, Mearns' quail roost on the ground in tall grass, huddling bobwhite-style, to conserve heat. The roost site varies each evening but is generally near a canyon bottom or small drainage. As the morning air begins to warm, the covey will leave the roost site and begin feeding in a close group.

HUNTING DESERT QUAIL

Desert quail are an important resource in the Southwest. More than one million Gambel's are taken in Arizona annually. These birds also account for 20 percent of California's quail harvest, and 200,000 birds are taken in New Mexico. Mearns' quail represent about four percent of Arizona's annual quail harvest.

Locating coveys is often hard to do. Gambel's, however, tend to be very vocal. Listen for the bird's assembly calls, beginning 45 minutes before sundown, to locate coveys. After you have a couple of coveys pinned down, follow them up the next morning.

If you can find and break up a covey, hunting singles with a dog can be a very enjoyable experience because the birds are *supposed* to hold. That doesn't mean they will. They're just supposed to.

Water holes are another good place to start. Work a dog around these areas in larger and larger loops, and you'll likely move some quail. Following stream cover also works to find quail. In addition, posting blockers at waterholes from early afternoon until an hour before sunset is a good idea. Gambel's will head back to water at this time for their daily drink.

Cruising roads until you mark a covey or find a concentration of tracks or other sign works well. Once a covey is located, you have a couple of options: You can rush in and try to flush the birds. This is where the idea that Gambel's are runners comes from. Frequently, the birds run rather than flush. A second tactic is a surround, where several hunters pool their efforts and converge on the covey from several different angles. This requires precise timing, understanding, and cooperation, something the average quail hunting party frequently lacks. However, it can be done. It also requires a well-developed sense of safety and knowledge of the country.

Gambel's quail shooting is not like trying to knock a pheasant down from the sky. A light, 1-ounce load of No. 7½s, 8s, or 9s work well from either a 20- or 12-gauge, choked improved cylinder through modified.

Gambel's dogs are frequently close working versatile breeds, like Brittanys and German shorthairs. Huggler writes that some hunters train their dogs to stay within 20 yards, which ups the shooters' bag, one reason such close workers are preferred.

Bill "Web" Parton, in *Wingshooter's Guide to Arizona*, says the best Mearns' quail hunting is on birds feeding in the thick grass understory, from noon to 3 P.M. Coveys will hold well, but flushed singles will "run like jackrabbits," writes Parton.

Mearns' quail are not early risers; they start feeding about 10 A.M. (Oxalis bulbs and sedge tubers are most of the birds' food from October through June.) Mearns' quail will be in the trough at the bottom of a canyon, loafing and feeding until about 3 P.M., when the birds move back up the hill to roost. In the mornings, look for Mearns' quail on the flat tops of hills, in open valley floors, and along the edge of trees. Also, look for roosting birds, Parton writes.

Mearns' quail hunting is not all that productive in numbers, according to Jim Heffelfinger, of Arizona's Western Gamebird Alliance. The average Mearns' bag is 2.7 birds per day. Arizona hunters averaged over two hours per bird during the last 5 years. Of 1,130 hunter-days recorded at wing barrels from 1988–1993, only 6 (0.5%) resulted in a limit of birds. Hunting does not affect the annual population fluctuations of this gamebird. Heffelfinger offers good excuses for this (a good skill for any quail hunter to develop): The rough topography of Mearns' habitat is hard on hunters; the oak overstory offers protection for birds on the covey flush; and the thick cover prevents gunners from seeing where singles sifted back into the grass.

"If you want to hunt in this country you would be well-advised to practice shooting your shotgun with one hand because you'll need the other to hang onto a tree trunk on the steep-sided canyon," Heffelfinger writes. For this reason, "Dang! I wasn't ready . . . " is the Mearns' hunter's rallying cry.

Mearns' quail are known for hunkering down and holding tight in cover when approached, a trait that earned them the "fool quail" nickname. "It is not uncommon to nearly step on these cryptic birds before they blast out of the oak leaf litter and remind you where your heart is," Heffelfinger writes.

Dogs are a necessity for Mearns' quail. Big running dogs will run past Mearns' quail. Close working, methodical dogs—such as German shorthairs, Brittanys, and Vizslas—are best at finding these birds.

As a target, Huggler writes, Mearns' quail will "without warning pogo-stick into the air, then zoom away at 45 miles per hour." Parton recommends that gunners don't look for the covey to come up off the ground, but take the birds as they appear.

Most Mearns' shooting will be close, so a 12- or 20-gauge choked improved cylinder and loaded with light 1-ounce loads of No. 7½ or No. 8s should work well.

8

PHEASANTS

The pheasants of the opening weekend were overwhelmingly birds of the year, callow juveniles that rose clattering in the air within easy gun range. Those birds went home with opening day hunters. . . . The birds that remain are either sagacious old roosters with long spurs, or smart young cocks who won their spurs during the first week of hunting. Such pheasants have much in common with the remaining hunters. Each tempers and hones the other in a process of mutual refinement.

John Madson

It is fitting that the bird that would come to represent everyman's upland gamebird in North America is not native to the continent. According to United States Fish and Wildlife Service figures, more upland bird gunners call themselves pheasant hunters than anything else, nearly 2.3 million people. There are 100,000 more pheasant hunters than turkey hunters; 800,000 more pheasant hunters than quail hunters; and 700,000 more pheasant hunters than dove hunters. Rooster, the numbers say, is king of the heap.

Given the magnificent things that can be said about so many other gamebirds—sage grouse, prairie chickens, and sharptails embody the spirit of the prairie; the wildness of place and bird associated with ruffed grouse; the gentlemanly elegance of bobwhite hunting—why did pheasants come to epitomize upland gunning in North America?

Timing played a role. Efforts to introduce North America to *Phaisanus colchicus* go back to 1730. However, it wasn't until more than a century later that the blind date between pheasants and North America sparked a love affair that continues today. This same time period also marked the emergence of the United States, and the North American continent as a whole, as unique entities, worlds apart from the "Old World." Also, North American population growth and changes in the nature of the social classes, especially the emergence of a middle class who now had time and

money for leisure activities like pheasant hunting, coincided with the arrival of a gamebird that suited this group's needs.

Another element of the rise of Rooster is the bird's association with farmland. Between the late 1800s and recent decades, agricultural would have been an apt description of most of the land east of the Mississippi River. And if agricultural land includes grazing lands and range lands, this could also have applied to the land between the Rocky Mountains and the Mississippi River. By their nature, pheasants are farmland birds, particularly linked to small farms, the type of operation predominant in North America until corporate agriculture reared its ugly head in the mid-1970s. Agricultural land and human beings are also in close contact with one another: Humans live around farms, farms feed cities. So pheasants, the middle class, and agriculture all came together with one another at the right time, in the right place, under the right circumstances.

According to Fish and Wildlife Service figures, nearly 2.3 million people hunt pheasants in the United States, more than any other game bird.

One more influence in Rooster's number one upland gamebird status is his ability to fill so many different niches. Pheasants, as a bird family, are basically Asian. Specifically, ringnecks are Chinese critters. Natural ringneck habitat, according to Chinese biologists and historical accounts, are areas with shrubs, forest edge, and farmlands. Yet pheasants pop up across the world in a variety of habitats, from Utah deserts to Iowa cornfields, from British pastures to Austrian farmlands.

Jason and the Argonauts supposedly brought the first pheasants to Europe, propagating them in the Phasis Valley, in modern-day Georgia. (No, Bubba, that ain't Atlanta, it used to be part of the Soviet Union.) This area is on the northern fringe of the bird's natural range. These pheasants were mostly dark-colored birds, not ringnecks. The Greeks and Romans, who admired Jason's birds as table fare, probably traded with the Chinese for ringnecks along the Great Silk Road, which brought trade from China to Europe. Populations of wild-reproducing pheasants (crosses between a variety of unique pheasant species) were well established in Italy, France, and parts of Germany before the fall of the Roman Empire. Pheasants appeared in Scotland and Ireland during the 1600s and later in Wales. British birds bred with other species of pheasants and developed into a unique subspecies of pheasant over time. Introductions of pheasants to North America began in the late 1700s with British birds, but failed. However, an attempt a century later, using birds directly from China, succeeded. The diversity of habitat in all of these places is astounding. Yet Rooster can adapt and actually thrive in places not naturally its home. Like German and Scottish brown trout—as well as not-so-nice Norway rats, starlings, parakeets, and a host of other introduced wildlife species—pheasants filled a vacant habitat niche in North America.

A final thought on the pheasant's rank as North America's number one gamebird has to do with something in the human psyche and the nature of Rooster that is linked. During the last 5,000 years, pheasants have been associated with human beings and have prospered along with man. Perhaps there is some primordial relationship between pheasants and human beings. You can see this link plainly in people who enjoy hunting pheasants. Not the blunt-spurred kids of opening day, but Rooster, the quintessential pheasant, the old veteran of the 10-man milo field drives, marsh-mucking with Springers, and more springtime breeding ground cockfights than we'd all care to know about. The opportunity to play field chess with Rooster sparks new life in tired legs. To cross sabers with Rooster, people travel incredible distances, hunt in biting wind and stinging snow, and hunt themselves to the brink of joblessness, divorce, and financial ruin. Rooster is also why, after nearly everyone has given up on pheasants as a thing of the past, a few hard-core hunters continue the November ritual in once pheasant-rich places like Pennsylvania, Indiana, and Michigan.

I saw this spirit in my German shorthair, Jack. Roosters were his bird, his passion, the fire in his eyes and heart. Say rooster to him, and he would leap and cavort as though you offered him a lifetime of bacon grease over French fries, not dog kibble. As a young dog, he hunted thick weed fields by bounding through them, *sproinging* up above the weed tops like a gazelle every now and then to see where he was going. Somehow he learned how to cut pheasants off at the pass, slipping out of a field to sneak along the edge and pin the birds that I would push into him. Sometimes, I

Despite the decline of pheasants in formerly pheasant-rich states such as Pennsylvania, Indiana, and Michigan, the opportunity to hunt Rooster annually renews the tired legs of hard-core pheasant hunters across the country.

swear he just *willed* pheasants to appear. We would hunt fields a line of drivers without dogs had just been through, and bingo, Jack's got a bird pinned. As an older dog, I saw him drag himself, leg spasms preventing his running, across a field to hunt roosters on a preserve. And this was after already having spent the morning pointing and fetching 27 huge cockbirds. Nothing could sate Jack's pheasant lust. He had it bad . . . or was it good?

* * * *

NATURAL HISTORY

The first attempts to bring Rooster to North America go back to 1730. One of the earliest records notes how, in 1790, New Jersey Governor Wentworth and Richard Bache, Ben Franklin's son-in-law, introduced English pheasants, *Phaisanus colchicus*, to Wentworth's New Jersey estate. George Washington is supposed to have liberated some birds on Mount Vernon. These and other attempts failed.

It wasn't until nearly a century later, in 1882, in Oregon, that the first successful introduction of pheasants occurred in North America. By this time, the conditions for pheasants were just about perfect. Farmland, the proper habitat for pheasants, was abundant.

In 1881, Judge Owen Nickerson Denny, American Consul General to Shanghai, brought 60 birds, *phaisanus colchicus torquatus*, wild-trapped ringnecks, to the United States aboard the *Otago*. Judge Denny's $300 efforts were well-intentioned but unsuccessful. The birds crossed the Pacific in small cages and were in poor shape when they disembarked.

Judge Denny was a determined fellow, however, and a second effort was made in 1882, this time using more comfortable bird quarters aboard the bark *Isle of Bute*. Judge Denny released 10 roosters and 18 hens on his property in Linn County in the Willamette Valley, then returned to China for 2 years. When he came home in 1884, the birds had spread into two adjoining counties. By 1894, some 50,000 pheasants had established themselves solidly, and pheasant hunting in North America began.

Parallel efforts took place in the East: In 1887 Rutherford Stuyvesant liberated a number of English birds on his estate in Allamuchy, New Jersey. English pheasants were also released in Massachusetts and elsewhere. Thanks to proper habitat, these stockings also worked.

Fueled by the success of these efforts, North America embarked on a pheasant stocking frenzy during the early 1900s. Birds were released in all kinds of habitat, from Rocky Mountain forests, to Great Basin deserts, to Deep South swamp. Other states used Oregon birds for releases. Also, game farm pheasants, some raised from Oregon stock, were released across the United States after 1911. In 1916, for example, Colonel Gustav Pabst made Wisconsin's first pheasant releases in Waukesha and Jefferson counties in southeastern Wisconsin. A decade later, Wisconsin was pheasant hunting.

Almost everywhere Rooster went, success followed, especially in the Midwest: A pheasant population study on Iowa's 2,500-acre Winnebago Study Area in 1941 counted an incredible 400 pheasants per section! Pheasants were even starting to be considered pests. Iowa contemplated a spring pheasant hunting season in the 1940s because the birds pulled corn shoots from the ground. South Dakota never had a game farm to raise and stock birds. Yet Rooster came to South Dakota in 1898, was plentiful by 1908, and became game in 1919.

Huron, South Dakota, writes Lionel Atwill in *Sports Afield,* has three claims to fame: It was the hometown of Vice President Hubert Humphrey and actor Cheryl Ladd, and its 22-ton fiberglass pheasant statue, erected in the 1940s by the owner of the Plains Motel, proclaimed Huron to be "The Pheasant Hunting Capital of the World." When this fiberglass pheasant was created, Huron could rightly make this claim. In 1945, South Dakota had an estimated pheasant population of 40 million birds, and 114,000 residents and 84,000 nonresidents journeyed to farms in the eastern portion of the state to shoot more than seven million pheasants. Hunters could shoot 15-pheasant limits in those days. Some gunners boasted of bagging 240 roosters from a single 40-acre milo field.

The zenith of South Dakota pheasant hunting occurred in the late 1950s. Pheasant numbers began falling, but the Soil Bank, a land set-aside program similar to today's Conservation Reserve Program, kept bird numbers high. More than three million pheasants were bagged by hunters in 1961. Iowa and other big pheasant states showed similar declines, still, there were many birds to be had, and no one was complaining too loudly.

During the 1970s and 1980s, however, things changed. One spectre on the pheasant horizon was corporate agriculture and the federal government's charge to American farmers to feed the world. These ideas and federal policies changed Midwestern farmlands. Family-run farms were gobbled up by agricultural conglomerates and turned into land for production rather than remaining Ma and Pa's back 40-acres. The industrialization of agriculture resulted in larger, more efficient tractors and harvesters. Those nasty, game-rich hedgerows that once bordered each small field had to go so the big farm rigs could turn around. Kansas farmers had ripped out 10,000 miles of hedgerows by the early 1980s. Hen pheasants like to nest in alfalfa. Intensive alfalfa cuttings resulted in the loss of millions of pheasant chicks and hens. With corporate agriculture's emphasis on getting as much from the soil as possible, more pesticides, which kill the insects necessary for pheasant chick growth, and herbicides, which wilt bird cover faster than a July dashboard melts a chocolate bar, were used.

Iowa's Winnebago area that held 400 birds per section in 1944 dropped to 100 pheasants per section in the 1950s, rebounded to 235 pheasants per section in 1961, but in 1976 there were *zero* pheasants per section. Nesting cover was, according to Iowa's Department of Natural Resources, the main cause of the losses. In 1941, almost 60 percent of the 2,500 acres were considered suitable nesting cover. By 1980, only 9.7 percent of the area could be called suitable nesting cover.

The East has a similar story. My home state, Pennsylvania, is a shining example of how to screw up a good thing. We had the best pheasant hunting in the East from the 1950s until the mid-1980s. In my first pheasant season, in 1972, nearly 750,000 pheasant hunters shot over a million birds. About 250,000 birds were stocked by our state game commission. The rest were wild, long-tailed roosters, hobgoblins that roared out of the predawn darkness and scared the *bejesus* out of a 12-year-old walking his trapline. (Today's parents wouldn't let a 12-year-old out of the house with sharp objects like knives and hatchets to wander the woods and catch muskrats, coons, possums, and the like. Things were different back then . . .)

I remember that first hunt. . . . Uncle David, his brother Stevie, and a bunch of other, unrelated hunters, canvas-clad and toting hump-backed Browning autoloaders and Remington pump guns, working through a 5-acre patch of standing corn. I still hear me yelling to them that I can see what must be 20 birds, pushed by the drive, milling around in the corn ahead, and Stevie yelling back that I shouldn't shoot, as though the heady excitement of it all might make me forget hunter safety classes.

I feel foxtail, that coagulated tan growth that carpeted the bottom of every 1972 York County cornfield a couple of feet thick, swish cool and comfortable over new boot tops. And I smell moist, freshly fallen leaves rotting in prickly hedges threaded with miles of multiflora rose and honeysuckle.

But most of all, I remember the ruffled roar of pheasant wings.

"Johnny," Stevie tells me, "go on down there by the end corner of the field and wait. We'll push 'em out to you. Just don't shoot towards the barn."

Green grass, waiting for a hard frost, lies smooth under the soles of the new "clodhoppers" and nervous sweat forms the basis of what will become rust that will eventually ruin the little .410 in years to come. But Grandpa Taylor's old canvas coat feels right, reassuring.

The first bird comes up fast, a squawking blur, barreling straight at me. And in my mind's eye, he seems to float out there, a mirage that is tangible, yet intangible in the same instant. I see his magical colors etched in that lucid blue sky—the iridescent green of a craning neck, the wild red eye patch, a regal white neck ring, and the magnificent black and gold breast feathers.

The jerky hammer cocks, the little gun barks, and the bird sails on. And after a skinny red shell pa-thunks off the ejector and flips, smoking, in the grass, I fumble in big, deep coat pockets for another.

Moments later another rooster rattles overhead and I repeat the bang-miss-pa-thunk cycle. And in the background, other shotguns roar, and cries of "Good Shot!" ring out.

My destiny is to go skunked this day. Five additional squawking banshees rocket over my head within the next few minutes. Seven skinny red .410 shells lie empty, cluttered on the grass. And when the silence returns, I hear my name.

"Johnny, didn't you get any of those birds?" Stevie asks. The wet-behind-the-ears kid with the fancy popgun must tell him no, a response which brings a guffaw and a knee slap, Stevie's way of saying he understands.

From this experience a pheasant hunter was born: First a kid with a grudge match to settle. Then a teenager who needed to prove his skills. And finally, a man to whom a solid point from a dock-tailed German dog and the singularity of a rooster etched into an autumn sky was one step closer to heaven.

A more somber reality, however, greeted my generation of pheasant hunters as we matured. By the early 1980s, Pennsylvania's pheasant harvest fell to 700,000 birds, with 250,000 of those birds stocked by the Game Commission. Within a decade, harvest numbers dropped to 300,000 birds (200,000 stocked). Pheasant hunter numbers also fell to less than 300,000. Throughout the 1990s, Pennsylvania's pheasant harvest was a few birds over 250,000, with the Game Commission stocking 200,000 birds.

Other eastern states experienced a similar decline. Ohio and Indiana, both major pheasant states between the 1940s and 1970s, lost 96 percent of their pheasant numbers between 1958 and 1978.

Habitat was, and remains, the major pheasant issue in the East. In 1964, 900-square-mile York County, Pennsylvania had more than 3,800 farms comprising about 380,000 acres of farmland. By 1984, we lost more than 1,500 farms, 83,000 acres of land, which is more than three-quarters of all the public hunting land in our region of the state. York County is now less than half agricultural, a change which took just 20 years. We now grow more shopping malls, housing developments, and industrial parks than corn and pheasants.

It would be easy to lay blame for all of this on the state conservation agencies, farmers, predators, evil spirits, and an assortment of other handy scapegoats. However, we are all ultimately responsible for what has taken place on our lands. Some fault must be laid upon eastern conservation agencies for not pushing the Conservation Reserve Program (CRP) of the mid-1980s, a 10-year land set aside program, harder than they did. Habitat is the key to pheasants, and CRP has helped resurrect the Midwest's pheasant populations. Many eastern agencies, Pennsylvania in particular, got caught up in the hoped-for proliferation of Sichuan (Szechuan) pheasants, which were supposed to nest along woodlot borders instead of hayfields, where 90 percent of pheasant chicks and often the hens who sit on the nest are killed by hay mowing before June 15. At a time when promoting CRP would have done more for pheasants, Pennsylvania, for example, conducted a 5-year Sichuan study, which discovered that the birds, when offered hayfields or woodlot borders, chose hayfields for nesting. It wasn't until the renewal of CRP in the mid-1990s that the Game Commission got on the CRP bandwagon, which was a day late and a dollar short for Rooster in Pennsylvania, I am sorry to say.

* * * *

Pheasants don't do the gaudy dancing of prairie grouse, or make a racket like ruffed grouse. Yet a salacious cock pheasant full of hot, spring breeding-season blood, his cheek patches crimson, his gold, black, blue dun, and olive feathers puffed, his once-careful walk a strut, is a sight to behold. Rooster crows to attract hens—*any* receptive hen that enters his domain. A horny devil, Rooster usually breeds up to 10 females, although some roosters are monogamous . . . maybe hen-pecked?

After breeding, the hen constructs a nest—often in alfalfa fields or near tall grass clumps, shrubs, a fence post, reeds, cattails, or sagebrush—and lays about a dozen eggs, one a day until the clutch is complete. A 24-day incubation begins after the entire clutch is laid. Hens hatch only one brood per breeding season. If a nest is destroyed, the hen will continue nesting until she successfully hatches a clutch, loses a clutch late in incubation, or can no longer produce eggs.

As soon as their feathers have dried, the hen leads her chicks away from the nest. Pheasant chicks start developing wing feathers within a few days of hatching and are capable of short flights at 2 weeks of age. Chicks stay with the hen until they are 7 weeks old.

Mortality rates for young pheasants are high. Cold rain or hail storms, predation, road traffic, and farming operations take the bulk of the birds. Between hatching and 2 weeks of age up to 25 percent of young birds die. This increases to almost 50 percent by 9 weeks. Only about three out of 10 chicks survive to adulthood. A 2-year-old pheasant is an old bird.

Cultivated farmland interspersed with patches of brush or woodlots provide the best pheasant habitat. Fallow fields, brushy pastures, roadside hedgerows, cut-over lands, brackish and freshwater marshes, lakeshores, woodlots, and meadows are also important. Fencerows, roadside ditches, and field edges with vegetation serve as travel corridors between these areas.

Within these habitat areas, there are four distinct types of pheasant cover:

Nesting cover—Abundant nesting cover in early spring is important because early clutches and broods are larger than later ones. Nesting cover must shield both nest and hen. Vegetation remaining from the previous year gives the hen and her brood the best chance of hatching success. Grass and forb stands of at least 10 inches high are best, especially if the grass is upright, for overhead concealment. Railroad right-of-ways, fencerows, shelterbelts, tree groves, weedy grain stubble, lightly grazed pastures, marsh edges, stream and ditch banks, and abandoned farmsteads

Good habitat is the key to robust pheasant populations, and good hunting.

also provide good nesting cover. In Colorado, southwestern Nebraska, and Kansas, wheat stubble serves the same purpose. Roadsides are also important. In eastern South Dakota, 14 percent of all pheasants were hatched in roadside vegetation. In a Nebraska study area, roadsides represented only 1.4 percent of the overall cover, yet produced more than 25 percent of the birds. Also, not mowing roadside cover from year to year substantially increases nesting use and hatching success. Pheasant may also prefer narrow strip cover for nesting.

Brood cover—Brood cover must conceal the hen and her brood and provide food. Ideal brood cover is layered: thick from ground level to eight inches high and fairly heavy between 8 and 20 inches. Brood cover and home range change as the chicks mature. The first 3 weeks after the chicks hatch, brood-rearing centers on 10- to 30-acre hatching sites. By late August, South Dakota home ranges average 71 acres. How pheasants use brood cover during the course of the day changes, too. In early morning when the grass is wet with dew, broods use field edges, roads, and open areas to warm themselves. Short, open cover is usually feeding cover. Recently cut hay or grain fields are feeding areas. Dusting and grit picking is done in open areas. Tall, heavy cover is used for midday loafing. Grass and weeds are used for roosting. Small trees and shrubs are valuable to broods for shade in hot weather. Corn, sorghum, and soybean fields are not used extensively until autumn, when the grain has been harvested. Crop fields are used for resting, feeding, and dusting, from August through October. By this time, the broods have broken up and small groups of young birds are scattered throughout all available cover.

Loafing and roosting cover—Pheasants loaf where their comfort is best met. During the summer, shady brush thickets, shrubs, and tall weed patches work. On a warm fall day, it's more open areas. Woody vegetation with overhead protection is preferred during the winter, especially if food is nearby. If necessary, pheasants use the leeward side of shelterbelt snow banks for blizzard protection.

Winter cover—Food close to protective cover is the main priority for winter pheasants. Pheasants in South Dakota, Michigan, Wisconsin, Iowa, and Montana rarely travel more than a quarter-mile to feed. Wetlands and some shelterbelts provide most of the Midwest's winter cover. Sweet clover and tall stands of dense cattails, bulrushes, and other marsh vegetation are preferred when snow covers food sources. In North Dakota, pheasants require wide, dense shelterbelts that provide adequate cover from drifting snow. In Kansas and Colorado, wheat stubble with nearby plum thickets is used. Cattails and bulrushes in the Texas Panhandle, with adjacent wheat, corn, and sorghum fields, provide excellent winter habitat.

Pheasants eat a wide variety of plant and animal matter. Waste grains, weed and grass seeds, acorns, buds, fleshy fruits, insects, and occasionally snakes and small rodents make up the bulk of the birds' diet. Chicks live almost exclusively on insects. A Montana Fish and Game Department study of pheasants in the Bighorn and Yellowstone valleys in the 1940s found that farm crops furnished 77 percent of the birds' diet. Wheat, barley, corn, and oats were the most important items. Beans, peas, and sorghum were also eaten in small quantities. Wild fruits amounted to less than 3 percent of total food. During egg laying season, hens regularly eat snail shells and other high-calcium grit needed for eggshell production. During autumn, pheasants feed on corn, small grains, wild seeds, berries, succulent vegetation, and insects to build up deposits of fat for the winter. The fruits and buds of woody plants are important winter food.

HUNTING PHEASANTS

Despite the decreased number of pheasants in the East, there are still bird hunters who manage to find some wild pheasants in pockets of cover, places they guard better than any Yankee woodcock gunner. Monroe Busch, a York County, Pennsylvania farmer, Pheasants Forever chapter official, and avid pheasant hunter says he still finds enough wild birds to satisfy himself and his dogs. He networks among fellow farmers for hunting areas and does a lot of habitat improvement on his own lands.

For other pheasant hunters, it is a lease where habitat improvements and stocking result in both holdover birds and put-and-take shooting. Often, hunting clubs form specifically to lease land to develop into a hunting area. State conservation agency stocking programs fall in the same category. For example, New Jersey, New York, and several New England states release birds for hunters. Another modern form of pheasant hunting is shooting preserve birds, which, on a good preserve with realistic settings and flighty birds, can be fun. All of these things are still a shadowy imitation of real pheasant hunting.

If you want Rooster in any numbers, you'll have to go to the Midwest. Thanks to CRP and an increased awareness of the value of pheasants to the Midwest, pheasant hunting in South Dakota, Iowa, Kansas, and Nebraska is still very good. Nebraska's CRP is responsible for setting aside more than 1.2 million acres of former cropland from Nebraska's 43 million total state acreage. The state's goal is 5 million acres, a possibility since more CRP sign-up periods are scheduled. Even at 1.2 million acres the land set-aside under CRP covers 30 percent more acres than the peak average under the Soil Bank Program.

Other places where pheasants can be found in decent numbers include Montana, North Dakota, Missouri, portions of Texas and Oklahoma, southern Minnesota, portions of Michigan, Wisconsin, Illinois, and Indiana. California, Oregon, Idaho, Wyoming, Washington, and small portions of the desert Southwest have wild pheasants in pockets, usually along river systems.

* * * *

The two keys to successful pheasant hunting are locating birds and forcing a flush within shotgun range. This sounds simple, but Rooster has a plentitude of tricks to bollix up the best-laid plans of hunters and bird dogs. It's what makes chasing pheasants so much fun.

Locating birds involves figuring out what you want from pheasant hunting, then going after it. If you want wild birds and good numbers, head for the Midwest. If you're just interested in seeing some dog work and taking a couple of birds home for the pot, stocked pheasant hunting on public land, private property, or preserves could be the ticket.

Eastern pheasant hunters are suffering through hard times: By the 1990s, Pennsylvania's million-bird pheasant harvest fell to 250,000 birds (200,000 stocked by the Game Commission). Other eastern states experienced a similar decline: Ohio and Indiana, both major pheasant states, suffered significant losses.

Locating preserves and stocked public areas is not hard. Preserves can be gleaned from the phone book, searching on the Internet, asking around at sporting goods stores, or talking to fellow bird hunters. State wildlife agencies, especially in New England, publicize areas that are stocked with pheasants for hunters. Check your state's wildlife agency Internet site or give them a call.

Finding wild bird hunting is a bit more difficult. In the East, you'll need to scout hard, network with a lot of landowners, and get permission to hunt private property to find truly wild pheasants. (When asking for permission to hunt private property, give an information sheet listing your name, address, phone, auto license number, and hunting license number to the landowner. This says you take responsibility for your behavior, and has helped gain access to land usually closed to hunters.) Public areas may have some wild birds, but these birds vaporize come opening day. Another option is contacting fellow bird hunters with whom you might swap a hunt for game that is abundant in your area, say ducks for pheasants. Finding wild birds in the East can be done; it just takes time and a lot more work to get several good areas, let alone a season's worth of wild pheasant hunting.

In the Midwest, public land is fairly abundant, but realize that this gets pounded pretty heavily, especially during the opener and the first weekend or so.

Still, I've hunted public land pheasants in north-central Kansas and had it all to myself a weekend after the opener. Another option is a guided Midwestern hunt. These usually involve leased land managed partially for pheasants, and access to CRP plots on private property that the average traveling hunter would never see. Joe Seibert, a Landisville, Pennsylvania friend, misses our state's once-bountiful wild pheasant resource, so he takes his German shorthairs, Marta and Rose, to Iowa for a week of pheasant hunting each fall. He started with a guided hunt, and over the course of several years, established local contacts. He now hunts CRP lands and other private areas on his own.

In the remainder of pheasant country, hunting public land can work. Combining valley quail and pheasant hunting in California sounds like a wonderful option. The same could be done with Montana sharptails and pheasants—even sage grouse, chukars, Huns, and pheasants in Oregon.

Once you've found birds, the work begins. Getting pheasants to flush within shotgun range is often field chess, and Rooster has your Queen, especially after opening day.

There are three basic techniques to hunting pheasants:

The classic pheasant drive involves a group of hunters cooperating to push birds into shooting range. Under most circumstances, the hunters select a block of cover, a crop field, a weedy draw, or a creek bottom and send a portion of the group moving forward in a line to push pheasants to the end or out the sides of the cover. Standers or blockers wait at the end of the cover for the drivers to push birds into them. The standers do most of the shooting, although drivers on either side of the drive can safely shoot if the birds break right or left.

In South Dakota, a pheasant drive might involve a small army of hunters, but then the country is big, too. In the East, more than five people are unnecessary, often illegal. Sometimes, dogs work ahead of the drivers, especially flushing dogs or retrievers used as flushing dogs. Everyone should be wearing blaze orange as a safety precaution, and there is no shooting below the horizon. The last 50 yards of the drive is usually when pandemonium reigns, because most of the birds in the field will be in the air. Smaller variations of the pheasant drive involve dogs—pointing dogs could work here—working the field in front of the driver with no standers. Usually, pheasants will bunch up at the end of the cover before flushing. Smaller patches of thick cover usually work best for small drives.

The second basic technique is working cover with dogs. Similar to the drive, this involves a couple of gunners and their dogs moving through cover to find pheasants. The dogs do most of the work. The gunners are mainly there to push birds into the dogs and do the shooting.

Lone-wolf pheasant hunting is a challenging and enjoyable way to hunt pheasants. It involves a single hunter, or a hunter and his dog. Basically, a solo hunter walks pheasant cover, stopping from time to time to unnerve pheasants, or move birds into corners of cover where they have no choice but to fly. The lone hunter has to outthink pheasants, and guess or imagine what the bird will do—how it will respond to the hunter working the field. I gunned small, dense weed fields on public land this way and shot some pheasants by zigzagging quickly through the field, stopping erratically, and jamming pheasants against openings to make them flush. When puppy Jack came home, we would play the same game, only he would point the birds for me.

Opening day pheasants are usually easy, as pheasants go. Blunt-spurred juveniles make up the bulk of the population, and they are usually cooperative—holding for pointing dogs; allowing themselves to be pushed into corners and flushed *enmasse* by a line of drivers; or squatting low until the flushing dogs can roust them out of the weeds.

However, opening day pheasants are the calm before the storm. Rooster's time begins about a week or so after the opener. Jack and I found Rooster on a mid-November hunt on Pennsylvania state game lands, when I witnessed a cockbird sneak under an overhanging mass of multiflora rose in a hedgerow. Jack pointed the bird, but Rooster squatted under the roses until I was on top of him. This cool customer didn't move until the toe of my boot touched the thorny roses about 2 inches away from his wing. Then he squirted out of an unseen hole in the thorny mess and flushed out the other side of the thick hedge cackling with laughter, offering no hope for a shot. *Woyonihan rooster!*

Midseason pheasants require a different approach. Ask yourself how other bird hunters are likely to do things, then do the opposite—something entirely unexpected.

"Almost any piece of cover can be hunted with a new approach," Tony Caligiuri and Bill Miller write in *Modern Bird Hunting.* "It may not be the most convenient way to cover a patch of ground but the results are usually worth the extra effort. Careful attention to details can make or break any approach to a hunting area in midseason. Avoid unnecessary noise or talking. Keep the dog at heel until you are absolutely ready to hunt and shoot. Take the time to hunt every piece of cover thoroughly. Take every opportunity to use a blocker and to use natural barriers that prevent birds from running ahead."

Late season pheasants require a lot from a hunter. With crops down, weed patches trampled or bowed under snow, birds can be easier to find. However, these are the survivors, super-Roosters. Hunt the thickest cover, especially marshes in the Midwest, dense woodlots in the East. If possible, hunt the edges of storms, when pheasants are out feeding, tanking up for a blow. Large drives can again be successful during the late season.

You should respect the bird, too. Several years ago, I read a story by a well-known outdoor writer about shooting late-season South Dakota pheasants after a major blizzard socked the area. The writer recommended taking advantage of weakened pheasants, pursuing them relentlessly and probing any standing cover where the birds might hide. As I read this, I wondered if it was really all worth it. Was shooting a couple of birds worth stressing who knows how many birds more than normal when they were already under duress? Why not just let the birds be, in the hope that it will result in a couple of extra chances next fall?

SHOOTING PHEASANTS

Steve Grooms, author of *Modern Pheasant Hunting,* knows Rooster. Grooms offers this advice on pheasant shooting: "Experience, particularly the experience of successful shooting, improves shooting; fear and panic destroy it. The best way to get the intensive, repeated experience that leads to good shooting is to take one or more trips to excellent pheasant country. . . . In other words, it is mighty hard to learn pheasant shooting if you only get shots at three or four birds a year in Illinois, Pennsylvania, or Michigan. It pays to really 'go to school' by treating yourself to an orgy of fine pheasant hunting in Kansas, Iowa, South Dakota or wherever else pheasant populations are healthy."

Pheasant shooting is relatively easy during the first couple of weeks of the season. But as the birds wise up, this changes rapidly. "By the second or third week of the season, most birds run instead of flying. You might have to run, too, perhaps taking a snap shot after dashing 80 yards. Sometimes the only shots you might get will be long pokes at wild flushers. Since the birds will be in heavier cover, you'll often be shooting through brush, and smart roosters know how to use brush to keep you screened. Cold weather will numb your fingers, and high winds will make the birds nervous on the ground and fast in the air," Grooms writes.

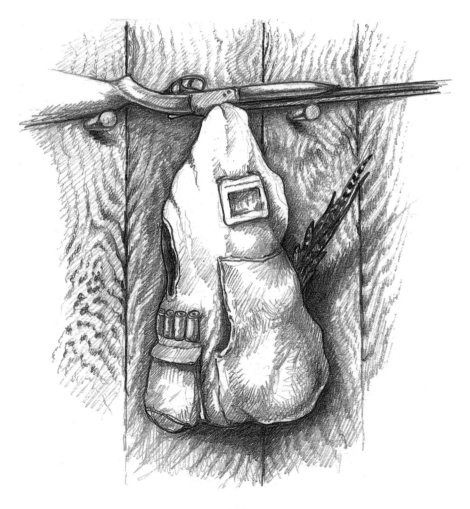

"A flushed rooster slants upward before gradually leveling off into a flat flight when he gets high enough to feel safe, about 10 to 20 yards up. Experience taught me this, but I've verified my impressions by studying films of flushing birds. How high a rooster goes depends on wind conditions and on how far they mean to fly."

Unlike many other gamebirds, pheasants are predictable: An experienced gunner knows where birds are going to break. "Knowing that, he'll make every effort to be in a good position to shoot. Experienced hunters are rarely caught down in low areas or behind screening brush when birds flush; at key moments, they'll scramble where they command a better field of fire," says Grooms. Veteran hunters also know that pheasants instinctively flush towards protective cover, and position themselves accordingly.

Reading the dog is also important. "The animated behavior of the dogs is the tip-off of an impending flush. You need to be able to read your dogs, and only training and hunting them will give you that."

Grooms recommends a 12-gauge if the shotgun is strictly for pheasants. He notes that hunters successfully use 16- and 20-gauge guns for pheasants. However, a 12-gauge handles 1-ounce or 1⅛-ounce loads with less spotty patterns and shot stringing. He also likes an improved cylinder choke because it delivers a deadly, evenly dispersed pattern from 19 to 38 yards, where the normal spectrum of shots occur.

Research shows that pheasants require at least 1.75 foot pounds of pellet energy to be taken cleanly, the amount of energy delivered by three pellets from the average shotshell load. A No. 7½ load will retain that energy out to about 35 yards. No. 6s will go up to 40 yards with the same energy. Grooms' choice of loads to handle pheasants would be a high velocity load of copper-plated No. 6s. This offers a dense swarm of pattern-filling shot, adequate penetration and enough knockdown power to go out to 40 yards.

My own experience says Grooms is right. I experimented one season with several one-and-an-eighth-ounce 12-gauge loads using No. 7½s versus No. 6s. For birds that were pointed, or shot under 30 yards, the No. 7½s were deadly. Yet the one cockbird that haunts me is a 35-yard bird that broke in front of Tim Hoff, Molly, his shorthair, and Jack and me. That bird scooted out from under midfield points by both dogs; then, near the end of the weed field, flushed wild and broke left, my side. Flustered, I missed with the Daly's bottom barrel, then recovered and hit solidly with the modified bore. Feathers flew like that bird was plucked, hit as solidly as so many other dead pheasants I had seen. But somehow the pheasant kept right on flying. Yet that same afternoon, I saw Tim take a 40-yard bird with his 20-gauge using copper-plated No. 6s. The lesson was plain: Either limit shots to pointed birds under 30 yards, or switch to No. 6s.

PHEASANT DOGS

Hunting with a well-trained gun dog is the surest way to find and bag more pheasants. Many breeds have the prerequisites for making good pheasant dogs: a good nose, strong retrieving desire, persistence, intelligence, and a sturdy physique. The prevailing wisdom holds that the ultimate pheasant dog is a springer spaniel or a

Jack doing what put the fire in his eyes. There isn't a finer pheasant dog around than a good German shorthair—yes, I admit, I'm biased.

Lab used as a flushing dog. Either breed makes a fine pheasant dog. Yet I'm biased as blazes here, and there isn't a finer pheasant hunter around than a good German shorthair. There is something in the persistent (stubborn), methodical, almost military way a good shorthair works a pheasant field that will produce more birds than any of the other breeds I've seen.

There is also something in the electric intensity of a buzz-tailed shorthair working bird scent, thinking about what Rooster is up to, and outwitting the bird that makes hunting over shorthairs unique.

To be somewhat fair, I've hunted pheasants over Labs, springers, setters, pointers, and even a Weimaraner. I've also hunted pheasants over a number of different German shorthairs, not just Jack. And what I saw still leads me to believe that shorthairs are the best choice for pheasants. Rooster and shorthairs go together like setters and grouse, pointers and quail, Brittanys and chukars. Outfoxing Rooster is drilled into the shorthair's genetics. From a strong natural instinct for retrieving, to sturdy physique, shorthairs have it all. All a trainer has to do is develop this, and express his own joy about pheasants, and the shorthair will pick up on it.

To be more specific, a shorthair from primarily hunting (but not field trial) bloodlines will make the best pheasant dog. Field trials, walking shooting trials, and a lot of those other events where Pup can earn letters behind his name are neat little man-games played with dogs. They do result in better dogs by determining who's good and breeding good with good. And it's nice to learn training tricks to get the dogs to perform some of the Herculean feats expected of them in these kind of events. However, most have little relevance towards real-world hunting. I've also seen some shorthairs that were little more than dock-tailed field trial pointers, running around the world and back in the time it took to hunt an area and get back to the truck. So go ahead and write nasty letters, but I'll take a good hunting bloodlines Kraut for pheasants any day.

Springer spaniels or setters would be my second choice—tradition and beauty fighting it out here. The springer was created for pheasant hunting. And setters, well, nothing makes my heart sing like my DeCoverly Kennels dogs.

The only problem with setters and springers is their hair. Whenever I hunted pheasants with Nash, we did well, and I was in awe of his beauty. What was unpleasant was picking a truckload of burrs, briars, weed stalks, and other junk out of his silky coat. A 45-minute training session in pheasant country meant an hour's deburring. One day while training my DeCoverly puppy Shana in pheasant country, I bumped into Chris Baldwin and his two springers. His dogs had more burrs than ear on their ears.

With shorthairs, you just hunt 'em and hose 'em off. . . . And someday old Kraut, when I come to join you on the other side, we'll be back out in Kansas, in that milo field, with the sleet starting to fall and the fog rolling in, and you pointing Rooster, your every muscle quivering with the love of it, that fire in your eyes.

9

THE PARTRIDGES: CHUKARS AND HUNS

They laugh at you from the tops of the most Godforsaken crags in the country. They run effortlessly ahead of you and flush out of range. They leave you cursing, aching, battered and birdless. And determined. You are addicted. Chukars were invented to squash egos.

Tom Reed

Thinking about this portion of our little romp through North America's uplands, I remembered the television show "The Partridge Family" and that little ditty they used to sing in the beginning . . . "C'mon get happy! . . . Whole lotta lovin' is what we'll be bringin', . . . Come on get happy!"

I also wondered if a hunter sliding *bass-ackwards* down a talus slope while chasing chukars in Idaho, or the hunter whose Brittany, frustrated with wild-flushing Huns, breaks and busts the only covey that might have offered a chance all day, believes that the partridge family of gamebirds is going to bring him "a whole lot of lovin'."

Judging by what fellow outdoor scribes have to say about North America's partridges, especially chukars, the answer to this question is a loud, defiant NO.

Paul Quinett, writing in *Sports Afield*, had this to say about chukars: "Upon hearing their call, the greenhorn charges uphill after the covey (which gives the illusion of a casual retreat), only to be brought down by any number of perils—poor footing, landslides, cactus spines, overheating, snakebite, wrenched knee, cardiac arrest, and sometimes something quite painful. Make no mistake, this is a cold-blooded bird.

"Only the best footwear should be worn in chukar terrain unless, of course, you are comfortable crawling. I've often come across some wretched chukar hunter with his boots off, inspecting the remains of his feet through teary eyes. I always offer the sensitive counsel: 'Don't shoot yourself,' I say, 'it's what they want.' Most evenings

you will find parties of chukar hunters sitting around campfires taking bets on who has the biggest blisters."

Special chukar equipment, Quinett writes, includes: ". . . mountain boots, 100 feet of high quality climbing rope, a hawk whistle, chukar call, snakebite kit, field glasses, canteen, a supply of minor tranquilizers, a crying towel and a weak mind."

Some sportsmen use a hawk call to make chukars, who have a reputation for being leggy devils, freeze. Quinett writes, "Years ago, however, this clever bird learned to discriminate between the cry of a real hawk and the wheezing screech produced by a panting chukar hunter through one of these devices. Nonetheless, I can recommend their use. I use mine to signal companions when I'm stranded on a cliff or have been caught in some misfortune."

So why would people want to torture themselves chasing after heathen Huns or contemptible chukars? Probably for the same reason otherwise sound minds enjoy chasing ruffed grouse up and down Appalachian sidehills, or wading into mesquite and cactus after bobwhites, or trying to outrun scaled quail—because we're bird hunters!

CHUKAR

The chukar, *Alectoris chukar*, is a native of Eurasia, the same broken-county grassland steppes Ghengis Khan and the Mongol hordes crossed to invade Europe.

There, chukars evolved to fill a special niche in a harsh land. Chukars came to North America from India and Turkey in the early 1930s.

The birds get their name from their call, *chuka, chuka, chukka*. In chukar country, this sound echoes from canyon to canyon. It is a siren's song to many gunners, luring them back up the canyon just one more time, another reason gunners call chukars the "devil bird."

Chukars are about 14 inches long and weigh up to 1¼ pounds. A covey bird and a superb athlete on the ground, chukars are able to run uphill and climb rimrocks and talus slopes like mountain goats.

Almost every state and Canadian province tried to stock chukars in the hopes of creating wild-reproducing populations of birds. Idaho's Fish and Game department, for example, first introduced chukars to Nez Perce County in the early 1930s. However, the first stocking that "took" was a mid-1930s Nevada effort. Nevada held the first open chukar season in 1947. By the mid-1950s, chukars were well-established in several other states.

Today, Idaho and the desert parts of Nevada, Oregon, Washington, Utah, and Wyoming have the largest chukar flocks. British Columbia, Colorado, California, Arizona, Montana, and New Mexico also have smaller populations of chukars.

"Recognizing their mistake too late, game departments throughout the West now allow generous bag limits and long seasons in hopes of slowing down the (chukar) invasion," writes Quinett.

Oregon chukar hunters take about 60,000 birds annually. Idaho hunters average between 70,000 and 80,000 birds. In 1999, Nevada's Division of Wildlife harvest models expected chukar hunters to take more than 110,000 birds for the first time since 1980.

Chukars live a "communal" lifestyle, according to Leonard Lee Rue. In March, chukar flocks, which are composed of several family groups that have been together since the hens nested and hatched chicks the previous spring, break up and the birds begin pairing off for mating and nesting. By April, the birds have mated and the females are incubating clutches that average 15 eggs each. Initially, chukar males break away from the nesting hens and form bachelor bands. They later return to help with the young.

Unlike most native North American birds, chukar broods do not break up in the fall. Instead, the birds stay together until spring mating season. Three to four family groups of birds come together to form a covey of chukars, which average 30 to 50 birds—100 birds in ideal habitat. Chukar populations fluctuate widely due to weather conditions during spring nesting season and winter weather.

Preferred chukar habitat is dry country, a steep canyon, where a stream or river provides a water supply. Here, the birds will roost in rimrock, talus slides and brushy draws. Ideally, the steep canyon slopes will have cheatgrass, talus, and cover such as rabbitbrush, sage, and bunchgrass. Wheat fields on the plateau above the canyon and a year-round stream below would make life perfect from a chukar's point of view.

In arid habitats, chukars are closely tied to water, making daily or twice-daily trips to water sources necessary until autumn rains and snow bring moisture to the high rims and slopes. Birds make their way to water first thing in the morning, then feed moving up the slope of a canyon. In the afternoon, the birds will feed, preen, and loaf on the slopes before moving back down to water prior to roosting in rimrock, talus, or other cover.

Chief in the birds' diet are the seeds and leaves of weeds. Shrub buds, fruits, berries, bulbs, and waste grain in cultivated areas also figure into their diets. Cheatgrass is important to chukars. Not a native grass species, cheatgrass and Russian thistle have created problems for native species by invading habitat; however, the plant is favored by chukars.

HUNTING CHUKARS

Remember the movie "Butch Cassidy and the Sundance Kid," when Newman and Redford are trapped on that ledge above the river and the Pinkertons chasing them "go for position" above the two outlaws, so they can shoot them or force them to surrender?

"Going for position" is what chukar hunting is all about. Chukars can run like hell. Although they tend to stay at the same elevation all day—find one and you could locate a bunch—these quirky birds generally run uphill and fly downhill. Working downhill on chukars forces them to fly.

Tom Reed, in a recent *Gun Dog* (July, 1999), disagrees: "Worn out old chukar hunters will tell you that chukars run uphill and fly down. Wyoming chukars fly both ways when they aren't running," he writes.

These strange habits earn chukars their "devil bird" moniker, according to Ken Retallic and Rocky Barker in *Wingshooter's Guide to Idaho*. Chukar hunting defies all the concepts of bird hunting that most Eastern hunters hold near and dear. A local contact for out-of-state chukar hunters, so hunters learn how to approach the birds, is important. Retallic and Barker also recommend bringing your dog, being in good shape, and planning ahead, working out who in the hunting party will hunt high, low, or in the middle of the canyon.

"Success in chukar hunting requires that hunters seek ground at or above the level at which the birds can be found," writes John Shewey, in *Wingshooter's Guide to Oregon*. "Such position can be accomplished in one of three ways: Early in the season, you can ambush the birds as they seek water at the canyon bottoms, typically at midmorning and again during late afternoon. Otherwise you have to get to their level by either walking up or hunting an area where you can drive to the top. . . . Otherwise you're stuck with the option of hiking up the steep slopes inhabited by chukar, which is one reason for the old adage that the first time you hunt chukars, you do so for the enjoyment of it, and every other time thereafter, you are motivated solely by revenge."

Once you reach the right level, Shewey says, start walking the contour, and give up altitude only begrudgingly. Chukars often hang out at the top of canyons, where they can feed on grain and buzz over the side when danger comes. A good tactic is to hunt along the edge of a canyon or just down from the edge.

"Chukar are easy to outwit if you take away their legs," writes Ron Mitchell, in *Petersen's Hunting*. "To do that, devoutly adhere to the cardinal, unamendable rule of chukar hunting: Never, but *never* hunt them uphill. If you do they'll run ahead until they reach the top, then slip over and fly to the next ridge. Instead, continue on a

quarter mile or so until you're out of sight, then climb up and come at them across the hillside so you'll be right on them or slightly above. If you're hunting with a buddy, send one man at the birds' level, the other about 50 yards above. The upper man will stop the running birds and get some flushing shots, while the lower man gets action as they sail down over him. It's futile for a human to chase chukar."

Early in the season, before autumn's rain and winter's snow, most chukar coveys will be close to water, especially a creek bottom in a canyon. Hot weather bunches birds in shaded gullies. Check the waterholes birds use before roosting.

"The gravy train grinds to a halt in late October," writes Mitchell, "when rains transform every cow track and pocked boulder into a watering trough. The chukar scatter to feast on newly sprouted cheatgrass, usually on north- and east-facing slopes where it grows thickest, and begin plying their tricks that separate the men from the boys. Only hunters well-schooled in chukar-hunting basics will be broiling birds at sunset over sagebrush campfires."

Big snows before Thanksgiving move chukars to south-facing slopes where the sun melts snow around rocks and exposes grass.

Use your ears when chukar hunting: The birds call and cackle to one another often and if you can locate the call, you might be able to follow up on it. Use binoculars to spot chukars on hillsides. Also, low, rounded hills allow the birds to see farther and outwit hunters. Sometimes it's better to hunt sharply edged canyons rather than hillsides.

"A hunting buddy of mine says you know when you are in chukar country when you are lowering your dog carefully off a ledge, praying that you don't drop him or yourself off a cliff face. When you start to think, 'Hey, maybe I better unload my shotgun' because you are clawing your way over rocks and brush, you had better get ready to shoot, because you are in chukar country. The only time I've ever wished for a 'sling for my shotgun is when I'm chukar hunting. That way I could have both hands free for climbing," writes Tom Reed.

One of the prime locations for chukar gunning is southwestern and south-central Idaho river country and the Owyhee Mountains. Good chukar country is also found along the Salmon and Snake rivers. One uniquely Idaho option is a "cast-and-blast" float trip down Hells Canyon, where sports can fish for sea-run steelhead, and hunt chukars.

However, remember what happened to three Hawaiians in Idaho. In 1818, Donald MacKenzie, of the Hudson Bay Company, sent three Aloha boys into Idaho's wilderness to scout for beaver trapping grounds. When they found beaver, they were to return to Fort Boise. They never did. The Owyhee River and the Owyhee Mountains, 11,000 square miles of dust, sagebrush desert, and chukars, were named for these brave souls. The moral of this story: People who wear grass skirts should stay the hell out of Idaho, because all the mountains already have names.

CHUKAR GUNS, LOADS, AND DOGS

Chukars are quick flyers, reaching 40-mph flight speed in a hurry, then gliding away down through the canyon. John Shewey says the bird's flight is quail-like. Chukars often follow the contours of the land around the point of a ridge before alighting.

Chukar gunners should look for a light gun, with a modified choke, shooting moderate (trap) loads of No. 5, 6, or 7½ shot.

"A good dog or dogs help immensely in finding chukars, especially later in the season when the birds appreciate the value of stealth and silence," says Shewey. "Pointing breeds are especially well-suited to chukar hunting: The birds hold well for a dog and pointers can cover lots of ground while the hunter continues along the same contour, only walking up or downhill to flush birds in front of the dog. Also, speedy pointing breeds can catch up with birds running uphill, thus pinning them down until the gunner can get there." Hunter surveys show that hunters with dogs bag 200 percent more birds than hunters without dogs.

"Just often enough to keep you interested, a chukar flock will hold for a dog. Generally, the birds will be along rimrock, in sparse cover, and hunters work the gullies that serrate the rim. One trick, if you can steel yourself to do it, is not to shoot the first bird up, since it may be an outrider, a distance from the main covey which will then flush out of range," Joel Vance writes. Single birds usually hold better for a dog than a covey.

However, chukar country has its problems for bird dogs. Cheatgrass has barbed awls like porcupine quills, worse than sand burrs. Lava rock, what cheatgrass grows over, can shred a dog's feet. Water and cactus are problems, too. Boot your dog—or hunt when snow covers the ground—and carry tweezers and extra water.

HUNGARIAN (GRAY) PARTRIDGE

Ben Franklin's son-in-law Richard Bache, in addition to being one of the first people to try to get pheasant populations going in North America, also released gray partridges in the late 1700s. Like his pheasant efforts, the gray partridge releases failed. However, Bache cut a path others would follow throughout the next century along the Atlantic seaboard. The problem with stocking gray partridge in the East was that the birds, also known as Hungarian partridge or Huns, are not small farm birds. They are birds that belong in big, open, cold winter country.

Big, open, cold winter country is certainly an apt description of Calgary, in Canada's Alberta province. In 1908 and 1909, 207 pairs of Huns were released near Calgary, and the birds took a liking to the new country, especially wheat fields that stretched horizon to horizon. The success of Alberta's Hun propagation prompted similar "monkey see, monkey do" efforts.

In 1900 and 1912, western Oregon got its first Hun stockings. These failed, but later attempts were successful. In 1914, 6,000 Huns were released in Iowa. Although most ended up as fox bait, the bird flourished in the northwestern corner of the state, eventually expanding into southeastern Minnesota. This didn't stop Minnesota from augmenting the effort with 1,000 Czechoslovakian gray partridges in 1929 at the hefty sum of $6.25 a pop. (Never let it be said that conservation departments don't know how to spend money!)

Wisconsin didn't want to be left out, so beer baron Gustav Pabst, an avid hunter, angler, and houndsman, stepped in. Not content to leave suds as his sole legacy, from 1910 to 1927 Pabst imported and released 5,000 Hungarian partridge on his farm west of Milwaukee. "The birds took to Dairyland like Yuppies to sushi," writes Tom Davis.

Stocking Huns, like chukars, soon developed into a frenzy, and at about the same time. Hun releases worked wherever wide-open spaces, cultivated grain, moderate rainfall, and hard winters collided: North Dakota, Montana, Saskatchewan, South Dakota, Iowa, southwestern Minnesota, and northeastern Wisconsin. Here, Huns could live in places other birds would not—stubblefields, sparse fencerows, idle pastures, roadside ditches, cut hayfields, and the high lonesome prairie.

* * * *

The Hungarian partridge, *Perdix perdix,* (literally partridge partridge), is roughly twice the size of a quail, 13 inches long, with a 16-inch wingspan, and weighs around a pound.

Like chukars, Huns are covey birds. Summer's broods stay together and join with other families to form large coveys in the fall and winter. In early spring, the birds separate to mate. After breeding, hens scratch a shallow nest under bushes, long grass or other plant cover, line it with leaves, feathers, and grass, and lay 14 eggs. The eggs incubate for 24 days. Both hens and cocks help raise the chicks.

Huns occupy grain country bordered by grasslands, rolling hills, draws, grassy slopes and high shortgrass knolls. A mix of native grasses and brush are best. Frequently, Hun habitat overlaps pheasant and chukar habitat in wheat stubble, valley quail habitat near ranch and farm buildings, and sharptail habitat in brushy draws on grasslands and around grain fields.

Ben O. Williams, co-author of the *Wingshooter's Guide to Montana,* writes that he likes to think of a covey's home range as a circle. When habitat is excellent, covey circles overlap. In sparse years, circles become larger and don't overlap. Williams has hunted the same covey circles for over 30 years where habitat has not changed.

Huns are usually early risers, feeding in the morning, then seeking water, and a place to loaf, dust, and preen. A second feeding takes place in the afternoon. Seeds and grains, especially wheat, are the most important food items. Huns also eat insects (grasshoppers are a favorite) and greens. Water sources are dew, streams, seeps, and ditches. Grit comes from roadsides. Warm weather finds Huns looking for shady places.

HUNTING HUNS

"The gray partridge, like its gallinaceous cousin the sharptail, is a citizen of big country and one of its defenses is to flush wild and fly far . . . if it doesn't run like a jackrabbit," Joel Vance writes. "But gray partridge are unpredictable. They may hold tight for a dog one time, flush in panic the next. As a general rule, the birds feed early and late, like most seed-eating game birds. But, unlike quail, they are not cover-seekers when alarmed; rather they may run to the middle of a bare field, then flush."

Huns depend on unobstructed vision for their security. During the middle of the day, the birds are likely to covey in clumps of cover where it is cool. Work the cover thoroughly, especially cool, shady areas not clogged with low vegetation. The birds like to walk to feeding areas and usually feed close to their afternoon loafing spot.

If you flush a covey out of range, watch them until they land, then follow up on the birds. Huns usually flush straight, but will probably arc left or right before lighting. This could be anywhere from a quarter-mile to a mile away. Getting shots at the birds could take several flushes. However, if the birds land in heavy cover, they will be reluctant to run and could hold for a dog. Following Huns flush after flush, you're likely to end up back where you started from, as the birds often have set comfort zones they like to return to.

John Barsness says Huns are more like sharptails than quail. Agricultural fields (particularly wheat stubble) and fallow fields bisected by dry watercourses steeped in chokecherry, serviceberry, buffaloberry, and what the prairie people call "buckbrush" (stunted ash and willows); windbreaks; and grassy draws near springs are the places to find the birds. Hun coveys, like bobwhites, associate with particular places.

"I have never seen a bird more addicted to 'structure' than a late-season Hungarian partridge," Barsness writes. "Early on, they may be found anywhere in a mile-long stubblefield, but later they seem to adhere to stacks of haybales, fence corners, or an old homestead. Of course they evolved in eastern and northern Europe around the earlier grain-growing versions of most of our northern plains settlers—Slavs and Scandinavians and various Teutonic types—so surely they must have a particle of some chromosome dedicated to steppe agriculture. Finding a covey in the lee of an old homestead always makes me feel not exactly uneasy, but as if something else is going on here, some layer of time that runs counter to the ancient association between dogs and humans, perhaps that moment hunters first scattered the seeds of wild grasses, dogs became more companions than hunting partners, and the wild birds of the steppes started living close to our leavings in winter."

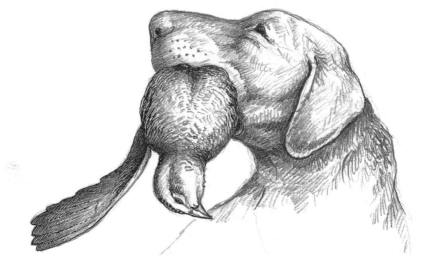

Ben Williams and co-author Chuck Johnson suggest looking for Huns in grasslands and dryland crops interrupted by draws, grassy slopes, and rolling hills; irrigated grain crops mixed with other cover types; grasslands with multiple types of vegetation that are not overgrazed; and CRP fields surrounded by cover and croplands.

Oregon's John Shewey says the best way to hunt Huns is to cover lots of ground with a good pointing dog. Birds can range widely across expansive tracts of good habitat, however, productive areas usually remain productive over long periods of time. The birds are most active in morning and late afternoon, when they feed. After feeding, Huns return to open areas to loaf. In warm weather look for shade, junipers, or chokecherry patches. Creek bottoms, bushy draws, and moist, cool areas are good at midday. In cool weather, look for rock outcroppings where the birds warm themselves in the sun. Breaking coveys into singles results in the best shooting. Singles will sit tight. Often, though, coveys will stay together despite multiple flushes. Hunting pressure and available cover are big factors in how well a covey will hold for pointing dogs.

SHOOTING AND HUN DOGS

"Partridge shooters need to be two things—quick and deliberate. If that seems a contradiction, so be it," is Joel Vance's shooting advice. "Few if any game birds flush more quickly, and considering that the bird is well-out when it flushes, it pays to be a quick shooter. On the other hand, because the shots are often at long ranges, many good partridge hunters use full-choked guns and the deliberate shooting techniques of good waterfowlers."

Shewey, however, likes an improved cylinder or modified choke, firing No. 6 or 7½ shot. Johnson and Williams agree, at least for the early season. Later, they might switch to a full-choked shotgun.

"A good Hun dog should hunt wide, for it has much land to cover," writes Charles Waterman. "It sounds like a job for an English pointer, and if I had to choose a Hun dog by breed, that's what it would be for me. I am aware that there are some circumstances where a close-working dog is best, but the overall picture calls for a big-goer. When you get close to the birds, a high degree of dog control is necessary because the Hun as a runner is in a class with chukars and pheasants. Only a few canine sages have learned deliberately to head off a sprinting covey, and I have never owned one of those treasures, although I have seen the miracle performed a few times."

Vance says, "The ideal partridge dog is also the ideal pheasant dog—one who knows how to handle running birds. If the dog can circle a running covey, chances are the birds caught between you and the dog will freeze and let you get close enough for easy shooting."

Johnson and Williams also prefer a wide-hunting Hun dog because there is a lot of country to cover. However, a close-working pointing dog can be outstanding if the birds cooperate. Also, flushing dogs and retrievers used as flushers can be effective, although these breeds tend to flush birds at greater distances and can't cover the open spaces like a pointing dog. They recommend dog handlers stick to the high points of hills, where they can see dogs work at a distance and get to dogs on point faster moving downhill.

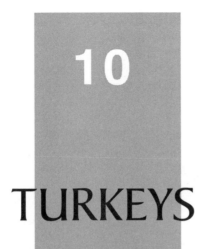

10

TURKEYS

A man really ought to learn turkey hunting in the fall. It will have a tendency to cure him of a great deal of the tippy-toe attitude that is normal with beginning turkey hunters. He will hear so many in the fall and see so many, that the sense of awe about turkeys that occasionally arises in the spring can be stifled. A turkey is, after all, only a bird. In the spring, because he looms larger than life, it becomes easy to overestimate him but you should not deify him. You are going to have ample trouble in your dealings with him without assigning attributes to him that he does not really possess. Fall humanizes him and lets you see him in what is really a state that is closer to his proper perspective.

Tom Kelly

The eastern sky shows thin bands of pink, yellow, and orange above the mountaintops on its horizon. Slowly, gently the sky will consume the shadow world of owls and whippoorwills, transforming shades of blue, black, and gray into rainbow hues. Sunlight will also spark to life a forest of buzzing insects, singing warblers, cooing doves—and a gobbling tom turkey, my hunting partner Bob Kerstetter and I hope. We seek an encounter with *Meleagris gallopavo silvestris*, the Eastern wild turkey, king of the springtime forest—discounting drumming ruffed grouse, of course, at least from my point of view. On the top of Tobacco Patch Mountain, we huff because the climb in the darkness was steep, our bodies still heavy with the accumulation of winter's inactivity. Between breaths, we listen for a gobble, stretching our sense of hearing far out into the forest, across the hills.

On the drive into the mountains, I joked with Bob about hoping to hear birds from the top of Tobacco Patch instead of across the valley, on the point of the opposite mountain. Earlier that season, I heard seven different gobblers from that mountaintop, all sounding like they were on Tobacco Patch.

I also tell him about "wrangler's disease": When I worked for the outfitter in Montana, we kicked the horses and mules out of the corral at night to forage in grassy mountain meadows. At first light, the wrangler's job was to track these animals and herd them back to camp for guests to ride. To help find the animals, cowbells were

strapped around the necks of two mares. When the wrangler got close to the herd, he heard the bells. After wrangling a couple of times, you'd listen for the bells. The problem was thinking you heard bells far ahead in the lodgepole. Ride toward the sound and it appeared to be closer. Yet at some point, the sound would stop, then reappear in the opposite direction, equally far off. Chasing sounds, a wrangler could ride on forever, consumed by the ghost bells of his imagination. I hoped we wouldn't suffer turkey hunter's disease, and go chasing the spirits of birds not really there.

The sky continues to brighten. Insects buzz. Warblers sing. A breeze, stirred by the warming land, tickles ears, and cools backs damp with the effort of the climb.

Then it comes, from far in the distance . . . *Gobble-obble-obble.* Our heads snap to the sound like a bird dog hitting fresh scent. Again, floating across the breeze . . . *Gobble, gobble-obble.*

"Too far," I whisper to Bob. He nods, we smear our faces with camouflage paint, wipe bug juice on hat brims and pants legs, and get ready for the hunt.

Then another sound . . . *yelp, yelp, yelp* . . . closer, comes to us. Bob suggests calling the bird.

Bob knows turkeys. The best measure is his ability to find and take turkeys each spring and fall, something he has done for a number of consecutive years. In the

The rising sun ends the shadow world of owls and whippoorwills, replacing it with a forest of buzzing insects, singing warblers, cooing doves, and a gobbling tom turkey.

woods, Bob becomes a turkey: He moves like a turkey, thinks like a turkey. The previous week, he took a nice gobbler in Huntingdon County, Pennsylvania. This morning he carries no gun.

We pick a position on a knob, where a bird answering our calls will have to pop up over the hilltop within shotgun range. We kick leafy duff away from the base of two large oaks, unsnap sit pads, settle in, and prepare for an incoming bird. Bob yelps, asking the turkey to join us. Initially, his calls are answered. Then the woods go silent, only the wind moves. We wait, call again, and wait some more. No bird.

Daybreak stretches into midmorning without action, and we decide to follow the trail across the mountain's spine, to a little flat near the point, where I heard a tom the week before. We walk the trail, throwing yelps and cutting down over the hill like a dog cast into cover, every 500 yards or so, but there is no response.

A carpenter ant mound marks the side trail down to the bird. We stop, call. *Cluck, cluck, cluck . . . purrrr . . . yelp yelp, yelp, yelp.*

Gobble, gobble-obble . . . says the reply.

Glances flash between Bob and me. Another set of yelps and clucks go down over the hill and the same answer thunders back, about 200 yards down the hill, and to our right. We move quickly to shorten the distance between the bird and ourselves. At about 100 yards from the gobbler, we get into position, Bob at the base of a gnarled oak, me about 15 yards ahead, more directly in line with the tom's likely path of travel. Bob will become a second hen, moving if necessary, to bring the bird to me. We are slightly above the bird, close enough to lure him, yet far enough out to avoid spooking him. The surrounding woods are fairly open, except for numerous mountain laurel patches between the bird and the two of us. We settle in—the heavy 10-gauge finds my knee, the camouflage mask covers my face.

I call again . . . *yelp yelp, yelp*—Gobble, gobble-obble . . . *Gobble, gobble-obble.* The tom "cuts" my calling, a sure sign, according to turkey pro Ben Lee, that this bird wants to "come up and see ya', rub up aginst ya'." I'm thinking that I would really like to "fix this bird up" as Lee describes it.

We call again, and the bird cuts the yelps another time. Then he double-gobbles, the sound shaking the earth. My knee wobbles. The camouflage face mask blows in and out with each short, excited breath. I worry the bird will spot these movements, but am reassured by another gobble. He is moving closer, then out; closer, then out.

Mentally, I see this bird below us—puffed up, taut fan spread for maximum effect, strutting his way up the hill, the midmorning sun catching each shiny black feather, the red, white, and blue periscope neck craning to find the little hen who talks so sweet.

I cluck sweet nothings at the bird and the tom gobbles back, moving again, swinging wide on the right, going towards the point of the hill, circling us. Bob crawls up behind me, tells me he will move backward, away from the gobbler, to lure him closer. Bob's slow, cautious-stepped gait on the leaves, *crunch-crunch,* sounds like a turkey. Then he yelps, clucks, and cuts. The gobbler likes this, double-gobbling his interest. Each time the tom's *Gobble, gobble-obble* sounds, I feel like I lift a foot off the ground.

Bob is 25 yards back now, above me, to the right. He settles in and stays put.

The bird continues gobbling, but swings to the right, as though he wants to put the morning sun above the mountain at his back instead of ours. We call, softer now, because the bird is closer . . . *Gobble, gobble-obble* . . . not more than 50 yards out.

I scan behind the laurel for the big black bird, listen for footfalls, check sunlit openings, expecting the tom to step into one at any moment. I know the bird is close, I can feel his magnanimous presence. But where? A soft cluck, another gobble . . . he's right on top of us.

Suddenly, there is silence, a pause, as though a pebble were dropped in the stillness of the pond of the woods. Either this bird is here, or the jig is up.

I wait, trying to turn stumps, dead branches, shapes in leaves . . . something, anything . . . into a turkey. Minutes pass, the silence continues, the ripples reach the shore. After about 15 minutes of silence, I call, a soft cluck. There is no response. I wait another five minutes . . . nothing. A chipmunk chirps. Doves coo. The best laid plans of turkeys and men have gone astray. I stand, wobbly, my heart still pounding. Damn . . . that was great!

The walk up the trail back to the truck is subdued. Bob says he thinks we had the bird in to about 25 yards, but at a spot where I couldn't see him because of some laurel and the lay of the land. Bob heard the bird's footsteps behind him, but never got a look, either.

I ask Bob if he is disappointed. He says no, and I see my friend—we've known each other 20 years, since middle school's fly tying club, I shot one of my first pheas-

ants with Bob—in a different light. Bob is in touch with the real reasons we came here—to see the sun rise, to hear gobbler music, to feel the incredible presence a tom turkey brings to a spring mountainside. I am also in awe of Bob, for his exceptional ability with turkeys, realizing more fully now how much it takes to outwit this bird. For this opportunity to rekindle an old friendship, for the morning, for the turkey, for the mountains, I am thankful.

* * * *

The restoration of the wild turkey to North America's uplands is one of modern wildlife management's greatest success stories.

Nearly 10 million wild turkeys roamed the virgin forests and wild places of the United States when Europeans first landed in the New World, according to Fish and Wildlife Service estimates. Original turkey range included 39 states, Ontario, Mexico, and Central America. Archeological records show that native people had been hunting turkeys for 4,000 years. The wing bone turkey call, which uses a wing bone from the bird, is one of their legacies. Still, the bird's vast numbers and their ignorance of man often made turkeys seem more like "fool hen" grouse than the crafty woods wizard of modern times. Some native peoples considered turkey hunting beneath the dignity of adults and sent children to club or stone what they could find.

Pennsylvania founder William Penn, in 1683 and 1684, noted the abundance and size of turkeys: "Of the fowl of the land, there is the turkey, (forty and fifty pounds in weight) which is very great." Also, "The woods are supplied with a quantity of wild birds, as turkeys of an extraordinary size." Yet a description of Pennsylvania from 1770 notes, "Wild turkeys among the winged tribe, were formerly very plentiful, but now are scarce."

In 1804, Lewis and Clark reported seeing turkeys along the Missouri River in what is now Nebraska, Missouri, Iowa, and South Dakota. However, turkeys disappeared from Connecticut by 1813. John James Audubon, in the 1840s, noted, "The wild turkey is less plentiful in Georgia and the Carolinas, becomes still scarcer in Virginia and Pennsylvania, and is now very rarely seen to the eastward of the last mentioned states." Turkey was also not on the Thanksgiving menu in Massachusetts by 1851. Squanto, Samoset, Massasoit, and the Wampanoag were also pretty much gone by 1851, their lands absorbed by settlers in revenge for fighting between the Wampanoag and settlers in King Phillip's War in the mid-1670s. Eastern wild turkeys were gone from 18 of the 39 states in the bird's ancestral range by the Civil War. And by the early 1900s, turkeys were gone from the Midwest.

Habitat loss, particularly the cutting of the vast virgin forests where turkeys had evolved to live; to some extent, the chestnut blight of 1910; and uncontrolled year-round gunning destroyed this abundance.

Although Plymouth Colony enacted the first conservation law, limiting the cutting and sale of timber in 1626, the clearing of the vast eastern forest took less than a century, from the mid-1800s to the early 1900s. Market gunning for wild turkeys peaked after the Civil War and extended into the early 1900s. In 1881, for example, a St. Louis, Missouri exporting firm filled an order from London for 700 *dozen* wild turkeys. One naturalist in the early 1900s called the turkey "extinct as the dodo."

Some states responded to the decline in turkeys. Prior to the Civil War, Pennsylvania, for example, established seasons on turkeys in several counties. After the Civil War, baiting and traps were outlawed. By 1873, the first statewide closed season on turkeys was in place. In 1905, a fall-only hunting season was enacted, and in 1917 a one-bird-per-season bag limit was established.

By the 1930s, however, only 30,000 wild turkeys remained. It wasn't until the late 1930s that turkey restoration efforts began to come together. The Pittman-Robertson (PR) Act of 1937, which established federal aid for wildlife restoration, and cooperative federal wildlife research began efforts to restore wild turkeys.

Cooperative federal wildlife studies in Virginia, Alabama, Louisiana, Texas, and Missouri showed that one of the major problems in restoring turkey to their original range was finding seed stock. Initially, game farm birds were used. Pennsylvania even went so far as to build special pens where rangy wild gobblers could breed with wing-clipped game farm hens, the offspring released in the wild. However, 1942 Missouri studies showed few game farm turkeys survived. Game farm birds also brought disease and genetic dilution to wild turkey flocks. In Nebraska, for example, releases of more than 330,000 pen-raised turkeys on about 800 sites resulted in 760 failures. The pen-raised approach cost millions of dollars and, by one estimate, delayed the restoration of the wild turkey by almost 2 decades.

A 1949 status report showed Eastern and Florida wild turkey subspecies were present in only 12 percent of the birds' ancestral range. Birds were totally gone from 19 states, and populations were low in five additional states. Western turkey subspecies had fared better. Populations of native birds survived settlers and were increasing in some areas. This is where a major seed for the restoration of wild turkeys began growing.

In 1935, 15 wild New Mexico turkeys were released in Wyoming. These birds created a flock of 10,000 by 1958. South Dakota introduced turkeys from New Mexico into the Black Hills between 1948 and 1951. The population increased from 29 birds to 7,000 birds by 1961. Nebraska released 28 Merriam's turkeys trapped in South Dakota and Wyoming in 1959 in the Pine Ridge area. Although Merriam's are not native to Nebraska, the release succeeded, and the Pine Ridge population grew to about 3,000 birds in only four nesting seasons.

Also, there was a natural expansion of remnant wild turkey flocks into areas that had previously held turkeys. In Pennsylvania during the 1940s and 1950s, native turkey flocks in the south-central region began expanding. The birds followed the mountains, spreading north to the rugged north-central and northwestern portions of the state. These areas had also grown back into more mature forest habitat.

From the late 1950s through the 1980s, several things came together that made wild turkey restoration a success in all of the bird's former range.

The maturing of the East's second-growth forest was a critical factor, one that few wildlife agencies or conservation groups want to talk about. Most of the East's virgin forests were logged off between 1850 and 1920. A second-growth forest of oaks, hickory, beech, and similar species sprouted up between the white pine and hemlock stumps. Hardwoods take nearly 100 years to mature. Eastern wild turkeys, although they need younger forest for nesting and brood rearing cover, are primarily mature forest birds. Timber cut in 1870 was reaching maturity in 1970. This created prime habitat for the bird.

Using trap-and-transfer birds instead of game farm birds was also extremely significant. The successful 1935 release of wild turkeys in Wyoming showed biologists that turkeys (as well as other upland gamebirds) could be restored to areas of suitable habitat if *wild* birds were used. This helped modern trap-and-transfer programs become the cornerstone of returning turkey populations to all of their former range.

A third factor was the development of the National Wild Turkey Federation (NWTF) in 1973. Started with just 1,300 members, this group incorporates a system of local chapters, state chapters, and a national organization that serves as a rallying point for turkey enthusiasts. The local chapters do the bulk of the hands-on fundraising and habitat improvement work. The state and national units serve as lobbying interests and focus groups, and keep turkey hunting and turkey hunter interests before the eyes of wildlife agencies and politicians.

In most states, upland birds are low on the priority list. The wheel that squeaks gets greased. With the NWTF's 215,000 members, and considering that 2.5 million

people in the United States call themselves turkey hunters, squeaking today comes pretty easy. Also, since 1973, NWTF has raised $115 million to help wildlife agencies trap and relocate turkeys to areas of suitable habitat and improve forests.

Today, about five million wild turkeys roam North America. Turkeys are back in all of their former range. In Indiana, for example, 70 of 92 counties have turkeys, with spring densities of six birds per square mile. Nebraska ranks 48th in the nation in woodland acreage, but 19th in the harvest of wild turkeys. Turkey range has even been expanded somewhat, to include areas where turkeys were not native. Huntable turkey populations exist in every state except Alaska. Canada's Ontario province and Mexico also have turkey hunting.

NATURAL HISTORY

No one quite knew what to make of the uniquely North American wild turkey when it first came to the attention of Europeans. Turkeys were mistaken for peafowl in Asia Minor and given the Indian name for the birds, "furkes" or "firkee." Turkeys even confused Linneaus, the inventor of scientific nomeclature. In 1758, he called the turkey *Meleagris gallopavo*. *Gallinas* refers to guineafowl, and *pavos* refers to peafowl. This is a misnomer.

Five subspecies of wild turkeys are found in North America. A sixth subspecies, *Meleagris gallopavo gallopavo,* is thought to be extinct, although this is the bird from southern Mexico that is considered to be the root of domesticated turkeys. When Cortez and his conquistadors entered the Valley of Mexico in 1519, they found Aztecs raising turkeys for food. They shipped the birds, among other loot, home. Europeans discovered the meat was tasty and the birds easy to raise, so they domesticated the turkey and exported it throughout the world. In an interesting twist of fate, domestic turkeys found their way back to North America in the early 1600s, aboard the ships of English colonists.

Male wild turkeys all have beards—distinctive hairlike extensions from the breast that can grow to around 10 inches long. (Some females may also exhibit a small beard.) Males grow spurs that reach an inch or more in older birds. Identification among the subspecies is difficult, and, of course, the best advice is to know what turkeys exist on your hunting grounds. In states like Washington, however, where Merriam's, Rio Grandes, and Eastern wild turkey populations all currently thrive, this is easier said than done. Looking at the tips of the tail feathers can help, although it is far from foolproof. Generally, Eastern and Florida turkeys have brown tips; Merriam's, buff colored to white; Rio Grandes, yellowish; and Gould's, white.

The five subspecies include:

Eastern wild turkey (*Meleagris gallopavo silvestris*)—The Eastern wild turkey is the most widely distributed, abundant, and hunted turkey found in North America. It inhabits roughly the eastern half of the continent, from the mixed forests of New England and southern Canada to northern Florida, and west to Texas, Missouri, Iowa, and Minnesota. It has also been successfully transplanted in California, Oregon, and Washington. L. J. P. Vieillot first described and named the Eastern subspecies in 1817, using the word *silvestris,* meaning "forest" turkey. The Eastern wild turkey is large. A gobbler stands up to four feet tall at maturity and can weigh more than 20 pounds. Mature hens are nearly as tall but lighter, between 8 and 12 pounds.

Florida wild turkey (*Meleagris gallopavo osceola*)—The Florida turkey, also called the Osceola, is found only on the peninsula of Florida. W. E. D. Scott first described this bird in 1890, naming it for the Seminole chief, Osceola. (Osceola led his people against settlers in a 20-year war beginning in 1835.) Similar to the Eastern turkey, the Osceola is smaller and dark-colored, showing less bronze, more iridescent green and red than the Eastern—ideal coloration for Florida's flat pine woods, oak and palmetto hammocks, and swamps. Females are similar to males but dull and lighter-colored. Southern Florida turkeys gobble during warm spells in January, several weeks before actual mating. Egg laying is mainly in April, with peak hatching by May.

Merriam's wild turkey (*Meleagris gallopavo merriami*)—Merriam's turkey is a western bird, found primarily in ponderosa pine mountains. Named by Dr. E. W.

Nelson in 1900, in honor of C. Hart Merriam, first chief of the U.S. Biological Survey, Merriam's is a relatively new subspecies. The bird's historic range was probably Arizona, New Mexico, and Colorado. However, Merriam's has been successful in Nebraska, Washington, California, Oregon, Montana, and other areas. Merriam's are particularly susceptible to timber harvesting, overgrazing, or development. Merriam's are similar in size to the Eastern turkey, but have a blacker appearance with blue, purple and bronze reflections.

Rio Grande wild turkey (*Meleagris gallopavo intermedia*)—Native to the central Plains states, the Rio Grande turkey got its name from the same river that flows through the arid, brushy scrub country of the southern Plains, western Texas, and northeastern Mexico. Rios are comparatively pale, copper-colored turkeys, with smaller body size, like the Florida turkey. The Rio stands about 4 feet tall and has disproportionately long legs. The Rio likes brushy streams and rivers or mesquite, pine, and scrub oak forests. It may be found up to 6,000 feet and generally favors more open country. In some areas, the birds have distinct summer and winter ranges and form large flocks of several hundred birds during winter.

Gould's wild turkey (*Meleagris gallopavo mexicana*)—Gould's is the largest of the five subspecies, with longer legs, larger feet, and larger center tail feathers. Its body plumage is somewhat blue-green in coloration. A mountain bird, Gould's is found in very small numbers in the Animas and San Luis mountains of New Mexico and in the Peloncillo Mountains of Arizona. Larger flocks occur in northwestern Mexico's Sierra Madre Occidental Mountains and in Chihuahua, Sonora, Sinaloa, Durango, Zacatecas, Nayarit, Jalisco, and Coahuila. The Arizona Game and Fish Department, U.S. Forest Service, the Centro Ecologico de Sonora, the National Wild Turkey Federation, and other agencies are cooperatively reintroducing a strong Gould's population first into Arizona and then into other states where suitable range exists.

* * * *

A turkey's pattern of life is keyed to the seasons. During late winter turkey flocks divide into three distinct segments: hens, young gobblers or jakes, and mature gobblers. This division is a preparation for spring's mating season. While mature gobblers work themselves into a frenzy getting ready for mating, hens seek out suitable nesting territory—primarily young timber with grassy areas and dense brush.

Like the prairie grouse, turkey mating rituals are high theatre. In addition to gobbling, mature toms strut, flex their fans, puff up, and vibrate their tail feathers to make a drumming noise. Hormone-hot blood surges through the bird's neck and head, making it look red, white, and blue.

Gobblers compete for breeding territory where several hens' nesting territories overlap. These "my beard's bigger than yours" fights establish a pecking order for opportunities to gather a harem of hens, breed them by midmorning, then look for more hens. Meanwhile, the jakes hang around watching this scandalous stuff, learning the trade, and occasionally breeding a hen while two or three boss toms are duking it out.

After mating, the hen lays a dozen eggs, seldom leaving the nest during the 28-day incubation period. Chicks can fly at 2 to 3 weeks. Insects are the chicks' high-energy food source, although adults like bugs as well. By late summer, however, the bulk of the birds' diet is wild fruit (especially dogwoods, greenbrier, sumac, and grapes), roots and tubers, green leaves, and seeds.

By fall, gobblers have segregated themselves in small flocks off in the hills, and the hens and the young-of-the-year spend most of their time together, roaming in search of good food. Mast crops, especially in the East, become important fall foods. Turkeys prefer beechnuts and acorns. One sure sign of turkey activity in mast-bearing timber or around grapevines are scratchings, where the birds scratch away fallen leaves to find nuts, grapes, or tubers. Waste grain augments natural food where turkey country adjoins farmland.

Turkeys have good winter survival skills. The birds' strong legs can scratch through most snow cover to reach acorns and other foods below. Conifer roosts offer shelter from the wind and snow. Spring seeps and other water sources offer aquatic plants, some greens, and invertebrates like salamanders.

Wild turkeys have few predators. Coyotes and golden eagles are the only predators large enough to handle adult birds, and even then with trouble. Turkeys are built for speed: Flight speeds can reach 42 mph, as fast as a red-tailed hawk. On the ground, turkeys can outrun all but the fastest human runners. Great horned owls and foxes occasionally take young birds. Skunks, raccoons, and opossums can destroy nests. Still, human beings are one of the few predators willing to take on the birds' sharp eyesight, excellent hearing, and uncanny knack for sensing danger. If turkeys had a whitetail's nose, they would be impossible to hunt.

HUNTING SPRING GOBBLERS

The basic idea behind spring gobbler hunting is that the hunter becomes a hen turkey and convinces a love-struck tom that this hen desires the thunder in his roaring gobble. The catch is that this hen must convince the gobbler to reverse the natural order of things, come running to the hen, rather than the hen running to the gobbler. You've got to whisper the kind of sweet nothings in the gobbler's ear that will create a sense of urgency in the bird. Make it so he wants to rub up against you.

Spring gobbler hunting is also a sound game, a position game, a game of luck (sometimes things happen at the right time and place and it all works out perfectly), a game of skill (knowing where birds are and how to work them), and a game of cunning and wits.

Ordinarily you would think that the human brain could easily outwit a bird whose gray matter could fit in the bottom of a coffee cup. But this isn't so—no shame on human beings. The wild turkey is a cunning, savvy critter, a bird with the eyes of a hawk, the hearing of an owl, and the sixth sense of psychic Sylvia Brown. Turkeys can sense that something is up when they walk into a caller's siren song. It's like they can read your mind, like they know the Trebark-covered lump in front of that old tree has bad intentions for Mr. Gobbler.

The first step is to locate some toms. Across most of the continent, turkeys begin gobbling well before the actual mating season. Increasing spring sunlight triggers hormonal developments, causing turkeys to feel the urge to make more turkeys. Many spring gobbler hunters like to spend the first really warm, still days of the year scouting and listening for gobblers, especially at dawn and dusk. Here in Pennsylvania, March and April are prime times to scout for turkeys. Other dates apply farther north and south. Closer to breeding season, when the birds are really getting worked up, owl hoots, gobbler calls, a car door slamming, distant thunder, or nearly anything in the right frequency range will start a tom gobbling. Pinpoint these birds for future hunts. The more turkeys located before turkey season, the greater the odds of bagging a bird. If you can locate a gobbler's roost the night before you hunt—actually put the bird to bed—you stand an even better chance first thing in the morning.

That morning, be in the woods and in position well before dawn. Get as close to the roosting tom as possible—but not too close or you'll bump him. In the East and South, 100 yards is the rule. In the West's more open country, distance increases.

Choosing a spot from which to ambush a tom takes some planning. Ideally, you should stay on the same elevation or higher than the bird. Turkeys usually don't work downhill or across an obstacle, like a creek, road, fenceline, or railroad track very well. They also have trouble crossing another tom's turf. The area should be open, yet not so open that a gobbler looking for a hen can see no hen—unless you plan to use a decoy. Chose a spot that offers a 40-yard field of fire within the likely route the turkey will take to come into you. Also, be sure to have a good background behind you. This camouflages your calling position by breaking up the human outline, and offers some protection from other hunters who might sneak a bird you are working or movement shoot. In the East and South, a tree wider than your shoulders is the right background. In the West, a boulder, a fence post, trees, even the land itself could work.

Get comfortable, because you could be there a while—or only a short time. This is why turkey vests with the shell loops, pockets and a fold-down sit pad in the rear are worth the money. Some hunters start with the gun up on their knee, ready to shoot; others wait until a bird gets close to get their gun up.

Next comes the calling. Which calls are best? That all depends on the particular bird you're working. Some birds respond best to box calls, others like a raspy mouth call. A West Virginia turkey hunter survey showed that 88 percent of hunters preferred a diaphragm, 40 percent chose box calls, and 36 percent used slate calls. (Many used more than one call.)

The basic manual on turkey hunting says that once you are set up on a roosted bird, some tree yelps—three or four gentle yelps—are the ticket. Some hunters like to simulate the sound of birds coming off the roost by flapping their hands against their legs (wings beating) and rustling the leaves (a bird landing and walking). This can add realism, sometimes the extra touch that convinces a turkey to come in.

If the tom answers the tree yelps, you're in good shape. You've probably connected with a bird that is looking for love and will soon be headed your way. However, know that the gobbler could be with hens. He could be at the edge of his territory and won't come to you, he could simply expect the hen to come to him.

A 12-gauge pump gun or autoloader with 3- or 3½-inch chambers, screw-in chokes to accommodate an extra full turkey choke, and a short barrel, is an ideal turkey gun. Stuff it with magnum loads of No. 4 or No. 6 copper-plated shot.

Again, the basic turkey hunting methodology says after the tree yelps, you start working a turkey up a little with some cutting (purrs, clucks, and other small turkey sounds), maybe a cackle, maybe working two calls at the same time, a slate and a mouth call. Calling styles vary by region. Southerners tend to enjoy giving a tom some hot and heavy hen "ye'ppin," as Ben Lee described it. Yankees are cooler, sparse callers, offering vague, soft suggestions of love, but not too much. Westerners, if they're not aligning a rifle's crosshairs at the base of a gobbler's neck, like loud calling to carry across the canyon.

According to a West Virginia survey, the average turkey hunter spends nine days in woods, hears 10 gobblers, calls to two or three birds, and sees five turkeys. Most turkeys, nearly 70 percent, were shot before 9 A.M. Hunters also heard .35 gobblers per hour, 1.27 birds per hunt.

Some callers like to work as a team—one gunner, one caller. Some like to move and call, so the bird thinks a hen is responding in the natural way. Movement calling can manipulate a tom's path, but in a crowded turkey woods, it can also be very dangerous. There are a million variations on the basic theme, each the option of the caller and the birds.

Say you've got a turkey coming in. Sit still. Pull that camouflage face net down, and get your gloves on. Movement is the first thing turkeys see, especially hands and a hunter's bare mug. If you don't already have your gun up, slide one knee up and rest your shotgun on it. Get everything ready to shoot so there is no movement when the bird steps into the picture.

Hunters who don't get a response from a tom at dawn have several options. If you feel confident a tom is roosting in the area, you can wait. Some birds come in silently. Another possibility is that the tom already has a hen. When he's done with her, usually by midmorning, he might come your way. You can also try to find another gobbler. Walk small backwoods trails, calling a bit every 500 yards or so, to imitate a hen meandering through the woods, looking for a gobbler.

In the West Virginia survey, the average turkey hunter spent nine days in the woods, heard 10 gobblers, called two or three birds, saw five turkeys, and seldom missed or crippled a bird. Only six birds of 201 called in were crippled and only 15 were missed. Most turkeys, nearly 70 percent, were shot before 9 A.M. Hunters also heard .35 gobblers per hour, 1.27 birds per hunt. They heard the most gobblers on Saturday of the first week of the season, Friday of the second week, and Thursday and Saturday of the last week of the season. About 10 percent of the overall harvest was taken on opening day, and the first Saturday accounted for 8 percent.

FALL TURKEY HUNTING

Hunting autumn turkeys takes a number of different paths. The traditional path, a product of the South, involves calling singles scattered from a flock within gun range. The way it works is that the hunter scouts likely turkey territory for sign of a flock of feeding birds, usually several mature hens and their young, which include both juvenile gobblers and young hens. Fall turkeys, especially in the Appalachians, are very grape- and mast-oriented (acorns and beechnuts in particular) and these are two good places to scout for sign. Fresh scratchings, droppings, and feathers under the grapes or on feeding benches, and groves of beechnut or acorn trees, indicate the hunt is on.

Say you find fresh sign at the top of a small, grape-tangled ravine in the middle of a main mountainside hill. The sign indicates the birds are feeding and moving down the ravine, heading towards a creek bottom. The hunter loops around the ravine, scurries down the mountainside, then swings back into the bottom of the ravine where it joins the valley. If he plays his cards right and the Red Gods smile, he'll outmaneuver the turkey flock and intercept them at the bottom of the ravine. There, he charges the flock, whooping, shooting into the air, to scatter the birds, like a covey of quail. If it all works right, and the hunter is successful in truly scattering the birds, within an hour or so, the flock will start to regroup at the place they were separated. The hunter finds a good spot to call from, waits a bit, then starts to use the high-pitched "kee-kee" assembly call, which, in tempo, sounds like a man whistling for his dog. Hens use the same call to regroup the flock. This will lure single birds back into the area until the hunter gets a shot. Usually, a shotgun is used, although many states allow rifles in the fall, something most turkey purists abhor.

A variation on this theme is simply ambushing birds at the cut-off point. Sometimes when a small flock is moving across a mountainside, or the point of a mountain, it makes more sense to ambush birds instead of trying to break up a flock. Rifle hunters use this technique, much like a deer hunter would slip up over the top of a mountain and down the other side, to ambush a deer herd looping around the front face of a mountain.

A third style of fall turkey hunting, used mainly in the West and the Appalachian Mountains by rifle hunters, involves just getting into turkey country and trying to get within rifle range of the birds. Some hunters still-hunt feeding benches and grapes where there is sign, hoping to intercept birds. Others glass mountainsides for turkeys, then go for position.

HUNTING SAFETY

Increasing wild turkey numbers have also upped turkey hunter numbers. Where large human and turkey populations overlap this creates a safety issue, especially where there is no strong turkey hunting tradition to enforce a code of ethics. Even in West Virginia, which does have a strong turkey tradition, 45 percent of 80 hunters surveyed said they had someone interfere with their hunts. In 68 percent of these cases, another hunter snuck between the turkey and the caller and killed or spooked the bird. In 10 percent of the cases, there were simply too many hunters in the woods. And in 5 percent, one hunter called up another.

I've been stalked by hunters twice, a frightening experience, and I know several people who were mistakenly shot during turkey season. Research on turkey hunting accidents shows the person most likely to be involved in an accident is an experienced hunter who is feeling pressure to bag a bird to keep up with his buddies. No turkey is ever worth a human life. Follow the rules of safe hunting, especially positively identifying your target, and there is no reason for anyone to shoot another hunter. Still, things happen; judgment fails. Regardless of where you hunt, defensive turkey hunting is smart, and a key part of being a safe hunter.

Safety Tips

- Never stalk a turkey, and never attempt to approach closer than 100 yards to a roosting turkey. The chances of getting close are slim; the chances of an accident increase.
- Eliminate red, white, and blue, the colors of a gobbler's head, from your turkey hunting gear.
- Never move, wave, or make turkey sounds to alert another hunter to your presence. Movement may draw fire. Yell "Stop" and remain hidden.
- Make your position known to other hunters. Pennsylvania requires hunters to wear 100 square inches (a cap) of fluorescent orange, visible 360 degrees,

when moving. And it is strongly suggested that a fluorescent orange band be displayed within 15 feet of the calling location.

- Select a calling position where you can see what is happening 180 degrees in front of you. Eliminating movement—not total concealment—is a key to success. Also, choose calling positions that offer a background as wide as your shoulders, to protect you from the top of your head down.
- Camouflage conceals; it does not render you invisible. Remaining motionless is the most effective camouflage. Both turkeys and hunters could be watching. Think and act defensively. Avoid all unnecessary movement.
- Positively identify your target. Be sure the shot path to the bird and beyond is safe before pulling the trigger. Never shoot at a sound or movement. Assume every sound is another hunter. Never shoot at part of a turkey. Preselect a zone of fire. Shoot at a turkey only in the predetermined zone, and only when you're certain it's safe. Once you pull the trigger, you can never take that shot back. A good rule of thumb: Shoot only when you can clearly see the gobbler's eye.
- Be extremely careful using turkey decoys. Place the decoy on the far side of a tree trunk so that you can see birds approaching from all directions, but cannot actually see the decoy. This prevents being directly in the line of fire should another hunter mistakenly shoot at your decoy.
- People in the same hunting party cause many accidents. Hunting is not a competitive sport. Peer pressure to bag a bird leads to poor judgment. Discuss hunting safety techniques with your companions. Be sure of everyone's location. Never assume that you are alone in the woods, even on private property. Also, never assume that other hunters are acting responsibly.
- Always keep your gun pointed in a safe direction. Keep your gun unloaded until you are set up in the field. Keep your finger off the trigger until you are ready to shoot.
- Use a flashlight when walking in the dark.
- Make sure your headnet does not obscure your vision.
- Respect property rights and secure permission before hunting.

GUNS, LOADS, AND GEAR

Spring turkey shooting is not the same as swinging on a rising covey of bobwhites. The sport requires a shotgun that can shoot more like a rifle. Turkeys are also big, tough birds, able to handle a lot of shot and still run or fly away. Maximum clean-killing turkey range is about 40 yards (or it ought to be). So you need a shotgun that throws a tight, dense, hard-hitting pattern.

Several years ago, in a turkey gun-testing mood, I compared similar No. 4 magnum patterns, using turkey head paper targets set up at 10-yard intervals from 15 yards to 40 yards, from both a 12-gauge pumpgun and my Harrington & Richardson 10-gauge single shot, both choked full.

The 10-gauge turned out to be the paper winner. Any turkey within 40 yards of the big 10 was going down. It saturated patterns with shot. At 15 yards, it would have decapitated a bird centered in the pattern. At 30 yards, it was perfect—tight little No.

Basic spring gobbler hunting gear: calls, camouflage make-up, shotgun, etc.

4 holes all over the place. At 40 yards, I could count on at least a dozen lethal head and neck hits.

The problem was that it "killed on both ends," muzzle and butt pad. Those big 3½-inch artillery piece shells kicked like a Missouri red mule. After the seventh consecutive shot, I was jelly, with a headache and a case of the jitters. I also wondered about what would have happened had I shot this gun with my shoulder hard against an oak tree. I never had a chance to use it on a real turkey, but I have used a ported 10-gauge autoloader on geese recently. It shot like a 12-gauge.

For an all-purpose gun—one that could double for waterfowl or even pheasants—I think it's hard to argue with a 12-gauge, with 3- or 3½-inch chambers, screw-in chokes to accommodate an extra full turkey choke, and a short barrel, under 28 inches, to make it a brush gun. I would also choose a pumpgun or an autoloader to double for waterfowl, because follow-up shots are sometimes necessary. Stuff it with magnum loads of No. 4 or No. 6 copper-plated shot; No. 2 steel could also work.

Rifle hunters might want to look at small, flat-shooting, fast calibers such as a .243 Winchester, .257 Roberts, 6mm Remington, and .223. These calibers can cleanly take a turkey without destroying too much meat, like a larger caliber deer gun might. Another option, especially useful for fall turkey hunting in states that allow rifles, is an over-under boring, with a .243 or .222 barrel over a 12-gauge. This way, you can select the shot based on the need.

11

THE DOGS

The greatest pleasure of a dog is that you may make a fool of yourself with him and not only will he not scold you, but he will make a fool of himself too.

Samuel Butler

There is no psychiatrist in the world like a puppy licking your face.

Ben Williams

Having a gun dog in your life induces a great many tears and copious amounts of laughter, and, thankfully, they tend to balance each other out on most occasions.

The laughter comes from things like "flying buttresses," the thing my year-old DeCoverly Kennels setter, Shana, does when she is bored, wants to play, or get my attention.

The house, Shana's opulent kennel, is longer than it is wide. Dog mental processes see this geometric reality as a great opportunity: She starts in the television room, at the far end of the house, gets a good run going, rockets through the dining room, streaks into the living room in the front of the house, and ... "Uh-oh, wall coming up, gotta turn around," she thinks. To accomplish this, she vaults the ottoman in the front corner of the living room and ricochets off the seat back of the overstuffed chair behind the ottoman, gaining energy and speed. This delights her, because after three of four bounces she gets quite a bit of momentum going and the faster she goes, the more she likes it. Usually, by the fifth time, she's not making me happy. I let her know about this, and she stops, a bit contrite. She's a good puppy. Watching that little devil rocket through the house, consumed with herself, how fast she can move, how much fun it all is, makes me laugh. Part of me wishes I could be a dog down there with her, running, leaping into the ottoman, bouncing off the chair back, and flying

forward faster than when I came in, but only for a moment or two, when the adult me remembers how much overstuffed chairs cost.

Tears come far too easily, days when you feel the silky-headed ghost of an old dog, long in the ground, rub across your fingertips and wish he were there again.

I'll take the tears, laughter, and everything in between, because life isn't right, it wouldn't be bird hunting, without a dog. For many upland gunners, the dog is the main focus of our sport.

Dogs are a very emotional thing for those who own them and are owned by them. You bond with a bird dog in a way that people who haven't hunted over dogs just can't understand. Hunting together creates a symbiotic relationship between dog and gunner; you become one, a team. The gunner relies on Pup's nose and instincts to put birds in the pot, to make the cycle complete. The dog relies on his gunner for care, feeding, and some loving, although dogs really don't expect too much from human beings. Perhaps they should. Many times, if you look at it from the dog's perspective, it seems like the dog is getting shorted in the dog/human arrangement.

Still, you can insult a bird hunter's intelligence, his choice of coverts, his vehicle, how he shoots—anything—but don't tell him his dog is worthless. Those are fighting words. He may well have a pot-licking, tire-wetting, meadow muffin-rolling canine disaster who couldn't point a pheasant if his life depended on it. But his owner might love that dog with all his heart, and if they're happy, well, so be it.

DeCoverly Kennels setter, Shana, where new dreams begin.

(I'll bet if you look close, you'll start seeing a lot of similarities between dog and owner.)

Also, as you read further, please keep something in mind: Many of the ideas expressed are my opinions. Although they are based on experience, I'm as biased as they come. I've been very much in love with all of my dogs and all of their flaws ever since we chose each other.

THE MODERN GUN DOG

To understand the modern gun dog, it is important to understand something about the relationship between dogs and their owners during the recent past. Since the 1940s, major changes have been taking place with the dog/owner relationship. What we expect a dog to do is far different today than it was in 1940.

During the 1940s and 1950s, the average gun dog was kenneled outdoors, his associations with human beings limited to feeding time, kennel cleaning, hunting, training sessions, and an occasional day out. Training was more properly described as "breaking," because the emphasis was usually more on heavy-handed force, at least by today's standards, than gentle coercion. Pup, however, could count on seeing a fair number of wild birds during this time, regardless of whether he was a Georgia pointer hunting quail, a New England grouse setter, or a South Dakota pheasant springer. (Retrievers were still more waterfowl-oriented back then.) The average gun dog owner, like most people of that time, lived in a rural, by today's standards, setting. He kept a quail call-back pen in his backyard, trained in a field down over the hill, and hunted on land in back of the house. Also, veterinary medicine was far behind where it is today even with simple things like vaccines, something modern gun dog owners take for granted. Dogs, like their people, lived shorter lives.

The 1960s and 1970s were a transition period for dogs, their owners, and even veterinary medicine. Dog owners lived in a more urban environment. The nearby farms were sold, replaced with housing developments. They had to start traveling to find good bird hunting—initially to the edge of town, and later, maybe an hour out. Dogs started coming indoors, being part of the family, if only part-time. The breeds available to the average hunter expanded to include many breeds once found only in Europe. Innovations in training tools, like electronic collars and the use of the dog training table, and other techniques flourished. This was also when retrievers started spending more time in the uplands, especially in the West, which created a new concept of versatility. In addition, ways of measuring a dog's suitability for breeding were changing from field trial wins to hunter-oriented organizations like the North American Versatile Hunting Dog Association (NAVHDA), the National Shoot To Retrieve Association (NSTRA), the North American Hunting Retriever Association (NAHRA), and others. Also, great strides brought about by plastics, new drugs, and other advances in human medicine were coming to veterinary medicine. Yet there were fewer birds, thanks to urbanization.

Between the 1980s and today, many new beginnings were in store for gun dogs and their owners. One of the best things that happened was the introduction of dog psychology to dog training. People stopped breaking dogs and started training them, using a dog's own nature to pull out Pup's best behaviors. A good example is Bill Tarrant's philosophy compared to descriptions of how many old-timers trained. This trend continues today, with no-stress techniques that allow dogs to train themselves, taking pressure off both trainer and dog.

The worst recent change is increasing urbanization. Shopping centers and housing are replacing bird fields at alarming rates. Dog owners have to travel much farther to find training grounds, let alone wild birds. The early 1980s were also a time of crashes in many wildlife species, especially for the East's pheasants and quail. Veterinary medicine has become capable of doing almost anything for dogs that can be done for people. In the 1940s, chemotherapy for an old dog with cancer, or a hip replacement operation, would have been absurd. Today, you can buy pills that eliminate both fleas and ticks, and dogs have dental floss. Pup has never had it so easy.

Pup is definitely a larger part of the family, only today he is more house dog than bird dog. His home environment, grass and trees and fences and the kids' toys, is far different from the hunting environment, something that wasn't so 60 years ago. Perhaps it's also why dogs get allergies to things like grass. Pup doesn't get nearly as much bird contact as he used to, especially with his owner being expected to multi-task spouse, children, family, career, organizations, and other responsibilities. This also limits hunting time. Between needing to drive farther to find birds and having less time to do it in, bird hunting hours are sparse. So Pup is a more frequent visitor at a nearby preserve or other kind of pay-to-hunt area to help keep him sharp.

The modern gunner still wants his dog to hunt with enthusiasm, to produce game and perform as he should for his breed and type, to handle commands and obedience.

Couch potatoes! Jack and Nash.

But we're also more inclined to lean towards form over function than in the past. We like pretty dogs, not skanky mutts. A lot of gunners get caught up in trends, buying dogs that are "hot" at the moment. We've also expanded our dog horizons in terms of breeds.

Before World War II, gunners had four basic bird dogs to pick from in the United States—English pointers, three kinds of setters, some Springers, and Brittanys. Retrievers were waterfowlers, not involved in the uplands. After World War II, GIs started coming home with the European dogs, especially the versatile breeds—dock-tailed German dogs, more Brittanys, and everything from Weimaraners and Vizslas to Munsterlander pointers and the old English, Welsh, Irish, and Scottish setters. Suddenly, North American gun dogs started becoming far more international looking. In addition, some of the old breeds, like the American water spaniel, were revived. The arrival of the retriever breeds in the uplands was an enormous development. Once viewed mainly as a dog that fetched downed game in the uplands, retrievers gained far greater acceptance as bird finders and flushers.

There are many chicken and egg questions here: Did these changes reflect the hunting conditions or did the hunting conditions create an interest in breeds better suited to changes in the land and the birds? Given changes in time and land space available to most hunters, which is a better choice: one dog that can do everything, or a specialist? Pretend it's a rainy night in grouse camp, and we've got time to discuss things, like gentlemen and ladies. . . .

VERSATILE DOGS CAN DO IT ALL

The concept that a person can own one dog and have Pup perform *all* the functions necessary in any type of hunting is a European idea that took root in the United States shortly after World War II.

Most gun dog breeds can trace their ancestry back to a variety of hounds and spaniel-type dogs that were crossed and mixed together in random (by modern standards) couplings designed to breed the good hunting traits of an individual dog with the good hunting traits of another individual dog. Breed standards weren't a consideration because there were no standards. As time continued, geographical areas produced a particular type of dog, such as the Gordon setter of Scotland, which tended to breed true to type.

In the Europe of kings, feudal lords, and castles, a different dog breed was used to hunt each type of game. Specialized kennels for these individuals kept a number of breeds true to type. And since hunting was limited to the landed gentry and kings, they could afford to maintain these kennels.

However, seventeenth and eighteenth century political revolutions that ousted the monarchies in favor of more democratic forms of government and the economic changes wrought by the Industrial Revolution of the nineteenth century changed all this. A middle class formed with enough time and disposable income to hunt. These people couldn't afford to keep large kennels of highly specialized dogs, so they developed dog breeds that could do everything.

The German shorthaired pointer is a good example. In the seventeenth century, a crossing of imported Spanish pointers, of predominantly hound blood, and the old

German bloodhound, produced a bulky, heavy dog known as the German pointer. The German pointer pointed birds and rabbits, trailed larger game when necessary, and was very popular among poachers and on baronial estates. However, in the mid-1800s, breeders wanted to improve the breed, make it sleeker, with more scenting ability. So American and English pointers were brought in and bred to the German pointer. In 1872, the German shorthaired pointer was a registered breed in the German Kennel Club Stud Book. And by the early 1900s, shorthairs were widespread and well-liked across Europe. Some were imported into the United States among German families in the Hudson River valley in New York, and Dr. Charles Thornton began breeding shorthairs in Montana in 1925. But it wasn't until after World War II that the breed's popularity soared.

Today, shorthairs are very popular gun dogs across the world. American Kennel Club (AKC) registrations for the shorthair in 1999 numbered 12,325 dogs, ranking it the most popular AKC pointing dog, and 24th among all the dogs AKC registers. (Labs and Goldens were No. 1 and No. 2.) The reason the shorthair is so popular among bird hunters is its ability to truly do it all.

Most shorthairs are efficient, hard-working, close-hunting "meat" dogs. They love to fetch any kind of downed game—they can even track and help hunters find downed furbearers and big game. Affectionate dogs, most tend to bond strongly to a single master, yet they are great around children and in a family. They also make good protectors of home and hearth. Training most shorthairs is not difficult. Minimal training produces very good results. Better trainers can get miracles out of a shorthair. However, in all honesty, shorthairs, especially males, lean towards being stubborn. This quality is great in the bird fields, when single-minded determination produces birds. It's not so great after the fifteenth time you tell the dog to get off the damned sofa and he just keeps hopping up there, looking at you like he owns the joint and he's not doing anything wrong.

Jack, my shorthair, hunted most of North America's major gamebirds—pheasants, ducks, doves, ruffed grouse, woodcock, and bobwhites in Pennsylvania; pheasants, scaled quail, bobwhite quail, and prairie chickens in Kansas; and grouse and woodcock in both Minnesota and Michigan. He handled all of them well. I never found a bird Jack really couldn't handle, although he didn't like waiting around for ducks—too cold. His motto was the T-shirt slogan, "Patience my ass, I'm gonna kill something." He was a true "meat" dog, he loved to fetch downed game. Dove hunting's shooting and fetching were fun to Jack. Sometimes, I swear that dog pointed just so he could fetch downed birds, and prance around like some hotshot. He truly shined on pheasants; they were the fire in his eyes, his passion.

Jack could be counted on to produce birds when other dogs failed, hunting under a variety of conditions, from dry sandsage prairie on the Cimarron National Grasslands in Kansas, to hot, dank Pennsylvania dove fields. He was a close-working dog, rarely moving out beyond 100 yards (except to chase turkeys), even on the wide-open prairie. Shorthairs have a habit of ground-scenting, or trailing game more than a setter or pointer, who work with a high head. Yet I rarely doubted his scenting abilities, and when he pointed, I felt very confident there would be a bird coming up very soon.

Today, shorthairs are very popular gun dogs across the world. American Kennel Club (AKC) registrations for the shorthair in 1999 numbered 12,325 dogs, making it the most popular AKC pointing dog, and 24th among all the AKC registers.

Most shorthairs are efficient, hard-working, close-hunting "meat" dogs. They love to fetch any kind of downed game—they can even track and help hunters find downed furbearers and big game.

The things I didn't like about Jack were not too big, really. Although he was wanted and loved very much, Jack was a compromise. Ever since I was a kid, and a tick-infested Irish setter hung around the house for a couple of weeks—my mother and father didn't want that bull in their tidy china-shop home—I wanted a setter. I chose Jack because I didn't have space for a specialist, and I knew shorthairs could do it all. Jack was very hard to see in the grouse woods, except in the snow, even with a wide blaze orange collar. He was a more traditional, dark-colored shorthair, not like so many of today's mostly-white dogs. Although Jack was one of the most handsome Krauts I ever saw, the plodding way he moved, the way I related to him in cover, couldn't hold a candle to the beauty of my setter Nash's fluid movement. The main thing, however, was his stubbornness. Patterns set in puppyhood remained there forever. (A tip for shorthair owners: start the dog right.) For example, Jack would never heel properly for me. He had to walk out in front a bit. I tried every training technique I could, even a spiked choke collar that looked like a medieval torture device. That dog just wasn't going to do it—*Nein!* So I accepted his good points for what they were, his faults for what they were, and decided the next dog would be more biddable, softer, mostly white, primarily a grouse and woodcock hunter, since that was the fire in my heart.

Is there a versatile dog that can do it all? Yes, I owned one and would recommend shorthairs to anyone who is willing to understand them for what they are. Versatile dogs can also include all of the "continental" hunting breeds: all of the German pointing dog varieties (Pudelpointers, wirehairs, large and small Munsterlanders, Griffons), Brittanys, Vizslas, Weimaraners, and some of the more obscure breeds, like the Italian Spinoni.

Versatile breeds should also include the flushing dogs—Springer spaniels and the retrievers—because they can assist a hunter in everything from ducks to pheasants. Springers are a joy to hunt over and fun to be with. They combine great dog beauty, lots of heart, and that dandy movement they have. They always seem so happy when hunting, always so busy.

I've hunted over several retrievers in the uplands and recognize that they make good versatile upland dogs, outstanding bird fetchers, but I'm also a traditionalist, with reservations about upland *specialists* using dogs developed to fetch waterfowl, over a versatile pointing breed or a springer. If you spend 90 percent of your time hunting ducks, 10 percent in the uplands, a retriever makes sense. Otherwise, I'd stick with a more traditional upland dog.

Versatile dogs are big business today. They have become popular in the show ring, in field trials, in hunt-to-shoot events, and as house pets for the trendy. Popularity is dangerous. It usually does the breed, the bloodline, and the dog little good. A good example is the Irish setter. Once primarily a keen hunting animal, it was swallowed up by show breeders and turned into a beautiful but air-headed glamour dog. (Recent efforts to bring the hunt and good sense back into the breed, now called the Red Setter, have been successful.)

When choosing a versatile puppy, stick with bloodlines of primarily hunting stock. Avoid a lot of field trial dogs, because they can be, like show dogs, bred for the purpose of impressing judges, not producing birds for a foot hunter. A good place to

Shorthairs are affectionate yet tend to bond strongly to a single master. Minimal training produces good results. Better trainers can get miracles out of a shorthair.

Denny Burkhart and his Brittany, Lady. Lady was an exceptional woodcock dog.

start looking for a pup is with people in dog organizations like NAVHDA, NSTRA, and NAHRA. Avoid those who immediately talk about how many titles their dogs have; some play the title game like the field trial game. Look for someone who has hunting stock, maybe a little show for good looks, and so much the better if they've won a few titles. Also, it is a good idea to look for a line of dogs bred to hunt the birds you favor. Shorthairs bred for generations to hunt big country, for example, may do fine in the thick Eastern grouse woods, but a better choice would be a kennel that produces proven grouse dogs through successive generations.

THE SPECIALIST: AHH . . . JOY!

Ross Steinhauer's English pointer, Smoke, looked like a dog stepping out of a William Harnden Foster illustration when we hunted grouse together late last fall. All we would have needed were some canvas coats, an older double for Ross, fedoras, and high boots, and we could have easily blended into one of Foster's images with Smoke and those wonderful coverts Ross had. Smoke and Ross are specialists.

Specialization . . . a fisherman starts with a cane pole, graduates to a spinning rig, and eventually becomes a dry fly purist. So will the seasons in an upland gunner's life lead him or her to find one particular bird and hunt it over most others. You experiment until you settle on something that suits your nature, then want a dog that matches this interest. There is a different level of dedication to the sport for the specialist, a deeper commitment, an esoteric search for beauty and excellence, something unique, rare, and special. Once found, you can't be satisfied with something less.

Who are the specialist dogs? Specialists, by our definition, are dogs specifically bred to do a specific thing. George Bird and Kay Evans' Old Hemlock English setters were developed as a result of their love of the dogs and ruffed grouse and woodcock hunting. Old Hemlock dogs carry in their bloodlines a human lifetime's worth of line breeding for characteristics that meant better grouse and woodcock dogs. Bob Wehle's Elhew pointer line is another example. Although Elhew pointers hunt nearly everything, they are specialized in the sense that they are highly refined dogs, the pinnacle of English pointer breeding.

Not that the specialist can't or doesn't hunt other birds or do some of the things versatile dogs do. They just seem to do one thing best and other things with the same grace and style, but maybe not as well as the one thing they do best.

Nash, son of DeCoverly's Miss Bliss and October Joy, was my first specialist. Nash's roots come from the Massayed Kennels in Wales, and the Sir Roger DeCoverly setter line of the late 1800s.

In 1916, near Wilkes Barre, Pennsylvania, George Ryman and his wife, Ellen Kernan, a prominent name in bench setters, set out to create their vision of the perfect English setter using dogs from several prominent English setter lines, including De-Coverlys. The Rymans were very selective in breeding practices and chose dogs that possessed the hunting abilities found in the older setter field trial lines, mixed with the good looks and temperament of bench stock. The Rymans succeeded greatly in this effort, producing a large number of extremely fine English setters. Ryman sold his interest in the kennels in 1931 to Carl Calkins, of Monroeton, Pennsylvania.

DeCoverly Kennels Nash, the author's grouse specialist. Nash represented a deeper commitment, an esoteric search for beauty and excellence, something unique, rare and special.

Calkins continued the bloodline under the Ryman Kennels name until the mid-1970s, when Ken Alexander came into the picture. Alexander, on his honeymoon, bought a puppy from Calkins, and in 1975, ended up buying the DeCoverly line from Calkins. Since 1975, Alexander has been breeding fine DeCoverly English setters.

Recently, Alexander, with the help of business partner Bill Sordoni, a true gentleman and a bird hunter, built one of the finest dog breeding and training facilities available in Pennsylvania's Endless Mountains, near Wilkes Barre. The several hundred-acre facility features the kennel, training grounds, clay target ranges, and other amenities of interest to upland gunners.

Alexander chooses each pairing from among more than 70 adult dogs, superb specimens of what an English setter should be, all on the premises. All breeding stock is University of Pennsylvania Hip (PennHip) tested against hip dysplasia, and all dogs are sold fully vaccinated, with a six-generation pedigree. The kennels feature soundproof whelping rooms with in-floor and radiant heat, a computer-controlled air exchange system, and other features which contribute to a stress-free breeding environment and strong, healthy puppies. DeCoverly Kennels also has several hundred acres of training grounds that range from low fields for starting young dogs to grouse and woodcock coverts right on the property. Daron Kovolenus, the full-time trainer, uses his gentle ways to produce outstanding results. Alexander said he has never seen anyone work the dogs like Daron can. "He knows more in five years than I know in 20 about these dogs," Alexander said.

This pursuit of excellence doesn't stop when you take a puppy home. It extends to training help throughout the dog's lifetime, especially help getting puppies turned into young dogs that perform like gentlemen and ladies in the field and at home.

DeCoverly dogs have been placed all over North America. (Alexander is very particular to whom he sells dogs. He wants real upland gunners who will treat these great setters as they should be treated: with plenty of love, a good home, and many opportunities to hunt birds.) Most DeCoverly setters are found near grouse and woodcock country: Pennsylvania, West Virginia, New England, and the lake states. However, DeCoverly setters are also in Arizona, Florida, Idaho, California, and all over the Midwest.

Obviously, this is not the kind of satisfaction a backyard breeder or even a small professional kennel can offer. It takes a lot of capital to operate a kennel like this. Yet this is more of a labor of love for both Sordoni and Alexander than a purely profitable venture. DeCoverly dogs do come with a fairly high price tag, as English setter puppies go, but the money is well spent. You get far more than you realize you are paying for.

So what makes the specialist unique?

I can only speak from 11 years with Nash, and a year with Shana.

Nash was always the perfect gentleman. He was gentle in my home, great around kids, and a fantastic bird hunter, except for a couple of years when I just couldn't seem to put him into birds. At nine months, on his first big adventure in Michigan, he was pointing grouse and woodcock like a champ. When we returned home, my coverts seemed to dry up. (Until I ranged a minimum of 2 hours away from home, we didn't get into any grouse.) Any fault he had I would blame myself for, not the breeding or the dog. We hunted ruffed grouse and woodcock extensively all across Pennsylvania and in Minnesota and Michigan. We also found a few pheasants in Pennsylvania. I took him dove hunting a couple of times, but it wasn't his cup of tea, or mine, except for a few days in September.

The thing that made Nash so special was *how* he hunted grouse, the beauty in it. I loved following that dog, especially on a lead-colored November day when the leaves were down, the forest sparse in its simplicity, yet richly textured if you looked close and understood the whole story.

When Nash worked a grouse covert, he was liquid, flowing in graceful figure-eight casts out to about 75 yards, maybe more depending on the cover. A square-headed, long-eared, deep-jowled tricolor, his looks, at least to my eyes, were outstanding, a joy to behold. He carried himself with grace, dignity, and elegance. Put a grouse before his nose and you had a dog that was electric, alive with the kind of soul-deep passion for grouse that stirs artists to paint, writers to write. (Yes, he was named for Nash Buckingham. I wanted a link between the grouse and woodcock setter world of George Bird Evans, Buckingham's friend and compiler of *The Best of Nash Buckingham*, and the quail and farmland country of Buckingham himself.) Following the jingle of Nash's bell through our special coverts was like listening to a fine string quartet playing rich Bach and Vivaldi melodies. The cello was Nash's rich, smooth movements; the violins my heart singing with great joy at the beauty I had found in 65 pounds of tricolor belton English setter. Nash touched my heart deeply and certainly riveted my soul because we could share a love of grouse; we understood one another that way.

Nash didn't have this effect on everyone. But that is the beauty of specialization. You create your own sense of uniqueness.

Nash's faults were few: He didn't live nearly long enough. He should have had a better trainer (instead of me), and I should have worked harder with him on retrieving. Otherwise, he was exactly what I wanted in a dog.

Shana, my first female, is the great, great granddaughter of October Pal, Nash's father. At a year old, it is hard to say what she will become. I have high hopes. She's faster than Nash, softer than he was, more sensitive to some things, rough and tumble to others. I see all the right things inside her: She moves beautifully high-headed in the woods, she has beautiful pointing style, a strong desire to retrieve, and noses into everything. Yet she is still full of puppy and likes to play and steal socks and cavort through the house with sofa pillows, and all those fun things. I have a feeling she will be a better bird-finder than Nash was. There's more fire in her, she is faster-working, a bit more lively than Nash tended to be; but then I could be slowing down, too.

Here is where the skeptical versatile dog man says specialization is more in the mind than in reality. And this is probably true, but it's the specialist's gunning experience that counts, not what's in the game pouch. The drawbacks of specialization are many: I miss not having a dog to hunt other things with, like waterfowl and doves. Perhaps when Shana gets a bit older, I'll bring a Golden or another shorthair home. Also, there are some limitations on what the specialist can do. I dislike running a long-haired dog in most farm country because burrs are a pain to get out and damage their coat. I would also think twice about running a dog who carries the emotional

The search for excellence goes into making a specialist.

Nash was always the perfect gentleman: gentle in the home, great around kids, and a fantastic bird hunter.

attachment and the financial value of the specialist in snake country, or over chukar country's lava rock for fear of irreparable damage. (Perhaps we should think twice about running versatile dogs over the same thing.) Could the specialist turn out to be something other than what the gunner intends? If a dog senses that you really love hunting Rooster more than grouse or quail, Pup will probably reflect this. Dogs are more sensitive to their owners' responses to things than we give them credit for.

The bottom line is that there is room in the world for both the specialist and the versatile dog. Celebrate each dog for its own sake, and love it with all your heart. They are here for all too short a time.

DOG TRAINING

I once thought I knew a lot about dog training. Two easy-to-train dogs raised my confidence. A decade passed. And this fall, I came to understand how little I really know, and ended up taking Shana back to DeCoverly Kennels to have Daron get her started more properly, something I didn't do with Nash.

Most of Nash's life, we lived on my three-quarter-acre patch in the middle of 1,000 acres of farmland, three farms owned by Clayton and Mary Tyson, all deeded to the Tyson family in the 1700s. I helped round up their stray steers—for some strange reason, the steers liked the grass in my backyard—and they let me run my dogs on their land. I had a call-back pen and trained in the hayfield behind the house. It was great. A few years ago, however, I moved, then moved again and found the best housing bang for the buck was in an older neighborhood within city limits. It's a nice place, but I miss some amenities of rural life.

Many gun dog owners today face a similar problem. Juggling family, career, and keeping a roof over your head demands a lot of time and energy; and a lack of space for the accoutrements of dog training, such as bird pens and training grounds, creates challenges for people who want to produce good dogs. Breeders are seeing more people who are buying started dogs or are having puppies trained by professionals, according to Alexander. This is not a bad thing, just different from the way it used to be.

Still, once Pup comes home from the kennel, his owner and the family need to continue with the basic work. Obedience training is not hard; it just takes a lot of practice. At minimum, a dog should know come, heel, sit, stay, and steady or whoa. Each trainer and training book or video has a different way to teach all these things to a dog. Some trainers like training tables, others like working in the backyard. The best way is to find out what works for you and Pup and stick with it. Plan on spending 15 minutes a day just working on these basics with Pup. In a month or two you'll see great results.

The emphasis on dog training today is using dog psychology rather than brute force. This is a good development, because it works with rewards and the dog's natural desire to please rather than a fear of punishment. Outthink your dog instead of giving into heavy-handed tactics. Treat a dog as you would a child. There are times when discipline is required, but use it sparingly. Each dog's temperament is different; some boneheads require a firm hand, others are soft and gentle. Learn to recognize this and train to the nature of the dog.

Range—how far a dog works ahead of his hunter—is always something that has perplexed people. Range is largely a function of training in the flushing breeds. Flushing dogs need to work to the gun, within 40 yards of a hunter. In pointing dogs, however, range is more a function of the amount of birds in a covert and the way the dog relates to the land. A dog that is searching far and wide is usually having trouble finding birds; or the objectives (bird holding spots) are widely spaced, and Pup is cruising from one objective to the next quickly to find birds and please his master. It might be better to switch coverts to find one more saturated with birds than try to hack a dog's range closer.

I've always been a fan of close-working dogs, those who spend most of their time within 75 yards, because watching the dog move gives me the greatest joy in a covert. Some dogs have a natural range that is greater than this. Some grouse hunters I have shared coverts with, for example, had dogs that would spend most of the day running beyond 100 yards, while the hunter enjoyed a solo walk through the woods. We listened for the beeper collar to sound, then ran for the point. They claimed it was more effective to hunt this way. I didn't enjoy it so much because when I hunt, I like to see a dog work, so I can vicariously run with the dog, nose to the wind, trying to catch some bird scent.

For today's coverts, a close-working dog is usually a better choice, especially in hunting the East. The farm trails that once dotted agricultural land have become hard-surfaced lanes leading back into a housing development, and the big-going dog that can't be controlled is asking for trouble when he hunts a well-populated area. Most of the versatile dogs and many of the specialists lean towards the close-working side of range. Learn to keep a psychological check cord between you and pup, loose but under control. A good place to start learning how to train your dog is with the breeder—many offer "puppy kindergarten" classes—or with dog training groups.

Nash and the author, in Sliding Rock covert, in Nash's last days. (Photo by Richelle Holland)

* * * *

Shana and I visit "the boys," Jack and Nash, up on the hill where their markers are placed, from time to time. We sit and reflect and sense their presence. It is a comfort to imagine a wet, black nose lifting my hand for more attention, or feel a thumping stubby tail whacking my pants leg, even if it is just the ghost—a *wanagi*—of a dog come calling. I was honored to have two such fine dogs in my life. I miss my boys.

DOG CLUBS AND OTHER USEFUL INFORMATION

North American Hunting Retriever Association (NAHRA)
P. O. Box 5159
Fredricksburg, VA 22403
Telephone (540) 286–0625
FAX (540) 286–0629
Website: http://www.nahra.org/

North American Versatile Hunting Dog Association (NAVHDA)
P.O. Box 520
Arlington Heights, IL 60006
Telephone (847) 253–6488
FAX (847) 255–5987
Website: http://www.navhda.org/links.html

National Shoot To Retrieve Association, Inc. (NSTRA)
226 N. Mill Street, No. 2
Plainfield, IN 46168
Telephone: (317) 839–4059
FAX (317) 839–4197
Website: http://www.nstra.org/
Email: nstra@indynet.com

National Hunting Dog Association (NHDA)
P.O. Box 40
Derby, KS 67037
Telephone (316) 686–2505
FAX (316) 683–8559
Website: http://www.nhda.com/

For more information on dogs, including training seminars, videos, dog breeders, and dog gear manufacturers, try two magazines, *The Pointing Dog Journal* and *Gun Dog*, available on newsstands.

Also, there are numerous webring sites on the Internet that can offer links to other clubs, including specific breed clubs and a variety of information on dogs, dog training, upland bird hunting, and other topics. Search using "gun dogs." Be sure to visit the American Kennel Club's site: www.akc.org.

THE GUNS

To be a first-rate shot necessitates the combination of two distinctly opposite con-
ditions: a highly strung nervous temperament which keeps you ever on the alert, a
cool head which enables you in moments of excitement to fire without recklessness
or undue haste. This combination is naturally rare. That 'practice makes perfect'
is in the case of shooting only true to a certain extent. For a man must be born
with a certain inherent aptitude to become a really first-rate shot.

Lord Ripon

Three shots—close, long, and medium—taken in the North American uplands say a lot about the ground a shotgun for this continent's birdshooter must cover. . . .

FIRST SHOT

The Canadian River snakes through dry western Oklahoma giving life, in the form of moisture, to everything it touches. Cottonwoods grow along its banks, interspersed with patches of grass and other thick vegetation. Bobwhite quail are fond of this riparian zone, finding sustenance in the weed seeds and shelter in the grass, brush, and cottonwoods along the river.

A dark German shorthair snuffles through this cover, working the vague scent of birds seen only in pronged tracks in the sand. Suddenly, the dog slows, peers ahead in the brush, nose and head casting side to side, then bounds forward, low to the ground, intent on something. A moment later, two gunners round a dense turn of brush and see a dog statue, frozen in a point, save for a quiver of his front legs and the twitch of his tail.

Two steps forward. A 30-bird covey roars up 15 yards away, flying in a dozen different directions. The gunner on the right focuses on a single bird speeding that direction, feels the Daly's comb touch his cheek, barrels tracking the bird for a moment, and hears the gun roar, the bird falling in a puff of feathers. The left gunner is startled by the sheer number of birds and tries to choose one then another and ends up sending a pair of salvos at the ghosts of bobwhites sailing off out into the prairie. Chuckling and calling himself a "true conservationist," he remarks how close the birds came up, they were so close. . . .

SECOND SHOT

Clay County Indiana's Eel River borders one of the prettiest farms in the state, in the eyes of one pheasant hunter, who, despite overall low pheasant numbers, keeps finding birds in isolated patches of weedy growth that border the river. Opening day was 3 weeks gone when an opportunity to revisit the farm came up one Saturday afternoon. Not one to miss opportunity, he takes the autoloader from the gun case, calls for Cassie, the chocolate Lab, and bids his wife goodbye, saying he'll be home at "dark-thirty."

On opening day, the weedpatch he wanted to hunt was still bordered by standing rows of tan corn, and the pheasants, when they got to the edge of the weeds, ducked into the corn and vanished, as those cagey birds will, when given a chance. Today, however, the corn is down and he believes his luck has turned.

Cassie drives hard into the weeds, quartering magnificently, working scent. It all feels so right, and confidence is high, but Rooster is unpredictable, and a true 40 yards from the end of the weed patch, a magnificent old cock thunders into the afternoon, *ba-cuuk,ba-cuuk,ba-cuuk*. Long is the word that travels through the gunner's head the moment the comb of the 12-gauge touches his cheek. Yet something inside says taking this bird is possible. The gunner sees the bird's tail over the shotgun's rib, swings past it, through the body, past the white neck ring, to the tip of the beak, and pulls ahead a couple of feet, what looks right, then touches the trigger. It seems like an eternity, but Rooster falls in a flurry of feathers, evidence of a solid hit. Cassie is on the bird in a moment, and she comes trotting back with 3 pounds of long-spurred wild pheasant in her very happy mouth. The copper-plated No. 6s did their job.

THIRD SHOT

Two Oregon gunners are anxious to get free for a weekend with Huns, pheasants, and chukars over their Brittanys. Gilliam County's wheat stubble, near the Columbia River, calls. So they answer.

Near the brushy end of one stubble field the fast-working orange and white Brits, traveling full-bore throughout most of the field, suddenly drop pace, become stiff-legged, then one slips into a picturesque point with the other backing. The gunners trot to close the distance, but not before the covey of Huns are wise to the approach of danger. The birds flush, swinging left, about 30 yards out. The left gunner finds one bird, puffs it, then swings on a second and takes it with equal grace. The dogs come trotting back happy. This portion of the cycle is complete. "Good shooting," says his partner.

* * * *

Choosing the ideal bird gun for North America's uplands is a daunting task, especially given the range of shots, the variety of types of shooting, and the circumstances involved. A shotgun well-suited for the Vermont grouse woods could be very out of place in a late-season Iowa cornfield or in Idaho, gunning chukars. Shotguns are very much like dogs in this regard, there are qualifications that might make one gun versatile enough for nearly everything; yet, there is certainly room for the specialist shotgun, or perhaps two guns are the answer. It all depends on what you're hunting, where, and how.

One thing the ideal shotgun ought to do is match the gunner's tastes and style, and fit him or her properly. We all have certain eye appeal items that make us choose one style or make of shotgun over another. This should be taken into account. I'm partial to old side-by-sides. You might like stack-barreled Browning over-unders, while your buddy might prefer Benelli autoloaders or a pumpgun. Regardless of the type of gun that "trips your trigger," it is imperative that it fit you properly.

Each of our bodies is different and shotgun fit needs to take this into account. A custom-made stock, created from measurements taken by a properly experienced gunsmith or shotgun expert—shooting schools often offer this service—is the ultimate mating of shotgun to person. This luxury is often out of most shooters' price ranges. Still, it wouldn't hurt to get the proper measurements and compare them to

Tailor your gun to the birds you're hunting, the type of cover you're in and, most important, your personal preference.

the guns on the rack, if you can do so. Trap and skeet shooters often hold gun events where you can be measured, or perhaps your gunsmith or sporting goods store has an adjustable stock measuring device available. If so, take advantage of this. It is worth the effort.

A third thing a shotgun should do is take gamebirds cleanly, provided the shooter does his part, at the ranges normally encountered. This involves a combination of patterning and ammunition choice, variables that can make things interesting. If all birds were chukar-sized and went up at 35 yards, choosing a choke and shotshell would be easy. But they're not. Close birds, under 25 yards, include grouse and woodcock and just about any pointed bird. Medium range birds, 25 to 35 yards, include the prairie grouse and just about any bird taken using flushing dogs. Long range birds, 40 yards-plus, can include any western game, pheasants, chukars, and huns. This is not to say that you won't find days when grouse are going up at 35 yards or chukars won't grace you with a 15-yard flush. The law of averages applies here.

Another thing the ideal shotgun should do is accommodate a variety of loads, to make it more versatile, so you can hunt pheasants with No. 6 magnums one day, grouse with light No. 8s the next. It should also be light enough to carry comfortably all day, yet heavy enough to track well on longer shots using sustained lead techniques.

Is there a shotgun that can handle all of these conditions? If you like doubles and have some money to spend there is: A 12-gauge English light game gun has been the choice of bird shooters the world over for more than a century. This shotgun has been in various stages of development since the flintlock fowling pieces of the late 1600s. It reached the zenith of its development in the early 1900s, with hammerless side-by-sides, and has reigned supreme in Europe since that time. Doubles along the same lines were very popular in the United States from the late 1800s through the 1940s, when the pumpgun and the autoloader became America's most popular shotguns. However, doubles made along classic English lines have experienced a renaissance since the mid-1970s.

The English light game gun is more than just a pretty side-by-side with lots of fancy checkering and engraving on the sideplates. It is also a highly functional tool for taking birds. It has a natural balance and swing to it that is unmatched in other shotguns. Usually weighing about 6½ pounds, you can carry one all day and not get too tired. Its 26- or 28-inch barrels are finely tapered to offer a wide sighting plane, yet one that is not intrusive. These guns are just as efficient in the woods or dense brush as they are in the open field shooting battue on driven pheasants. Typically, the barrels are bored with chokes equivalent to improved cylinder and improved modified. And in the hands of a skilled shooter, these shotguns are deadly.

The stackbarrel over-under, a largely American improvement on the English light game gun, is another alternative. Several gun makers, notably Browning, offer light over-unders with very similar specifications to the English light game gun. There is also an advantage to the narrow, single rib sighting plane on stackbarrels: Everything is a bit more precise, especially on crossing shots.

Southern quail hunters and others who are small bore enthusiasts will probably disagree with the 12-gauge as the selection of choice. Carry a 12-gauge into some southern quail plantations, and you'll be told, very politely of course, to "git on home, Yankee."

There is no doubt that 16-, 20-, and 28-gauge guns can handle just about everything a 12-gauge shotgun can. Even the .410 in the right hands can perform as well as the 12-gauge under certain conditions. However, a reality of physics in shotgunning is that smaller diameter bores build up higher breech pressures, which lead to deformed pellets. Ideally, shotgunners want a uniform spread of pellets throughout the pattern. Deformed pellets spread a pattern out and can create open areas in the pattern. Shooting heavy loads in small-diameter bores also increases shot stringing.

Two Oklahoma State University professors, Dr. George C. Oberfell and Charles E. Thompson, who conducted thousands of tests on patterns, penetration, and extrapolations of data from shooting live birds under laboratory-controlled conditions, explored this idea many years ago. "It is the shot load that kills, not the gauge," they wrote in *Mysteries of Shotgun Patterns.*

They worked out a rule of thumb for effective shotgun ranges when all other conditions are equal (ounces of shot in the air, choke boring, pattern, pellet velocities, etc.) For a .410 with ½-ounce of shot the effective killing range is 30 yards; a 28-gauge, 35 yards; the 20-gauge 40 yards. The 12-gauge with an 1¼-ounce shot load was given a 45-yard range, about the same as a 3-inch 20-gauge load.

Availability is another factor in favor of the 12-gauge. The factory loads available in a 2¾-inch 12-gauge shotshell are incredible, everything from ⅞-ounces of shot, to as much as 1¾-ounces of shot. A 3- or 3½-inch chamber allows you to approach 10 gauge status. And just try to find 28- or 16-gauge loads in Joe's Hardware or even a sporting goods shop in a small Kansas town.

Back to loads, a 1-ounce 2½ drams equivalent powder load is standard fare for the English game gun. Using English shooting techniques, gunners in battues have taken driven pheasants and red grouse flushed off the moors at ranges that would make Nash Buckingham and his 65-yard duck gun, Bo'Whoop, blush. Ballistic magic takes place in a 1-ounce 12-gauge load. It's an ideal mating of load and bore.

I like to keep things simple, one gun, one load for as much as it can reasonably handle. I experimented with 12-gauge reloads for targets and birds for several years and settled on a standard load that seems to work effectively in any 12-gauge gun I've tried. It's a 1⅛-ounce, three drams equivalent powder load that travels about 1,300 feet per second—basically a fast trap or skeet load. Top it with No. 8 shot and you're good for clay targets, grouse, woodcock, doves, and quail. I've used 7½s effectively on pointed pheasants and late grouse. No. 6s work on prairie grouse and pheasants. By standardizing everything, I came to know the boundaries of my gun and load combination, something that helps me take more game.

Those wishing to explore the mysteries of shotgunning further to come up with their own conclusions should read two books: Bob Brister's *Shotgunning: The Art and the Science,* Winchester Press, 1976, and *The Orvis Wing-Shooting Handbook,* by Bruce Bowlen, Nick Lyons Books, 1985. Brister offers a concise yet thorough, no-nonsense look at shotguns and shotgunning from butt pad to muzzle in language that is easy for a non-technical person to comprehend. Bowlen details the English method of training shotgunners to shoot better.

* * * *

Lofty ideals and eternal truths are noble things; they keep the human race reaching for what might be and push us on to strive for the best that can be. However, when it comes time to deal with reality and get down in the trenches, most North American bird gunners are not toting light English game guns. We carry an interesting collection of shotguns out into the quail fields, the grouse woods, and the prairie. George Bird Evans recommends a shotgun "with a history" for gunning birds, to make the shooting experience more meaningful. Many gunners possess this, although it might not be in the class of the famous Purdey that George inherited from his friend Dr. Norris.

In one corner of North America's gun cabinet sits a hump-backed Browning autoloader. Purchased in the 1960s, it was Uncle Ed's pheasant gun. Carrying this gun while wearing his canvas hunting coat and brush pants, Uncle Ed looked a little odd. The old Browning has a 30-inch barrel, designed to get the maximum powder burn and push the paper-wadded, 2¾-inch, No. 5 high-brass loads he shot out of the barrel faster, so they brought down those cackling long-tailed birds a bit more precisely. Yet Uncle Ed was a short, thin man with a Belair cigarette perpetually dangling from his lips, his blaze-orange Jones cap jauntily cocked to one side. When he walked those weedy November cornfields with the Browning it often looked like David wrestling Goliath. Today, the Browning belongs to Uncle Ed's grandson, Ryan, who hunts pheasants with it, too. Briar scratches in the stock, worn bluing on the action, and a hand-worn forearm tell of Uncle Ed's years with the Browning. Ryan says there is something about seeing Rooster suspended above the long rib of this shotgun that is magic. Touch the gold trigger, Rooster comes down—it is that simple.

Remington is the name stamped on the barrel of Bob's Model 870 pumpgun. Bob works down at the plant and wanted a gun that would cover all his bases, from pheasants and waterfowl to the turkeys he lives to hunt. So he chose the plain-Jane version of the 870, with a Parkerized finish, so it would not scare sharp-eyed turkeys or ducks away. Three choke tubes, modified, full, and improved cylinder came with the gun, but Bob bought a fourth, extra full, for his turkeys, and a camouflage sling, to make it easier carrying it in and out of the woods. The number of turkey fans and beards and feet with spurs that grace Bob's living room attest to the gun's effectiveness on turkeys. Yet there is a bit of mud still in the butt pad from the time he came pheasant hunting with Jack, the German shorthair, and me, and to his surprise brought home an old, long-tailed pheasant, the kind we used to find when we were kids. There are also memories of dove hunts, sitting on a camouflage stool along a field edge on a flyway leading into the roost, when the barrel got hot and the shells were gone too quickly. Grouse have fallen to the Remington's spell, too, Bob remembers, puffing his pipe, contemplating days gone by. Yet the gun still looks fairly new because it is one of the things Bob treasures, cares for.

Harrington & Richardson is a familiar name to a lot of gunners because H&R Topper was the stamp on the barrel of their first bird gun, a single shot with a hammer. Matthew, 14 years old, stood below the Trius trap set up in the cut wheat field for practice, self-conscious, and a bit edgy about the feel of the new shotgun, a New England Arms single shot with a tight hammer and an equally hard trigger, in his hands.

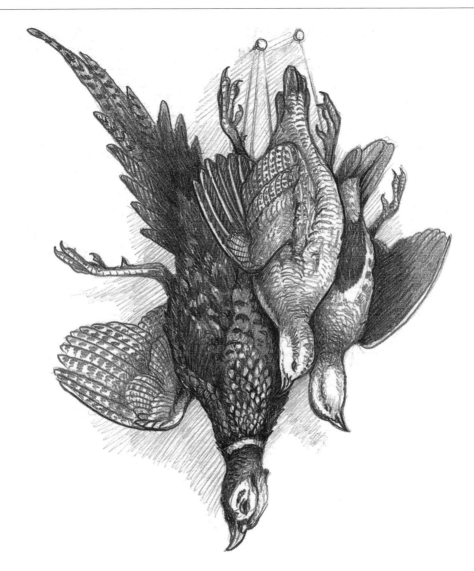

Shell, his aunt, threw targets for him. I tried to offer a little instruction on how to shoot, but not too much. Finally, a target went off the trap's ledge, sailed out over the field and puffed under the single-shot's spell. Matthew's confidence was suddenly inspired and he went on to find three more targets that afternoon. In September, we tried the dove fields. He was a bit worried about shooting the wrong birds, but after watching me a little bit, I heard the gun bark a few times down on his end of the field and hoped that he was learning something about hunting. I smiled, too, remembering "Black Bart," the little .410 H&R single with a chromed action and stock and forearm painted black, that was my first bird gun. Seven pheasants and I couldn't hit one of them!

A shotgun with a history certainly describes the Lefever Nitro Special, No. 165378, an old side-by-side that accompanies me bird hunting. It originally belonged to a relative of my grandfather, on the Taylor side, who sold it to my grandfather in the 1930s. A single stamped duck flushing up off a cattail swamp, its body rubbed smooth and silvery from more than 70 years of hands cradling this shotgun, flies away on the sidewalls. Gouges in the stock, darkened by gun oil and time, are a road map of long-gone rabbit hunts and quail and pheasant flushing. The checkering is simple, functional, yet pretty. A small bulls-eye marks the thumb of the cocking lever near the safety. I guess it weighs about seven pounds, with 28-inch barrels originally bored modified and full, because a dime wouldn't fit in the right barrel. A few years ago, I had them rebored to skeet chokes to make the Lefever more useful in my grouse woods.

My grandfather, Walter Taylor, was a gentle, dark-haired man of the earth, who loved black-eyed Susans, picking fox grapes, making wine, and fishing the Susquehanna River and the Chesapeake Bay with a cigar in his mouth. He probably hunted rabbits and groundhogs with his shotgun, before the arthritis in his knee got bad. Grandpa Taylor gave me my first traps for Christmas in 1972, the year before he died, and sent me down a path that, although it has been hard at times, is one I cherish. He never got to hunt with me, but I like to think that we walk together through the woods, especially in one covert that has plump purple fox grapes. My father, Gene Taylor, also hunted with this shotgun. I can see Dad carrying it, trudging through November cornfields rank with foxtail, his kid ravenous about pheasant hunting. Dad lacked interest in small game—a bad experience with a landowner over a bird that fell just a few yards over his fence after my father shot it on public land. I treasure having a father like I had, and hope I can match his patience, the great love in his heart. Now I hunt with this gun. Someday I will pass it along, too.

PEOPLE WHO HUNT

If a man does not keep pace with his companions, perhaps it is because he hears a different drummer. Let him step to the music which he hears, however measured and far away.

Henry David Thoreau

Carleton Coon, in *The Hunting Peoples,* a 1971 Nick Lyons book, writes about how, in the ancient past, man formed relationships through hunting. Families joined forces to make food-gathering chores easier, which allowed denser population centers to develop and gave man more spare time. In time, establishing relationships for mutual benefit extended to the animal kingdom, with dogs, horses, and other domesticated beasts. Group hunting efforts soon became the norm. A common thread joins Masai tribal lion surrounds in Africa, medieval lords using human drivers to push fowl and other game into the waiting falcons, and two guys heading out for the bird field with their dogs.

Who hunts the North American uplands? Is he your hunting buddy, the guy who shares a musty camp, a car always ripe with the fresh scent of wet, muddy dog, food that would choke a goat, and the long, tired, yet ultimately satisfying walk back to the truck at the end of the day with you? Is it the couple down the road with the brace of Brittanys who don't seem to be home much in autumn, according to your wife? Is it the single Mom, new in town, whose son wants to hunt but doesn't know anyone willing to take her boy? Is the North American upland hunter your age, older than you, younger than you?

Actually, the North American upland bird hunter is all of these people and more.

Statistically speaking, the "average" upland bird hunter in the United States is a white male, age 40-something, with a college degree, who earns about $40,000 per

year. According to Fish and Wildlife Service figures, there are currently 14 million hunters in the United States, a figure down 300,000 from 1996. They spent $565 million on licenses, and 47 percent of these hunters were from the "Baby Boom" generation, people born from 1947 to about 1960.

Some of the largest numbers of hunters hunt in Michigan, 934,000; Texas, 911,000; Pennsylvania, 879,000; Wisconsin, 665,000; and New York, 642,000.

Individual state counts by interest in a particular species show that 10 to 15 percent of all hunters do some bird hunting. Pennsylvania, for example, with nearly a million hunters, shows about 150,000–200,000 ruffed grouse hunters on average. In Wisconsin, the figure is higher, with 150,000 grouse hunters for 665,000 general hunters. Minnesota has about 140,000 grouse hunters.

With other species, the numbers are smaller, but equally interesting: Missouri has 55,000 quail hunters and 15,000 pheasant hunters. Pennsylvania, which once had 750,000 pheasant hunters, is now down to under 200,000 according to recent statistics. Pennsylvania woodcock hunters number about 15,000. Keystone dove hunters number 60,000.

Who is the typical North American upland hunter? It's you, me, anyone, from any walk of life.

Organization involvement offers another track on the trail of who the upland bird hunter is: Quail Unlimited boasts 44,000 members across the United States, but especially in the South. Pheasants Forever has 85,000 members. The Ruffed Grouse Society has nearly 25,000 members.

Still, statistics don't really flesh out human beings.

George Bird Evans, in *The Upland Shooting Life* (Alfred A. Knopf, 1971), classifies upland bird gunners into a number of groups: Old-timers, Social Hunters, The Loner, The Fair Shot, The Long-Shot Addict, The Gadgeteer, The Reporter, and The Purist.

Evans had a special fondness for old-timers and their stories of days gone by. He remembers meeting Riley Warden, an 84-year-old "living in the glories of the past . . . always about to smile," Mel Heath in his red and black Woolrich shirt, and Cliff Springer, who also hunted grouse until he was 84.

Evans enjoyed gunning with a few select friends, Les Crowl, Dr. Charles Norris, and Obie Conaway, but didn't go for group hunts—no more than two grouse and woodcock gunners, this "Combination-of-Two" being a relationship ". . . as delicately balanced as marriage, occasionally lasting longer."

Evans also had a great deal of respect for female hunters, The Fair Shot, especially those who went it alone. He chuckled at the way The Gadgeteer strapped himself down with numerous accoutrements. He found the Long-Shot Addict a problem, because the Long-Shot showed no consideration for what he may be doing to the birds. And he seemed to bear The Reporter a lot of understated wrath for ratting out favorite coverts.

Evans described himself as a Loner, someone who appreciates a feeling that "... an undiluted immersion in beauty and tension and action" in the glorious wilderness "is there just for him and his dog." He went on further to call himself a Purist, a subspecies of the Loner. The Purist, Evans wrote, "... is on a cloud when things go well; when things don't happen according to his standards—his dog's work, his shooting—he would be best let alone, for no one is a deeper griever. If the Purist were any more exacting he wouldn't hunt at all, yet all this raises his enjoyment of shooting to a plane perhaps higher than the average gunner's, simply because when events occur in such a rare combination as to satisfy him, angels hum softly."

I've enjoyed sharing the field with both friends and family, as well as many days alone. Evans is right about hunting alone. It is the best way to develop a gun dog. Also, under the right circumstances—and I would have to share his idea of being a Purist as well—hunting alone is a spiritual experience. Yet I strive to find a balance between gunning alone and with friends, hoping I can make those angels hum softly more often.

* * * *

Overall, the number of hunters is falling, a disturbing trend. Of greater cause for concern is that hunter recruitment (bringing new people into the sport) is too low to keep up with attrition of older hunters. About 18 percent of all hunters are 55 years and older. Most studies show that 50 is the age at which most people start dropping out of hunting. Still, there are some new trends taking place among those who hunt, especially upland bird hunters, that are interesting.

One is the influx of women into the sport. According to the National Shooting Sports Foundation, five million women participate in the shooting sports in the United States. This includes about 1.2 million ladies who hunt, most between 25 and 54 years of age. So don't be surprised the next time you round a corner and come across a carload of Fair Shots out for some upland sport.

Actually, this could do a lot to boost the image of hunting in general by getting the "scratch and sniff" male element to clean up a bit of their act because the girls are around.

I've been privileged to share the field with several ladies. I remember being somewhat surprised at seeing Jill Hoff, Tim Hoff's daughter, enjoying pheasant hunting as much as Tim and I did with his shorthair, Molly, back in the early 1980s. Jill was a teenager then, and she went on to pursue a career in wildlife and natural resources. A second cousin, Cynthia Taylor, shared a couple of deer camps with us—her father, Clark; my father; her brother, Scott; and I. Standing on top of a beautiful snow-covered mountain one morning, Cynthia thanked her father for showing her the beauty of the mountains, for being there, something that touched Clark deeply.

The Becoming an Outdoors-Woman program is an effort by state wildlife agencies and concerned lady gunners to teach women basic outdoor skills, like shooting, fishing, bicycling, hiking, and camping for both their own interests and so they can pass them along to children. This is especially important to single moms whose kids want to learn outdoor skills but lack a contact to do so. Since 1997, the program has found its way to all 50 states and is growing.

Traditionally, fathers were responsible for passing along things like hunting to their children, especially sons. Today, with half of all marriages ending in divorce, and families joining and rejoining to form new families, and more single moms choosing to remain single, there are many children, sons especially, who won't benefit from the passing down of traditions like hunting. Many local sportsmen's clubs, shooting groups, and state wildlife agencies are going out of their way to attract youngsters to the outdoors, however.

Sharing your outdoor skills with a youngster is a rewarding experience. I've done it through Boy Scouts, family, and friends. It requires a good bit of time and effort on your part; however, the results are well worth it.

Starting a youngster bird hunting is not hard, just time-consuming. Start with a hunter's safety education course. Here in Pennsylvania, these include safe gun handling training and hunting safety. Both you and your young hunter should take it together. It never hurts to get a refresher course. Shooting is the next logical place to begin, because it is usually what holds a kid's main interest. Explain the gun, its parts, how it is used, how it works. A good example of basic gun safety rules speaks louder than all the lectures in the world. A portable trap in a farm field is a good way to get a youngster accustomed to shooting. No one sees his misses (be sure to make a fuss on the hits), and it's fun.

First hunting trips should be easy and feature a lot of action. A preserve is a good place to begin, if you have access to one and can swing the bird fees. A dove shoot might be a good alternative. Pheasants or quail hunting can follow. Save the hard hunting, like grouse or chukars, for later, when the youngster's interest is certain.

* * * *

Developing your own set of outdoor ethics is something that requires experience and a good guide. Sportsmen go through a series of stages: learning, putting the skills to use, proving those skills, and finally limiting themselves on how they hunt to give game more of an edge. For example, as a novice pheasant hunter, all I wanted to do was learn more about the birds, then go out and find more birds. As time went on, being able to put birds in the game bag mattered more, and on days when I could shoot a brace of pheasants, I considered myself quite the hunter. Later, this became less important, I sought out higher challenges such as hunting old roosters using a dog. During this process, I had many mentors and guides to show me the way.

Finding the upper levels of sportsmanship is an attainment some hunters never reach, probably because they don't strive to get there. Poor sportsmanship, however, is also the fault of those who continue to allow it—all of us who hunt—because we say nothing about gunners who park in farm lanes, shoot randomly, have poor gun handling skills, wound birds without following up on them, take risky shots, and do other things that are blatantly illegal in the name of shooting game.

On a dove shoot with Steve Snyder, from Harrisburg, Pennsylvania, and his Golden retriever, Peaches, we saw shooters breaking laws pertaining to how close to the road and houses they shot. They were winging birds without following up on them, and they didn't have permission to hunt the land, something Steve had worked hard to obtain. Being less afraid of armed confrontation than I, Steve accosted the shooters and they left, something that saved his hunting spot as well. Perhaps more of us should have more courage, myself included, about confronting less than ethical behavior.

The best gift you can offer other shooters, especially youngsters, is a good example.

* * * *

Part of this consideration of those who hunt has to center on the how we manage the resources we have. In order to continue to have upland bird hunting in North America, we need to conserve our current resources and leave something behind for the future. We've touched on a number of different issues in the chapters dedicated to individual birds. However, there are a couple of issues that are important on a larger scale that should be addressed here.

The single biggest issue facing *all* upland bird species today is habitat loss—particularly in the East. Part of the problem is people. There are 275 million people in the United States today. By 2100, there will be 571 million. Population growth, and the subsequent development of land, as well as changing land use, such as clean farming practices, threatens to pave over or poison what's left of the East's pheasant and quail fields, as well as reduce cover and birds elsewhere on the continent.

According to the United State Department of Agriculture, the development of rural land has doubled since the 1980s. Between 1982 and 1992, 1.4 million acres per year were developed. The rate between 1992 and 1997 was 3.2 million per year. Texas and Pennsylvania, two large hunting states, and Georgia lead the nation in development.

The South is a particular problem. Without the spotted owl to contend with, timber companies are harvesting up to 10,000 acres a year for a single chip mill used to produce pulpwood. Meanwhile, Atlanta is becoming one of fastest-spreading metropolitan areas in the United States. Its growth corridor has expanded from 65 miles around the city to 110 miles in a decade. Since 1973, Atlanta has lost 25 percent of its tree cover (350,000 acres).

The increasing human population and changing land use isolate bobwhite coveys into pockets of suitable cover, where the birds are more prone to predation and the effects of bad weather. This, together with a threefold increase in the use of cover-wilting herbicides since the 1960s, and the widespread replacement of native forbs with grasses and introduced plants gives birds a one-two-three whammy.

A curious corollary is how gray partridge numbers in Europe and Asia declined 90 percent since 1945. A British researcher, Nicolas Sotherton, trying to discover why, found that herbicide use could be a culprit. When just six percent of agricultural fields were not sprayed, Huns were able to raise enough broods to offset the normal mortality of 30 percent.

Overgrazing in the West is reducing once-rich coverts to barrenness. Although CRP land set-asides have been a benefit to many areas of the Midwest, they are far too often seeded with exotic grasses that are not good bird food. Lack of knowledge about what benefits wildlife best is often the problem, not the willingness of landowners to work with wildlife.

Another people issue that is also especially prevalent in the East is too much hunting pressure. Wildlife science has for years espoused the idea that hunting didn't have any appreciable influence on wild bird populations, that it was impossible to over-hunt game. Late season hunting may disprove that idea.

Noted grouse researcher Gordon Gullion and George Bird Evans both contended that grouse numbers can be damaged by long extensions to the hunting season. Taking birds moving into breeding habitat during the winter, especially after early January, under some circumstances, reduces grouse numbers in that area.

The Pennsylvania Game Commission recently ran a computer-generated population growth model using evidence from a grouse flush survey on study counties that were closed and open to late season hunting. Counties closed to a 3-week extension of grouse season would have more birds than those open to the late season if the model is correct.

Evans noticed visible results of reduced populations in his West Virginia coverts. I also saw it first-hand in my South Mountains coverts. Isolated by virtue of geography and surrounded by several large human population centers, the South Mountains got hit hard by hunters, especially during the late season, when they were less willing to venture too far from home. Also, the influx of former pheasant hunters into the grouse woods put added pressure on the birds. The limited number of coverts and additional people competing for them was devastating. In the early 1980s, I was moving about three grouse an hour there. By the 1990s, that number fell to a bird an hour. I quit hunting this area in the early 1990s because I didn't want to do any more damage to the birds.

Getting wildlife agencies to hear the cries of frustrated bird hunters is also getting harder because there are fewer of us. Wildlife agencies seem to have shifted management priorities from what needs to be fixed to what their "customer base," which is largely a deer and turkey crowd, want. This makes sense from a satisfy-the-customer point of view. But when an agency is charged by its charter with managing *all* the wildlife in the state, it fails to do so when pheasant populations drop from 1.2 million birds to about 50,000 more birds than the 200,000 birds the agency stocks. This was the case in Pennsylvania, and it's not uncommon elsewhere. Many young hunters were introduced to hunting through upland bird gunning. By eliminating these opportunities, we could be eliminating a lot of young hunters.

Wildlife agency and university interests in quail research and restoration have also shrunk in recent years. Only 12 states have quail research projects, and only 1.25 percent of the tax monies hunters voluntarily pay under the Pittman-Robertson Act, the Federal Aid to Wildlife Restoration effort, are being spent to study quail. Deer and turkey populations in the East are in great shape. Upland bird numbers are not.

Stewardship applied to the outdoors means taking care of our resources, preparing for the future with the actions of today. We, as bird hunters, need to become better advocates for upland game. We need to speak out. Joining an organization helps. More than that, take time to write your newspaper or legislator about things that might influence upland bird hunting in your area. Three national groups that are highly recommended are:

The Ruffed Grouse Society, 451 McCormick Road, Coraopolis, PA 15108; Telephone (412) 262–4044; Fax (412) 262–9207; Website: www.ruffedgrousesociety.com.

Quail Unlimited, P. O. Box 610, Edgefield, SC 29824–0610; Telephone (803) 637–5731; Fax (803) 637–0037; Website: www.qu.org.

Pheasants Forever, 1783 Buerkle Circle, St. Paul, MN 55110; Telephone (651) 773–2000; Fax (651) 773–5500; Website: www.pheasantsforever.

THE FUTURE

The future of upland bird hunting is a long way from cloudy. The bright spots include pheasants, prairie birds, and some quail areas in the Midwest coming back strong. Ruffed grouse hunting in the lake states remains excellent. Dove opportunities keep growing in the East.

The bird hunters who remain in the field are dedicated, not drawn by easy pickings, as was the case in the past. There seems to be a renaissance of interest in the old sporting traditions in bird hunting, hunting in classic ways with classic dogs, and this is a good thing, because it is the roots of the sport, the carrying on of traditions. It should be preserved.

Going into the twenty-first century, I see the privatization of hunting, the development of more pay-to-hunt areas, managed for dense populations of wild game. In Texas, for example, the state wildlife agency offers residents a $40 permit which grants hunters access to private lands enrolled in a state program to permit hunting, as well as the opportunity to get on public lands.

There are some positive signs for the future. In Montana, the state started a modest program called Block Management in 1985, which has grown to provide free public hunting access to over eight million acres of private lands throughout the state. Funds to enroll landowners in the program are generated through out-of-state bird hunting and big game license sales. Kansas started a similar program in 1995, Walk-In Hunter Access, that currently provides access to over one million acres of private land. As access to private hunting lands diminishes due to the proliferation of leased hunting rights, farm consolidation, and habitat loss, many states will likely continue to try to secure access for the hunting public that was once taken for granted.

In the East, things will probably go the European way, with clubs buying up large tracts of land and permitting only members access to the hunting there. This could be a problem for the hunter who has little spending money but a good heart and a willingness to work hard for his game.

I hope the interest in developing dogs for the foot hunter as opposed to impressing field trial judges continues. There is room for both, just as skeet, trap, and now sporting clays shooters shoot with different guns than they do in the field. The pendulum swung too far a few decades ago, doing the dogs a great disservice. Creating dogs that are dual dogs, sharing the best attributes of hunting blood and the best attributes of show looks and temperament is where it's at.

The tools of the twenty-first century are making a hunter's life a lot easier. Computers and the Internet can now offer immediate access to information once available only from a local contact. Tools like Global Positioning System (GPS) keep grouse hunters from getting turned around in the woods. And advances in shotguns, such as screw-in choke tubes, are expanding the range and versatility of firearms.

Still, upland gunners need to be vigilant. Our sport could vanish, should we not be careful with how we use land, how we hunt, how we represent ourselves in the field.

14

COMPLETING THE CYCLE

Completing the cycle is how a friend described what happened when his dog hunted, pointed a bird, and he shot it. The bird was the reward for his dog's completion of the hunt, find, point, shoot, fetch circle.

The cycle doesn't end there, however. The cycle is complete when the bird is properly handled between field and table, all utilizable parts of it put to some good use. For example, woodcock wing coverlets make the best nymph legs possible. They have excellent action under water and are one of the few things that naturally imitate the mottled brown color of most nymphs. I also use feathers from other birds for other flies, to decorate things, and in my Native American spirituality. Gunners have an obligation to make the most of every bird, a gift of the Creator.

FIELD CARE

Heat and bacteria can quickly ruin upland game for the table. Bacteria begin breaking down tissue in game birds immediately after death. And in some cases, this actually aids flavor and tenderizes the meat. The English, for example, hung their pheasants for up to a week to age the meat and create a better flavor. The main problem is that when heat creates the conditions for the rapid growth of bacteria and the breakdown of tissues, usually at temperatures of 65 degrees or above, decay sets in and this can sour the bird for the table.

Warm weather hunting situations—doves, any southern or western birds, early season grouse—require speedy handling so the bird can cool quickly and to preserve the flavor. Field dress birds and get them into a cooler as soon as possible whenever there is a question of spoilage.

In addition, birds that eat things that may lend a strong flavor to the meat should be handled differently. Sage and spruce grouse are the best two examples. Most gunners field dress these birds, removing the entrails immediately.

In cooler weather there is usually nothing wrong with keeping birds in your shooting vest's game pouch until you return to the car, then transferring them to a cooler or just keeping them cool in the vehicle.

At home, preparation for the table includes plucking or skinning birds, then proper storage until they are ready to be used in a meal. I usually skin my birds because I prefer this under most circumstances. The exceptions are woodcock and doves, which I pluck like waterfowl. This is time-consuming, but worth every effort. After the bird is feather free, rinse it well—especially the body cavity—making sure it is clean. Keeping birds cool but unfrozen in a freezer bag in the refrigerator can, like hanging game, help in aging the meat, but I usually put them directly in the freezer.

COOKING WILD GAME

A large part of the joy of upland bird hunting is enjoying the fantastic eating that results from well-cared-for birds. Game is truly the food of kings, if it is handled well and prepared gently—even better if you make an event of it, sharing a meal with friends and family. I'm remembering a George Bird Evans description of how his setters' pink tongues flashed while licking the juices of a roast grouse from heirloom silver with Mahler symphonies playing in the background. What a life! And if my grandmothers had witnessed Nash or Jack schlepping grouse drippings off their good silver, they would haunt me the rest of my days!

Three basic books that have proven invaluable for me in cooking game include:

Dressing and Cooking Wild Game, by Teresa Marrone, from the Hunting and Fishing Library, 1987, Cy DeCosse Incorporated. This book features field handling tips and recipes from Annette and Louis Bignami, Joan Cone, Bill Joe Cross, George and Kathryn Halazon, Teresa Marone, and Jim Schnieder, with special recipes from William Gregoire and Bill Stevens. Filled with photos of what your meal can look like, it is best used as a primer for novice cooks who aren't sure exactly where to begin. "The Basque Pheasant," "Pheasant with Apples," and "Baked Pheasant in Madeira" recipes are excellent.

Fish and Fowl Cookery: The Outdoorsman's Home Companion by Carol Vance Wary with William Wary, the Countryman Press, 1987, is another excellent source of recipes.

The L. L. Bean Game & Fish Cookbook, by Angus Cameron and Judith Jones, Random House, 1983, has a ton of good recipes for all kinds of gamebirds, as well as information on field care, hanging birds, and other Epicurean delights.

RECIPES

Taylor's Standard Gamebird Roast

This is a simple, free form (meaning you add things to taste, a pinch of this, a touch of that), yet enjoyable way to prepare any light meat gamebird, especially ruffed grouse and pheasants.

Two grouse or one pheasant
Small roasting pan
Several apples, carrots, mild celery, and cabbage (red, green, or Chinese)
Spices, honey or brown sugar, soy sauce, red wine vinegar
Bacon strips and/or orange peels (shredded and whole)

Start with a small roasting pan with a lid, and a pheasant or a couple of grouse for two people, more birds if company is coming. Chunk apples, carrots, onions, and mild celery into quarter-sized pieces, shred cabbage and mix together in a bowl, then use this to stuff the bird's body cavity and create a thin layer on the bottom of the roaster. Place the stuffed bird into the roaster, and use the remainder of the stuffing mixture to fill in the open space left in the roaster, covering all but the bird's legs and breast, if possible.

Add spices: Sprinkle soy sauce, red wine vinegar, brown sugar or honey to taste over the legs and breasts, then sprinkle sage, lemon pepper, a dash of red pepper, garlic powder, and a dash of grated orange peels over the breasts. Cover the breasts and legs with bacon strips (wrap the legs) and/or orange peels (breasts only) to maintain moisture. Roast long and slowly, about 325 degrees for an hour or so.

All Natural Michigan Flavor

As Bill Goudy and Denny Burkhart demonstrated when we hunted woodcock in Michigan, grilling birds in the great wide open over charcoal is a great way to enjoy game while camping, or for lunch. Better yet, it's simple: All you need are the birds, a grill, some briquettes, a safe place to make them, and that "all natural Michigan flavoring" that comes from any wild place.

In this case, it's usually better to leave the skins on the birds, something easy with woodcock, harder with birds like pheasants. For a variation, try quail over mesquite briquettes, or sharptails broiled over hardwood coals. Sharptails have "nut-dark" breast muscles, which are well fed by blood vessels, one reason they can fly so well and their meat is rich and dark compared to a pheasant.

Roger Marlow's Valley Quail Bake

Roger Marlow's recipe for valley quail set my mouth watering. Marlow and his hunting partner hunt valley quail near an abandoned apple orchard and fill a daypack with golden and red delicious apples, small from their reversion to wild fruit, but sweet and crisp. They bake quail with these apples, adding raisins and brown sugar. They serve this with brown rice, fresh asparagus, and a glass of Napa Valley white wine. Yowsa! Haven't tried it yet, but this would work great with grouse or pheasants, too.

Pheasant Salad

A favorite pheasant treat was a pheasant salad, made like chicken salad, only add mandarin oranges, pineapple chunks, marshmallows, walnuts, and raisins. Creative cooks can apply their own special additions to this and come up with a lot of variations.

Dove Breast Italiano

The Arkansas Fish and Game Commission web page holds this gem. Place dove breasts in a zip-seal plastic bag, cover with Italian salad dressing and marinate for 3 to 4 hours. Remove the breasts from the bag, slit the breasts along the bone with a sharp knife, and insert one or two slices of Jalapeno pepper in each slit. Season the breasts with garlic salt and black pepper, then wrap each in a half-slide of bacon and secure the bacon with a toothpick. Grill over indirect heat for about an hour.

15

WHERE TO GO

Searching for new bird coverts often seems like the quest for the Holy Grail. Only good knights, strong and true of heart, find the Grail, or at least the path to it. However, thanks to both old-fashioned research tools, like personal contacts and the telephone, and modern tools like the Internet, finding new hunting territory is not an insurmountable task.

Start with the basics. Here, the Internet is invaluable. You can do almost everything on the Internet, from purchasing a nonresident license to locating public hunting areas and learning about new regulations. Gathering vast amounts of information from the basic state wildlife agency website is also possible. Some websites are better than others. The Missouri Department of Conservation's website, for example, shows harvest information past and present, where bird densities are highest, contacts for both regions and across the state, and other important information.

The best place to begin is the Fish and Wildlife Service's website: http://offices.fws.gov/statelinks.html. This lists the individual websites for all 50 states as well as U.S. territories. Simply click on the state and you're on your way.

Lacking a computer, you'll have to go about it the old-fashioned way, requesting information via mail. One of the best comprehensive resources for information on federal, state, and local wildlife and environmental agencies, as well as a number of group listings, is the National Wildlife Federation's annual Conservation Directory. Contact the National Wildlife Federation, 1400 Sixteenth Street, NW, Washington, D.C. 20036–2266; phone: 800–432–6564.

State conservation department or fish and game officials are the next step down the trail. If this information is not already available on the website, state wildlife management agencies have a good handle on where bird numbers are highest within a given area, where production is poor, perhaps due to bad spring weather. Most are more than happy to help connect hunters with game.

Also, in the West, federal lands are often the bulk of the public land available. Get the National Forest Service or Bureau of Land Management maps from the federal government.

The next level of state or local government is another good contact source. For example, in Pennsylvania, an agency separate from the Pennsylvania Game Commission, the Department of Conservation and Natural Resources, via the Bureau of State Parks and the Bureau of Forestry, operate 2.4 million acres of state forest lands and 115 state parks open to hunting in most areas. Forestry officials, especially land managers who are familiar with timbering operations, have been exceptionally helpful finding new places to hunt.

Private landowners, such as timber or pulp companies, can also be a good source of information. Much of the best hunting areas in Maine, for example, are privately owned timber companies who allow hunting and are happy to direct hunters to their holdings, sometimes for an access fee. They will even provide maps to these areas in many cases.

Check the bookshelf for guides to individual states as well. Wilderness Adventures Press, 45 Buckskin Road, Belgrade, MT 59714, 800–925–3339, for example, offers a number of state-oriented guides for sale. The information there is very good.

Hunter organizations such as Quail Unlimited, Pheasants Forever, The Ruffed Grouse Society, the Western Gamebird Alliance, based in Arizona, and others are a good resource. Most can be found on the Internet. Also, get involved and ask some questions from local chapter members, regional representatives, or contact the national offices for help. Quail Unlimited, for example, puts out a quail hunting forecast each fall.

This should be enough to get you started. Below is a list of United States state wildlife agencies, with some information on bird harvest numbers as well as websites to get you access to Canadian provincial wildlife agencies.

WILDLIFE MANAGEMENT AGENCIES

Alabama Game and Fish Division, Department of Conservation and Natural Resources
64 N. Union Street
Montgomery, AL 36130–1456
Telephone (334) 242–3465
Bobwhite quail, doves, wild turkeys, and woodcock

Alaska Department of Fish and Game
Division of Wildlife Conservation
P.O. Box 25526
Juneau, AK 99802–5526
Telephone (907) 465–4190
Fax (907) 465–6142
Ptarmigan, blue grouse, ruffed grouse, spruce grouse, and harp-tailed grouse

Arizona Game and Fish Department
2221 West Greenway Road
Phoenix, AZ 85023–4399
Telephone (602) 942–3000
Gambel's quail, Mearns' quail, scaled quail, doves, blue grouse, chukar, pheasants, and wild turkeys

Arkansas Game and Fish Commission
#2 Natural Resources Drive
Little Rock, AR 72205
Telephone 800–364–GAME
Bobwhite quail, doves, wild turkeys, and woodcock

California Department of Fish and Game
1416 Ninth Street
Sacramento, CA 95814
Telephone (916) 653–7664
Pheasants, valley quail, mountain quail, Gambel's quail, doves, chukar, blue and ruffed grouse, sage grouse, and wild turkeys

Colorado Division of Wildlife
Department of Natural Resources
6060 Broadway
Denver, Colorado, 80216
Telephone (303) 297–1192
Sage grouse, wild turkey, blue grouse, ruffed grouse, chukar, snipe, sharp-tailed grouse, doves, pheasants, white-tailed ptarmigan, bobwhite quail, Gambel's quail, and scaled quail. Colorado re-opened a limited season for greater prairie chicken in 2000, the first since 1937.

Connecticut Wildlife Division
Main Office
79 Elm Street
Hartford, CT 06106–5127
Telephone: (860) 424–3011
Ruffed grouse, woodcock, wild turkeys, and pheasants

Delaware Division of Fish and Wildlife
Department of Natural Resources
89 Kings Highway
Dover, DE 19901
Telephone (302) 739–4506: Information and Education section
"Opportunities for upland bird hunting very poor in Delaware at this time," said H. Lloyd Alexander, Section Administrator. "Quail numbers in 1997 declined by 90 percent compared to 1987, less than 5,000 birds were harvested each season for the past three seasons. The outlook for pheasants even more dismal." Alexander said less than 1,000 pheasants were taken in the last 3 years, many of them escaped game farm birds. Deer or waterfowl hunting in Delaware is good, not upland birds. Doves and woodcock are present in huntable numbers.

Florida Fish and Wildlife Conservation Commission
620 South Meridian Street
Tallahassee, FL 32399–1600
Telephone (850) 488–3831
"Small game hunting is reasonably good, with the exception of quail," said Tommy Hines, of the Small Game Management Section. Dramatic declines have occurred in Florida quail populations. This is due to "the tremendous changes in land use that have occurred over the last 30 years," Hines said. "The only good quail hunting on private lands is on plantations where there are intensive management programs. . . . We are presently trying to develop a program to address the low quail numbers. However, even if we are able to achieve some success on both public and private lands it will still have a limited impact. Land use changes are so dramatic and driven by such strong economic forces that widespread changes are virtually impossible to achieve. As a result, it appears that quail hunting, in particular, will be a relatively expensive endeavor in Florida in the future."

In 1982, for example, 215,000 Florida gunners took 28,000 turkeys, 38,000 quail, 123,000 doves, and 2,000 woodcock. In 1997, 134,000 hunters took 39,000 quail, 55,000 doves, 401 woodcock, and 21,000 turkeys. Quail hunters in 1945 took 45,000 birds and in 1950, 67,000 birds . . . a sign of the times.

Georgia Wildlife Resources Division
Department of Natural Resources
2070 U. S. Highway 278, SE
Social Circle, GA 30279
Telephone (770) 918–6416: headquarters and hunting information
Bobwhite quail, doves, wild turkeys, and woodcock

Hawaii Department of Land and Natural Resources
Division of Forestry and Wildlife
1151 Punchbowl Street, Room 325
Honolulu, HI 96813
Telephone (808) 587–0166
Pheasants, chukars, francolin, valley quail, Gambel's quail, Japanese quail, doves, sandgrouse, and wild turkeys

Idaho Department of Fish and Game
600 S. Walnut
P.O. Box 25
Boise, ID 83707
Telephone (208) 334–3700
Fax (208) 334–2114 or (208) 334–2148
"Huns and turkeys are really up right now," said an official department response. Chukars are very strong, and hunters can be "overrun by quail" in some areas. (Perish the thought!) Pheasants are much lower than 20 years ago but doing better. Sage grouse are up from last year, but still in danger of being listed under the Endangered Species Act because of population declines. In 1996, hunters bagged 166,500 pheasants, 132,000 doves, 188,000 forest (ruffed and blue) grouse, 35,000 Huns, 82,000 chukars, 115,000 quail, 34,000 sage grouse, 14,000 sharptails, and 2,600 turkeys. Also check with the Idaho Bird Hunters, Inc., P.O. Box 6412, Boise, Idaho 83707, for more information.

Illinois Department of Natural Resources
Office of Resource Conservation
600 N. Grand Avenue W
Springfield, IL 62701
Telephone (217) 782–6384
Pheasants, bobwhite quail, doves, wild turkeys, Hungarian partridge, and woodcock

Indiana Division of Fish and Wildlife
Department of Natural Resources
402 W. Washington Street, Room W273
Indianapolis, IN 46204
Telephone (317) 232–4080
Fax (317) 232–4020
Pheasants, bobwhite quail, doves, wild turkeys, ruffed grouse, and woodcock

Iowa Department of Natural Resources
Henry A. Wallace Building
900 East Grand
Des Moines, IA 50319–0034
Telephone (515) 281–4687 or (515) 281-HNTR: special hunting line
Fax (515) 281–6794
According to Todd Bogenschutz, Upland Wildlife Research Biologist, on the 20-year outlook, Hun and turkey numbers are better; pheasants and ruffed grouse are down a bit; woodcock numbers are down; and quail are considerably lower. In 1998, 184,000 hunters took 1.2 million pheasants; 13,500 hunters took 25,000 Huns; 32,000 hunters took 100,000 quail; 38,000 hunters bagged 16,000 turkeys; 2,000 hunters shot 3,000 grouse; and 2,000 hunters took 1,500 woodcock. Dove season is currently closed.

Kansas Department of Wildlife and Parks
Office of the Secretary
900 SW Jackson Street, Suite 502
Topeka, KS 66612–1233
Telephone (785) 296–2281

Pratt Operations Office
512 SE 25th Avenue
Pratt, KS 67124–8174
Telephone (316) 672–5911

Randy Rodgers, small game biologist for Kansas, summarizes Kansas' bird hunting this way:

Pheasants—Down 50–60 percent in the western third of state; stable in central third; increasing slightly in eastern Kansas; the northwest has the most pheasants and the southeast, none. Kansas consistently ranks among the top four pheasant states (South Dakota, Iowa, Kansas, Nebraska). In 1998, 125,000 hunters took 680,000 birds.

Quail—Bobs are declining east of the Flint Hills, and increasing in the north-central and the western third of state due to CRP grasslands. Quail numbers have declined significantly, but are still in top three (Kansas, Oklahoma, Texas) with 115,000 hunters bagging 1.4 million birds. Scaled quail are also found in Kansas, but only in isolated hotspots in the southwest.

Greater prairie chicken—Rare east of Flint Hills, chickens have also declined significantly in their Flint Hills stronghold in 1990s. North-central Kansas chicken numbers are stable, and the birds are increasing in western Kansas due to CRP. Overall, chicken are declining moderately (Nebraska, Kansas still tops). About 11,000 hunters took 13,000 birds.

Lesser prairie chicken—Down slightly over the last 20 years, CRP in western Kansas is helping a lot. However, Kansas has a one bird per day limit, and FWS petitioned to put lesser on "Threatened" species list in 1995, stating that the listing is warranted, but precluded by higher priorities. Kansas is one of five states working to increase lesser chickens, but the decline was greatest in Kansas. About 300 hunters took 200 birds.

Ruffed grouse/sharptails—Ruffed grouse were reintroduced to eastern Kansas in the 1980s. This is a low-density population, and is not hunted. Its future is also questionable, due to increasing urbanization in northeastern Kansas. Sharptails, reintroduced in the late 1980s and early 1990s, are maintaining their populations. They are also not hunted.

Doves—Although one of the top dove producers, Kansas is too far north to be a player in large dove take numbers. Still, 73,000 hunters took 1.4 million doves.

Hunters should also check the department's website by mid-September for bird forecasts. Looking to the future, Rodgers said human habitation is hard on birds, especially in eastern Kansas. With help from federal farm bills, pheasants, bobs, and chickens still look fairly bright. "A return to the good old days isn't in the offing. We are working hard to instill in landowners a conservation ethic that, we hope, will leave room for healthy upland gamebird populations far into the future."

Kentucky Department of Fish and Wildlife Resources
#1 Game Farm Road
Frankfort, KY 40601
Telephone (800) 858–1549
Bobwhite quail, doves, wild turkeys, and ruffed grouse

Louisiana Department of Wildlife and Fisheries
Wildlife Division
P.O. Box 98000
2000 Quail Drive, Rm 223
Baton Rouge, LA 70898–9000
Telephone (225) 765–2850
Fax (225) 763–3510
Fred Kimmel, Biologist Program Manager, said generally there are fewer opportunities for hunting quail, woodcock, and doves than 20 years ago. With woodcock and quail, there are fewer birds. Restricted access to land has further reduced the opportunities for upland bird hunting. Twenty years ago there were still large areas of the state that were unposted. However, with the advent of leasing land for deer hunting, access to private land is much more difficult. With doves, the state still has good numbers; getting a place to hunt is harder, though.

Harvest figures show these trends: In 1978, 452,000 quail were taken by 41,000 hunters. In 1988, 19,000 hunters took 203,000 birds. In 1993, 7,000 hunters took 43,000 quail. And in 1999, 4,100 hunters shot 34,000 quail. Woodcock numbers are similar: In 1988, 39,000 hunters took 299,000 birds. In 1999, 5,700 hunters took 21,000 birds. For doves, in 1988, 95,000 hunters took 2.2 million birds. In 1999, 61,000 hunters took one million birds. For turkeys, about 20,000 hunters took 10,000 birds annually.

Still, Louisiana has one million acres of state wildlife management areas, and 400,000 acres of national forest. Kimmel sees the future of upland bird hunting in Louisiana as being mixed, depending on the species: Quail in the Pineland regions should maintain stable, albeit low populations. There is potential for improvement in agricultural areas if conservation practices such as buffer strips and field borders become accepted practices, Kimmel said, but he didn't anticipate much change in the status quo. He was more optimistic about habitat improvement conditions for woodcock: The Wetland Reserve Program resulted in the reforestation of 120,000 acres, most on the Mississippi River floodplain, which resulted in habitat restoration in an important wintering area. Turkeys were in most of the suitable habitat available right now.

Maine Department of Inland Fisheries and Wildlife
284 State Street
41 State House Station
Augusta, ME 04333–0041
Telephone (207) 287–8000: general information; (207) 287–8003: automated line
"Hunting opportunities have changed little in Maine over the past 20 years (with a few notable exceptions), although the posting of private land has become a concern, particularly in the southern portions of the state," said Andrew Weik, wildlife biologist. "The future of upland bird hunting is bright, although residential development and urban sprawl will continue to reduce the quantity and quality of huntable lands in the more populated areas of the state. Because Maine has relatively little public land, most hunting opportunity is on private land, and so it is very important that hunters seek landowner permission before entering private land."

Weik said grouse numbers are basically unchanged since 1980: 100,000 hunters take 400,000 to 500,000 birds annually. More than 8,300 hunters bagged 23,000 woodcock in 1998, with numbers down in southern and south-coastal Maine. Maturing forest and reduced habitat due to human population growth are problems there. Singing ground surveys are down 2.1 percent per year 1980–1999. Spring turkey hunting is growing. The birds were reintroduced in 1978. The first gobbler hunt took place in 1986, when 500 permits yielded 9 birds. And in 1999, 3,000 permits brought 890 birds.

Maryland Department of Natural Resources
Tawes State Office Building, E-1
580 Taylor Avenue
Annapolis, MD 21401
Telephone (410) 260–8540
Fax (410) 260–8595
TTY (410) 260–8835
Bobwhite quail, doves, wild turkeys, and ruffed grouse
Tom Matthews, of the MDNR's Game Management section, said pheasant and quail numbers have been down for the last 15 years. Quail hunting in Allegheny and Garrett counties was recently closed. However, some decent—but localized—quail hunting remains on the Eastern Shore. There is also some marginal quail hunting in the western counties. As elsewhere, habitat is the primary problem. For the future, DNR is hoping CREP will help some with creating habitat.

Massachusetts Department of Fisheries, Wildlife and Environmental Law Enforcement
100 Cambridge Street, Room 1901
Boston, MA 02202
Telephone (617) 727–1614

Division of Fisheries & Wildlife
Field Headquarters, 1 Rabbit Hill Road

Westborough, MA 01581
Telephone (508) 792–7270
Fax (508) 792–7275
Ruffed grouse, woodcock, wild turkeys, pheasants, and quail

Michigan Department of Resources
Stevens T. Mason Building
530 West Allegan Street
P. O. Box 30028
Lansing, MI 48909
Telephone (517) 373–1214
Fax (517) 353–1547
Michigan pheasant, ruffed grouse, and woodcock populations were stabilizing from 1992 through 1996, according to MDR. Nearly 132,000 hunters took 175,000 pheasants and 374,000 grouse. About 75,000 woodcock hunters took 229,000 birds. Bobwhite quail are present in huntable numbers in isolated areas of southern Michigan.

Minnesota Department of Natural Resources
Division of Fish and Wildlife
DNR Information Center
500 Lafayette Road
St. Paul, MN 55155–4040
Telephone (651) 296–6157 or 888-MINNDNR
TTY: 651–296–5484 or 800–657–3929
Fax (651) 297–7272
Minnesota gunners took 400,000 pheasants in 1998, with numbers down 36 percent in the east, and up 51 percent in the west. DNR biologists saw 21 Huns per 100 miles of survey route, a good number, comparable to 1991, a good year. Minnesota is the "house of grouse" with 650,000 birds taken by 140,000 hunters annually. Sharptail numbers were up 15 percent in the northwest and up 19 percent in the east-central regions. For more farmland wildlife research information, contact Minnesota Department of Natural Resources, Farmland Wildlife Populations and Research, Route 1, Box 181, Madelia, MN 56062–9744. Minnesota also has a thriving wild turkey population and strong woodcock numbers.

Mississippi Department of Wildlife, Fisheries, and Parks
P. O. Box 451
Jackson, MS 39205
Telephone (800) 354–5033
Bobwhite quail, doves, wild turkeys, and woodcock

Missouri Department of Conservation
Administrative Office
P.O. Box 180

2901 W. Truman Boulevard
Jefferson City, MO 65109
Telephone (573) 751–4115
Fax (573) 751–4467

Missouri quail numbers are way down in the last several years, with 1998 the lowest since 1967. The 30-year average harvest is two million birds annually; however, gunners took 677,000 quail in 1998. Also, about 19,000 hunters took 58,000 pheasants in 1998. Doves, wild turkey, ruffed grouse, and woodcock are also available.

Vicki Heidy, wildlife staff biologist, says one of the bright spots in Missouri's upland bird hunting is a new Department of Conservation division that will work with landowners who are interested in managing their land for wildlife. With more than 95 percent of the state in private land ownership, MDC is hoping this new group can have a positive impact on habitat improvement. Also, a Conservation Atlas lists all public areas and activities available on each. Check their website, it is one of the best in the nation.

Montana Department of Fish, Wildlife, and Parks
1420 East Sixth Avenue
Helena, MT 59620
Telephone (406) 444–2950

Pheasants, Huns, sharp-tailed grouse, sage grouse, blue, spruce and ruffed grouse, Merriam's turkey, doves, and a small population of chukars in the Pryor Mountains of southeastern Montana

Nebraska Game and Parks Commission
2200 North 33rd Street
Lincoln, NE 68503
Telephone (402) 471–0641

Scott Taylor, Upland Game Program manager, said that in a 20-year history of Nebraska bird numbers, pheasants have declined, bobs are stable to slightly declining, chickens are slightly up, sharptails are stable, Huns are declining, doves are stable, woodcock are up, and turkeys are up. In the short-term future of hunting, things will stay largely the same. Longer term trends are linked to global agriculture and economics and how they influence farming, which influences habitat. Taylor guessed that agricultural production would continue to intensify, and ". . . hence the habitat supporting farmland game species will become even more scarce. I hope I'm wrong."

About 77,000 resident hunters took 519,000 pheasants in 1998. Quail harvests were 251,000 for 36,900 resident hunters. About 9,500 residents took 44,000 chickens and sharptails in 1998. Hunters—26,000 residents—took 492,000 doves. And 470 resident hunters took 744 Huns. Also, 8,900 turkeys were tagged by 26,000 hunters (non-residents and residents).

Nevada Division of Wildlife
Department of Conservation and Natural Resources

Reno Headquarters
1100 Valley Road
P.O. Box 10678
Reno, Nevada 89520
Telephone (775) 688–1500
Fax (775) 688–1595

From an upland game status report, compiled by Norm Saake and San Stiver in 1999, comes this summary of state upland game harvests:

Sage grouse—Summaries show downward trends. Almost 28,000 birds in 1979 to 5,700 in 1998, with 3,200 hunters. (The average take is about 10,000–15,000 birds.)

Blue grouse—Only occasionally does NDW evaluate forest grouse numbers. There were 1,550 bagged in 1998, compared to a 1981 high of 2,900. The average harvest is 1,200, with 1,100 hunters.

Chukars—Appear to be holding their own in the 1990s; however, below the birds' historic high levels of the 1960s and 1970s. Hunters took 62,000 birds in 1998, compared to 218,000 in 1980. The average is 65,000, with nearly 11,000 hunters.

Huns—Hunters bagged 2,800 in 1998, compared to 9,600 in 1974. There are about 750 hunters in recent years.

Quail—California, mountain, and Gambel's are up. Hunters bagged 62,000 birds in 1998, compared to a 171,000 high in 1979, and a 55,000 average. There were 6,800 hunters in 1998.

Pheasants—Harvests depend on farmland. "Poorest in past 50 years," with 1,000 in 1998, 22,000 in 1966, average take of 1,200 birds, with 1000 hunters.

Doves—About 53,000 doves were taken in 1998, compared to 170,000 in 1969, and an average of 60,000 birds, with 4,800 hunters.

New Hampshire Fish and Game Department
Public Affairs Division
2 Hazen Drive
Concord, NH 03301
Telephone (603) 271–3211

Karen Bordeau, wildlife biologist, said 12,000 pheasants were stocked in 83 sites, with 6,200 pheasant licenses sold. The state is also involved in a habitat program for early successional forest on private and public land for grouse and woodcock. Turkey hunting opportunities will also increase with the establishment of statewide habitat projects.

New Jersey Division of Fish and Wildlife
P.O. Box 400
Walk-in at 501 E. State Street, 3rd Floor
Trenton, NJ 08625–0400
Telephone (609) 292–2965: information; (609) 292–6685: wildlife management
Bobwhite quail, pheasants, wild turkeys, ruffed grouse, and woodcock

New Mexico Department of Game and Fish
P. O. Box 25112
Santa Fe, NM 87504
Telephone (505) 827–7911
Fax (505) 827–7915
Gambel's, scaled, bobwhite, and Mearns' quail, pheasants, blue grouse, doves, and wild turkeys

New York Department of Environmental Conservation
Division Headquarters Offices of Fish, Wildlife and Marine Resources
50 Wolf Road
Albany, NY 12233–4750
Bureau of Wildlife
Telephone (518) 457–4480
Fax (518) 457–0691
Bureau of Habitat
Phone (518) 457–6178
Fax (518) 485–8424

Robert M. Sanford, wild turkey specialist, noted changes in the populations of both woodcock and turkeys as examples of changes in New York hunting. In 1979, 35,000 turkey permits were sold, with 3,000 birds taken. In 1999, 251,000 permits were sold, and 17,000 birds were taken. In 1984, 28,000 woodcock permits were sold, and 81,000 birds were taken. A decade later, 10,000 permits were sold, and only 25,000 birds were taken. Sanford said good habitat growing out of the proper age and old field habitat being consumed by development was the source of the woodcock decline.

Michael J. Murphy, wildlife biologist, looked at pheasants as an example of decline. In 1968, 272,000 hunters bagged 521,000 birds. In 1998, 38,000 hunters took 90,000 birds, many game farm birds released for put and take hunting.

Grouse show a similar story: In 1982, 172,000 hunters took 562,000 grouse. In 1998, 68,000 hunters bagged 171,000 birds. Again, the loss of habitat is the main reason for the declines. For grouse it is the loss of sapling/seedling timber.

Murphy said the future of New York's bird hunting is grim. "As the state becomes more woodland and more developed, wild pheasant populations will decline or disappear; quail will only be on Long Island and in few numbers, if at all. Grouse will decline without additional early succession stage timber, but should provide huntable numbers. Turkey are our best upland game."

North Carolina Wildlife Resources Commission
Division of Conservation Education
512 North Salisbury Street
Raleigh, NC 27604
Telephone (919) 733–3391
Bobwhite quail, doves, wild turkeys, ruffed grouse, and woodcock

North Dakota Game & Fish Department
100 N. Bismarck Expressway
Bismarck, ND 58501–5095
Telephone (701) 328–6300
Fax (701) 328–6352
Pheasants, sharp-tailed grouse, sage grouse, Huns, ruffed grouse, woodcock, and wild turkey. About 13,450 hunters are taking nearly 69,000 doves in North Dakota annually.

Ohio Division of Wildlife
1840 Belcher Drive
Columbus, OH 43224–1329
Telephone (614) 265–6300 (voice)
(800) 750–0750 (Ohio Relay & TTY only)
(800) WILDLIFE
Luke Millen of ODW, said Ohio's pheasant numbers dropped from over three million birds in the late 1970s and early 1980s to less than 250,000 birds today. CRP lands are helping to keep these bird numbers stabilized. Ohio hosts a population of about five million doves each fall, no harvest numbers. Hunters take more than 14,000 turkeys annually.

Ohio also measures quail numbers differently: in number of birds harvested per 100 hours of gunning, 3, up from 1993. They sent out surveys to 83 cooperators, who flushed 17 coveys per 100 gun hours (2½ weeks of work). This is the second lowest level since the late 1980s. Population estimates have fallen or stayed fairly flat since 1980, less than one quail per 1,000 miles driven (seen by rural mail carriers). Woodcock numbers are falling, less than one male per survey route stop. This has been declining since 1966. Grouse hunters had .8 flushes per hour on grouse in a cooperator's survey.

Oklahoma Department of Wildlife Conservation
Information and Education Division
1801 N. Lincoln
Oklahoma City, OK 73105
Telephone (405) 521–3856
Fax (405) 521–6535
Quail are the most popular gamebird in the former Indian Territories; 600,000 hunters bag 1 million quail annually in recent years, down from 2.2 million in 1990 and 3.3 million in 1992. Also, turkeys are now found in all 77 counties. Oklahoma is one of the few states with huntable populations of 3 subspecies of wild turkey: Eastern, Rio Grande, and a smaller number of Merrian's. Pheasants, doves, woodcock, and snipe are also present in huntable numbers.

Oregon Department of Fish and Wildlife
2501 SW First Avenue
Portland, OR 97207
Telephone (503) 872–5260: Wildlife Division

Blue grouse, ruffed grouse, sage grouse, chukars, Huns, pheasants, valley quail, mountain quail, wild turkeys, doves, snipe, and band-tailed pigeons

Pennsylvania Game Commission
2001 Elmerton Avenue
Harrisburg, PA 17110–9797
Telephone (717) 787–4250
Bruce Whitman, Chief of the Division of Information, said the loss of large continuous blocks of habitat is the main problem with Pennsylvania pheasants. While there is some natural reproduction, the current program is dependent upon the release of 200,000 PGC-raised birds on suitable public access areas such as game lands and private land enrolled in public access. About 158,000 hunters flushed 27.9 birds per 100 hunter hours.

"We still have a dedicated corps of woodcock hunters who spend as much time hunting places as they do actual birds. There is some action on some native birds, but for the most part it is driven by migrating birds and can be impacted by current and long-term weather." There are 13,000 hunters, 57.1 birds per 100 hunter hours.

"Personally, I think our grouse hunting is still pretty good, considering we live in a state with 12 million people," Whitman said. Success takes scouting time and effort. Bird numbers and flushes can be up in one area, below average in another location not all that far away. There are 183,000 grouse hunters, who move 18.5 birds per 100 hunter hours.

Turkey hunting is great in Pennsylvania. Spring 2000's season was forecast as the best ever. About 200,000 spring and 200,000 fall turkey hunters shoot 3.7 spring, 4.9 fall birds per 100 hunter hours.

Rhode Island Office of Fish & Wildlife
4808 Tower Hill Road
Wakefield, RI 02879
Telephone (401) 788–8168 or 789–3094
Fax (401) 783–4460
Ruffed grouse, woodcock; and Rhode Island is one of the few New England states that permits dove hunting.

Division of Wildlife and Freshwater Fisheries
South Carolina Department of Natural Resources
P.O. Box 167
Rembert C. Dennis Building
Columbia, SC 29202
Telephone (803) 734–3888
Bobwhite quail, doves, wild turkeys, ruffed grouse, and woodcock

South Dakota Department of Game, Fish, and Parks
523 East Capitol Avenue
Pierre, SD 57501–3182
Telephone (605) 773–6245 Foss Building

South Dakota's legendary pheasant hunting had 135,000 hunters bagging 1.1 million birds in 1998, with a total population of 4.4 million birds. Biologists observed 1.25 male prairie chickens, and 1.5 sharptails per square mile in recent surveys. Black Hills turkey hunters also have a 40 percent success rate. Huns, ruffed grouse, bobwhite quail, and doves are also available in huntable populations.

Tennessee Wildlife Resources Agency
Department of Environment and Conservation
Central Office
Ellington Agricultural Center
P.O. Box 40747
Nashville, TN 37204
Telephone (615) 781–6610
According to Mark Gudlin, small game program coordinator, the loss of habitat, the growth of the human population, and increases in lands leased to deer hunters, results in the loss of access to lands for quail hunting. However, don't overlook asking for permission to hunt on private lands. Yet access to lands with good quail habitat is not easy to find. About 90 percent of quail hunting still occurs on private lands. Between 1950 and 1990, Tennessee lost 6 million acres, a third of its farmland, a rate of 250 acres a day.

TWR, in the next 5 years, wants to increase bob numbers and convert 300 acres of fescue per county, per year to native grassland. In 6 years this would be 5 percent of the current fescue acreage. The agency would also like to convert 60,000 acres of crop/pastureland to wildlife-friendly buffers by 2006, and also increase the number of hunters (40,000 now) up to 46,000. In 1987, Tennessee gunners were shooting 1.3 million quail annually. Currently, there are 10 breeding birds counted per acre, the state would like to up this to 14 per acre by 2006. Harvests show this: In 1951, 125,000 hunters were shooting 1.5 million quail. In 1985, 81,000 hunters took 1.3 million quail. By 1998, 42,000 hunters were shooting 500,000 birds.

With other gamebirds, 53,000 turkey hunters in 1998 took 16,000 birds. Also, 142,000 dove shooters took 2 million birds. With grouse, 50 percent of grouse hunting occurs on public lands. There is a lot of public land in the eastern part of the state, where 12,000 hunters took 3,500 birds.

"The long-term outlook is not bright. We will have to make some significant habitat gains in the next decade to maintain any kind of quality quail hunting experiences for the general populace. All hope is not lost; there are efforts we are making strides in. Maintaining good grouse habitat on public lands will likely rely on our ability to keep small-scale clear cutting as a management tool on public lands. Already the percentage of young hardwood forest stages on the 652,000-acre Cherokee National Forest is declining. What happens in the chip mill industry in the future could impact (pro or con) grouse habitat on private lands. Mourning dove opportunities should be relatively stable."

Texas Parks and Wildlife Department
4200 Smith School Road
Austin, TX 78744
Telephone (800) 792–1112 or (512) 389–4800
Steve DeMaso, Upland Wildlife Program Coordinator, said turkey, quail, dove, and pheasant populations are stable. Lesser prairie chicken numbers are decreasing. Visiting hunters should pay careful attention to weather in spring and summer; it will play a big role in upland bird production. In 1999, 358,000 hunters took 4.5 million doves; 114,000 quail hunters took 600,000 bobs; 39,000 gunners bagged 170,000 scaled quail; 67,000 spring turkey hunters took 24,000 birds; and 23,000 pheasant hunters took 44,000 birds. Texas has bobwhite, Gambel's, and scaled quail and even a small huntable population of chachalaca (a small tropical gamebird).

Utah Division of Wildlife Resources
P. O. Box 146301
1594 W. North Temple
Salt Lake City, UT 84114–6301
Telephone (801) 538–4700
(Toll Free) Recorded Information (877) 592–5169
Fax (801) 538–4745
Dean Mitchell, DWR Upland Game Coordinator, notes that 13 species of upland birds are available, one of most diverse states in what people can hunt. About 54,000 bird hunters, 3 percent of Utah's population, hunted upland birds. (This was 6 percent in 1981.) Pheasants are the most popular species. The state closed columbian sharptail hunting in 1979, sage grouse hunting is also closed in some areas. Only four core areas permit sage grouse hunting. Sagebrush habitat is the key, if more is not available in next 10 to 15 years, hunting could be eliminated. Pheasants are also in trouble. CRP lands are usually found on dryland agriculture areas, not in the irrigated areas pheasants prefer. This link to habitat loss and degradation could be a problem. Doves, Huns, ptarmigan, continue into future as they are. Chukars, forest grouse, and turkey populations will probably increase.

In 1997, the following harvest figures applied: 208,000 doves were taken by 22,000 hunters; 23,000 chukars were bagged by 9,600 hunters; 37,000 hunters took 78,000 pheasants; 4,000 sage grouse were bagged by 4,000 hunters; 31,000 forest grouse (ruffed grouse and blue grouse) were taken by 10,000 hunters; 9,000 quail were taken by 3,600 hunters; 5,000 Huns were taken by 2,300 hunters; 339 spring turkey hunters took 81 Merriam's, and 229 hunters took 127 Rios; also 37 ptarmigan were taken by 18 hunters.

Vermont Department of Fish and Wildlife in the Agency for Natural Resources
103 South Main Street
Waterbury, VT 05671–0501
Telephone (802) 241–3700
Fax (802) 241–3295
John Hall, information specialist, said there were no harvest numbers, but

ruffed grouse and woodcock are in good shape, especially in the northeast quarter of the state.

Virginia Department of Game and Inland Fisheries
4010 West Broad Street
Richmond, VA 23230
Telephone (804) 367–1000
Turkeys, doves, and quail. Virginia's quail management plan, a joint effort by state legislators, the VDGIF, and concerned citizens, is looking to address quail numbers now and in the future. A number of programs have begun across the state. Ruffed grouse and woodcock are also present.

Washington Department of Fish and Wildlife
WDFW Main Office
Natural Resources Building
600 Capitol Way North
Olympia, WA 98501–1091
Wildlife Program (360) 902–2515 and (360) 902–2162
Pheasants, chukars, Huns, valley quail, bobwhite quail, mountain quail, blue, spruce, and ruffed grouse, doves, and three subspecies of wild turkey.

West Virginia Division of Natural Resources
Wildlife Resources Section
State Capitol Complex, Building 3
1900 Kanawha Boulevard
Charleston, WV 25305–0060
Steve Wilson, wildlife resources section, said increasing turkey populations are one of the good things happening in West Virginia. In 1966, 1,300 turkeys were taken; in 1999, 14,000 birds were taken. During the 1990s, the state averaged between 15,000 and 20,000 birds. Wilson said doves are stable; quail, grouse, and woodcock numbers, however, are declining. Quail numbers remain down due to unsuitable habitat. Grouse numbers are low due to maturing woods. Pheasant numbers are stable, but hunting is very limited.

Wisconsin Department of Natural Resources
Wildlife Management
P. O. Box 7921
Madison, WI 53707
Telephone (608) 266–8204
Fax (608) 267–7857
Woodcock, turkeys, and ruffed grouse. Wisconsin gunners average about 400,000 grouse each fall.

Wyoming Game and Fish Department
5400 Bishop Boulevard
Cheyenne, WY 82006
Telephone (307) 777–4600

In State Only: (800) 842–1934
Pheasants, chukars, wild turkeys, Huns, sharp-tailed grouse, sage grouse, blue and ruffed grouse

Canada Contacts
One of the best ways to get in touch with Canada's bountiful upland bird hunting opportunities—everything from Huns, sharptails, chukars, and ptarmigan to some fantastic grouse and woodcock hunting—is through the Internet.

One combined source of handy information can be found in www.huntinfo.com. This lists all the provinces individually and how to get access to the provincial agencies responsible for managing wildlife there. Individual websites are listed below. Also, check out what happens when you search for Canada hunting or a particular province and hunting.

Alberta, www.gov.ab.ca/env/fw/hunting
British Columbia, www.monday.com/hunting
Nova Scotia, www.gov.ns.ca/natr/index
Prince Edward Island www.gov.pe.ca/index
Quebec, www.mef.gov.qc.ca/en/index
Yukon, www.yukonwild.com
New Brunswick, www.gov.nb.ca/dnre/f&wca/natres
Northwest Territories, www.govt.nt.ca/RWED/index
Ontario, www.mnr.gov.on.ca/mnr/index
Newfoundland and Labrador, http://public.gov.nf.ca/
Saskatchewan, www.serm.gov.sk.ca/
Manitoba, www.gov.mb.ca/natres/wildlife/hunting

BIBLIOGRAPHY

This is a partial listing of some of the research that went into this book. What is not shown is the accumulated knowledge of reading years' worth of the writers in several periodicals—some cited in the text. These included: *Gun Dog, Wing & Shot, Petersen's Hunting, Sports Afield, Outdoor Life, Field & Stream, Shooting Sportsman, Audubon, Pennsylvania Game News, Pennsylvania Sportsman, Pointing Dog Journal, Shotgun Sports,* and others. It is also hard to account for the lessons learned via shoe-leather express and the school of aspen sprouts, multiflora rose hedges, and endless prairie skies. For all these teachers and pathfinders, I am a grateful student.

* * * *

Atwater, Sally, and Schnell, Judith, editors. *The Ruffed Grouse: The Wildlife Series.* Stackpole Books, 1989.

Barsness John. *Western Skies.* The Lyons Press, 1994.

Basket, Thomas; Sayre, Mark; Tomlinson, Roy E., and Mirarchi, Ralph E., editors. *Ecology and Management of the Mourning Dove.* Stackpole Books, 1993.

Bell, Bob. *Hunting the Long-Tailed Bird.* Freshet Press, 1975.

Bent, Arthur Cleveland. *Life Histories of North American Gallinaceous Birds.* New York: Dover Publications, 1963 (originally published in 1932 by United States Government Printing Office at Smithsonian Institution U.S. National *Museum Bulletin 162*).

Brister, Bob. *Shotgunning: The Art and The Science*. Winchester Press, 1976.

Caligiuri, Tony and Miller, Bill. *Modern Bird Hunting*. North American Hunting Club, 1990.

Coon, Carleton. *The Hunting Peoples*. Nick Lyons Books, 1971.

Cornelius, Geoffrey. *The Starlore Handbook*. Chronicle Books, 1997.

Duffy, David Michael. *Hunting Dog Know How*. Revised edition. Winchester Press, 1983.

Evans, George Bird. *An Affair With Grouse*. Old Hemlock, 1982.

———. *The Upland Shooting Life*. New York: Alfred A. Knopf, 1971.

———, editor. *The Best of Nash Buckingham*. Winchester Press, 1973.

———, editor. *The Upland Gunner's Book: An Anthology*. Amwell Press, 1986.

Farrand, John, Jr., editor, *The Audubon Society Master Guide to Birding, Volume 1, 2 and 3*. New York: Alfred A. Knopf, 1985.

Fergus, Charles. *The Upland Equation: A Modern Bird-Hunter's Code*. Lyons & Buford, Publishers, 1995.

Grooms, Steve. *Modern Pheasant Hunting*. Stackpole Books, 1982.

Huggler, Tom. *Quail Hunting in America*. Stackpole Books, 1987.

Johnson, Chuck and Williams, Ben O. *Wingshooter's Guide to Montana; Upland Birds and Waterfowl*. Wilderness Adventures Press, 1996.

Kelly, Tom. *The Tenth Legion*. New York: The Lyons Press, 1998.

Leopold, Aldo. *A Sand County Almanac*. New York: Oxford University Press, 1966.

Miller, Dorcas. *Stars of the First People*. Pruett, 1997.

Moon, William Least Heat. *PrairyErth*. Boston: Houghton Mifflin Company, 1991.

Morris, Desmond. *Dogwatching*. New York: Crown Publishers, Inc., 1986.

Norris, Dr. Charles C. *Eastern Upland Shooting*. Countrysport Press, 1989.

Parton, William. *Wingshooter's Guide to Arizona; Upland Birds and Waterfowl*. Wilderness Adventures Press, 1996.

Robertson, Peter. *Pheasants*. Voyageur Press, 1997.

Roebuck, Kenneth C. *Gun Dog Training: Pointing Dogs*. Stackpole Books, 1983.

———. *Gun Dog Training: Spaniels and Retrievers*. Stackpole Books, 1983.

Retallic, Ken and Barker, Rocky. *Wingshooter's Guide to Idaho; Upland Birds and Waterfowl*. Wilderness Adventures Press, 1997.

Schama, Simon. *Landscape and Memory*. New York: Alfred A. Knopf, 1995.

Shewey, John. *Wingshooter's Guide to Oregon; Upland Birds and Waterfowl*. Wilderness Adventures Press, 1999.

Sisley, Nick. *Grouse and Woodcock*. Stackpole Books, 1980.

Smith, Steve. *More and Better Pheasant Hunting*. Winchester Press, 1986.

Spiller, Burton. *Drummer in the Woods*. Stackpole Books, 1980.

Tarrant, Bill. *The Best Way to Train Your Gun Dog*. New York: David McKay Company, Inc., 1977.

———. *Gun Dog Training*. Voyageur Press, 1996.

Vance, Joel M. *Upland Bird Hunting*. Outdoor Life Books, 1981.

Waldman, Carl. *Encyclopedia of Native American Tribes.* New York: Facts on File Publications, 1988.

Waterman Charles F. *Hunting Upland Birds.* Winchester Press, 1972.

Webb, Sherman. *Practical Pointer Training.* Winchester Press, 1974.

Werenert, Susan J., editor. *North American Wildlife.* Reader's Digest Association, Inc., 1982.

Wehel, Robert G. *Wing & Shot: Gun Dog Training.* Scottsville, New York: The Country Press, 1964.

Winterhelt, Sigbot and Bailey, Edward. *The Training and Care of the Versatile Hunting Dog.* The North American Versatile Hunting Dog Association (NAVHDA), 1973.

White, William M. *Henry David Thoreau: Sweet Wild World, Selections from The Journals, Arranged as Poetry.* Charles River Books, 1982.

INDEX